Teaching and Learning in Further Education
2nd Edition

Further education colleges deliver education and training to more students than any other institution in the post-compulsory sector. This book provides a practical guide to teaching and learning within the context of the changing FE environment and addresses the diverse nature of the curriculum and of the student body for which it is designed.

This new edition contains fully revised material on FE funding, curriculum, assessment and teacher training to present the most up-to-date picture of further education in the UK. Drawing on a considerable research base, this book places FE teaching and learning in its social, economic and political context.

Topics covered include:

- the changing context, structure and funding of the FE sector
- the nature and range of FE students and staff
- teaching and learning strategies
- the assessment and recording of achievement
- continued professional development
- support available to FE teachers

Throughout, case study examples help you to consider differing student needs and how these might best be served. They also provide an opportunity to reflect upon how the changing policy context of FE impacts upon students, programmes and institutions. Practical activities are also included, which can be used as catalysts for questioning your attitude and approaches to work in FE.

Whether you are embarking on a career or already teaching, this book will help you review your approach and understanding of the process of teaching and learning in further education.

Prue Huddleston is Director of the Centre for Education and Industry at the University of Warwick.

Lorna Unwin is Professor of Vocational Education at the Centre for Labour Market Studies, University of Leicester.

Teaching and Learning in Further Education

2nd Edition

Diversity and change

Prue Huddleston and Lorna Unwin

RoutledgeFalmer
Taylor & Francis Group

LONDON AND NEW YORK

First published 1997
by Routledge
11 New Fetter Lane, London EC4P 4EE

Simultaneously published in the USA and Canada
by RoutledgeFalmer
29 West 35th Street, New York, NY 10001

Reprinted 2000
Reprinted 2001 by RoutledgeFalmer

Second edition first published 2002

RoutledgeFalmer is an imprint of the Taylor & Francis Group

© 1997, 2002 Prue Huddleston and Lorna Unwin

Typeset in Garamond by M Rules
Printed and bound in Great Britain by St Edmundsbury Press, Suffolk

British Library Cataloguing in Publication Data
A catalogue record for this book is available from the British Library

Library of Congress Cataloguing in Publication Data
A catalogue record for this book has been requested

ISBN 0–415–27146–0

Contents

List of figures   vi
List of abbreviations   vii
Preface   xi

Part I Further education in context

1 Where will I teach?   3

2 The student body: Who will I teach?   28

3 Diverse curricula: What will I teach?   39

Part II Teaching and learning

4 Approaches to learning   79

5 Teaching strategies   116

6 Assessment and recording achievement   140

Part III Professional development

7 Evaluation, reflection and research   165

8 Professional development   177

9 Networks and support agencies   190

References   199
Further reading   210
Index   213

Figures

1.1 National learning targets to 2004   11
1.2 South-east Derbyshire College   14–15
1.3 FEFC-funded full-time equivalent (FTE) students in sector
   colleges by mode of attendance, age-band and programme
   area, 1998–99   17
3.1 Fourteen areas of learning   40
3.2 National qualifications framework   45
3.3 Influences on curriculum design   46
4.1 Maslow's hierarchy of needs   96
4.2 Teacher–learner relationship   105
4.3 Types of aims and purposes in group teaching   107
4.4 College guidance map   109
4.5 Guidance team influence on learner's pathway through college   112
5.1 Teaching strategies continuum   120
5.2 Reflection exercise   122
5.3 Model for effective learning   133
8.1 FENTO Standards for Category A: Assessing Learners' Needs   183

List of abbreviations

ACAC	Curriculum and Assessment Authority for Wales
ACM	Association for College Management
ALBSU	Adult Literacy and Basic Skills Unit (now Basic Skills Agency)
ALF	Average Level of Funding
ALI	Adult Learning Inspectorate
AOC	Association of Colleges
APC	Association of Principals of Colleges
APL	Accreditation of Prior Learning
ATL	Association of Teachers and Lecturers
BTEC	Business and Technology Education Council (from April 1996 BTEC merged with the London Examinations Board to become EDXCEL)
CAD/CAM	Computer-Aided Design and Manufacture
CBI	Confederation of British Industry
CCEA	Council for the Curriculum, Examinations and Assessment (CCEA) in Northern Ireland
CEF	Colleges' Employers' Forum
CGLI	City and Guilds of London Institute
CPD	Continuing Professional Development
CPE	Continuing Professional Education
CPVE	Certificate for Pre-Vocational Education
CRAC	Careers Research and Advisory Centre
CVE	Centre of Vocational Excellence
Delni	Department for Employment and Learning Northern Ireland
DfEE	Department for Education and Employment
DfES	Department for Education and Skills
DTI	Department of Trade and Industry
EBP	Education–Business Partnership
EBPNN	Education–Business Partnership National Network
ELLD	Enterprise and Lifelong Learning Department
ELWa	Education and Learning Wales
EMA	Education Maintenance Allowance

ERDF	European Regional Development Fund
ESF	European Social Fund
ESTYN	Her Majesty's Inspectorate for Wales
FE	Further Education
FEDA	Further Education Development Agency
FEFC	Further Education Funding Council
FENTO	Further Education National Training Organisation
FESC	Further Education Staff College
FEU	Further Education Unit
GCSE	General Certificate of Secondary Education
GEST	Grant for Educational Support and Training
GNVQ	General National Vocational Qualification
HE	Higher Education
HEFC	Higher Education Funding Council
HMI	Her Majesty's Inspectorate
HNC	Higher National Certificate
HND	Higher National Diploma
HRD	Human Resource Development
ISR	Individual Student Record
ITE	Initial Teacher Education
ITO	Industrial Training Organisation
LEA	Local Education Authority
LEC	Local Enterprise Company (Scottish version of TEC)
LSC	Learning and Skills Council
LLSC	Local Learning and Skills Council
LSDA	Learning and Skills Development Agency
MSC	Manpower Services Commission
NATFHE	National Association of Teachers in Further and Higher Education
NCET	National Council for Education Technology
NCITO	National Council for Industrial Training Organisations
NCVQ	National Council for Vocational Qualifications
NIACE	National Institute for Adult Continuing Education
NISVQ	National Information System for Vocational Qualifications
NVQ	National Vocational Qualification
Ofsted	Office for Standards in Education
PGCE	Postgraduate Certificate of Education
PIU	Performance and Innovation Unit
QCA	Qualifications and Curriculum Authority
QTS	Qualified Teacher Status
RAC	Regional Advisory Council
RDA	Regional Development Agency
RSA	Royal Society for the Encouragement of Arts, Manufacturing and Commerce

SCAA	School Curriculum and Assessment Authority
SFEFC	Scottish Further Education Funding Council
SHA	Secondary Heads Association
SRB	Single Regeneration Budget
SSC	Sector Skills Council
TDLB	Training and Development Lead Body
TEC	Training and Enterprise Council
TFW	Training for Work
TSC	Training Standards Council
TTA	Teacher Training Agency
TUC	Trades Union Congress
TVEI	Technical and Vocational Education Initiative
WEA	Workers' Educational Association
YT	Youth Training

Preface

This book has been written primarily for people who are embarking on a teaching career in colleges of further education (FE) and for those already teaching who may wish to review their approaches to and understanding of the process of teaching and learning. It may also be of use to managers in FE and to people working in organisations which have a relationship with FE colleges.

The book attempts to encapsulate the dynamic and volatile world as experienced day in and day out by students and staff in the hundreds of FE colleges throughout the United Kingdom. For unless one is able to have some picture of these powerhouses of education and training, it is difficult to begin to envisage the nature of the teaching and learning that goes on within the FE sector.

To teach in an FE college at the start of the twenty first century is a very demanding job. At first glance, it would seem that the FE teacher shares little of the advantages enjoyed by colleagues in schools and universities. Unlike schools, colleges are open to their students from early in the morning to late at night, often at weekends, and, increasingly, throughout the traditional summer holiday period from mid-July to early September. Unlike universities, colleges are open to people of all abilities, from those adults who may be learning to read and write to those who are technically highly skilled and, again increasingly, to those who are following undergraduate and postgraduate courses. There is a heterogeneity about the student body, structures and curricular offerings in FE colleges which would send some school and university teachers running for cover. That very diversity, however, helps make FE colleges such stimulating and exciting environments in which to work as a teacher.

Since the first edition of this book was published in 1997, there have been major changes in post-compulsory education and training policy in the UK, all of which have and will continue to affect FE colleges. As authors of a book that seeks to present a comprehensive analysis of the FE sector, we face the challenge of trying to be as up-to-date as possible. We acknowledge, however, that given the way in which successive UK governments seem intent on re-organising some aspect of the architecture of education and training every few months, some of the initiatives covered in this book may have been further amended or even withdrawn in the time it takes for a manuscript to be published. All colleges struggle to incorporate externally imposed change in such a way as to cause as little disruption as possible to their students and staff. As we write, however, there are regular reports in the media of conflicts between staff and managers about contracts of employment, and battles between the organisations which represent colleges and government agencies.

Sometimes change affects the viability of a college and it is worth noting that since 1993, when colleges became independent from local authority control, 37 have been involved in mergers, either with other colleges or with higher education institutions. In addition, the status of colleges can change. In July 2001, sixteen colleges in England were declared Centres of Vocational Excellence, as part of a government plan to ensure colleges meet the needs of the economy (at local, regional and national levels) more effectively.

Working in any sector of education, however, means that one must be prepared for change and periods of upheaval, much of which may be imposed from outside one's sector or organisation. Despite the catalogue of concerns given here, the majority of FE teachers still spend much of their working day helping their students to learn, to progress and to achieve. Throughout this book, we have tried to portray the realities of college life in order to emphasise that FE teachers must be capable of adapting to many different situations and circumstances. In any one day, an FE teacher will employ a range of strategies, moving from a traditional didactic style in one lesson to being a facilitator of group work in another, from the company of mature adult students to a group of disaffected 14-year-olds, and from teaching and assessing in the college classroom to the variable conditions of the industrial or commercial workplace.

The book is divided into three parts: Part I: Further education in context; Part II: Teaching and learning; and Part III: Professional development.

In Part I, we describe in Chapter 1 the FE world, how it is funded and the external constraints which govern the ways in which colleges can go about their business. Chapter 2 examines the nature and scope of the FE student population and introduces the reader to some real students whose needs and expectations pose challenges for teachers and support staff. It also describes the different types of staff found in colleges and the multi-skilled nature of teachers. In Chapter 3, we discuss the rich diet that comprises the curricular offerings found in FE colleges from basic skills workshops through to higher education courses.

In Part II, we explore in Chapter 4 the relationship between teaching and learning, drawing on a number of theoretical approaches that can help teachers reflect on their work and be used as a basis for examining the problems they encounter. This underpinning theory is continued in Chapter 5 where we present a number of strategies for use in the different teaching situations found in a college. In Chapter 6, we focus on assessment and recording achievement.

In Part III, we see that, as in all teaching, regardless of the sector, professional educators never stop learning about their work and spend a great deal of time reflecting on how to improve and develop their competence and levels of creativity. In Chapter 7, we discuss the concept of the reflective practitioner as it relates to both teachers and students, and the extent to which teachers can also function as researchers. The possibilities for continued professional development are examined in Chapter 8, and Chapter 9 provides information about the organisations and resources upon which FE teachers can draw for support in their work. At the end of the book we indicate further reading material for each chapter that will help you extend your understanding of some of the complex learning and teaching concepts covered in the book.

In each of the chapters, we have included sets of questions and activities for you to consider. We have boxed these under the heading 'Reflections' and hope that you will find time to use them as catalysts for questioning your attitudes and approaches to your work in FE and for discussion with colleagues.

This book has been written in the spirit of sharing rather than preaching and, as such, reflects the philosophical basis of much of the teaching and learning that occurs in FE colleges. Our ideas come from our own experiences of teaching in colleges and, more recently, of working with FE professionals in a staff development and research capacity. We hope the book provides you with some useful and relevant information and ideas but equally we hope it provides enough challenging material to make you say, 'I think I would tackle that situation differently' or 'I can come up with a better way'.

Part I

Further education in context

Chapter 1

Where will I teach?

NATURE AND SCOPE OF FURTHER EDUCATION

This chapter describes the shape and scope of further education (FE) colleges and gives particular emphasis to their diversity. At the time of writing, there were some 440 FE colleges in England, 47 in Scotland, 27 in Wales and 17 in Northern Ireland. These figures are subject to change because, much more so than in the case of schools and universities, colleges are subject to merger and even closure. In 1999/2000, there were 3.8 million students enrolled in colleges in England, 434,435 in Scotland, 224,100 in Wales, and 150,000 in Northern Ireland. The vast majority of these students are over the age of 19 and studying part-time. In England, 80 per cent of FE students are over the age of 19 and the number of part-time students is increasing (LSC, 2001a). The FE sector comprises colleges which can be classified under five headings:

- general FE and tertiary colleges;
- sixth form colleges;
- specialist designated colleges;
- colleges of Art and Design and the Performing Arts;
- agriculture and horticulture.

The oldest of these colleges have their roots in the Mechanics Institutes of the mid-nineteenth century. Originally intended to provide technical education on a part-time basis for the growing numbers of technicians and craftspeople required by the industrialisation process, they grew and developed during the twentieth century to provide vocational education and training mainly on a day-release basis. For example, Huddersfield Technical College began as the Huddersfield Mechanics Institution in the 1840s, and became a technical college in 1896, whereas Lowestoft College, the most easterly college in Britain, traces its origins to evening art classes held in 1874 and courses in navigation for fishermen began in 1923. As Green and Lucas (1999, p.11) note, the growth of the FE sector was 'part of the formation of the modern state in the late nineteenth century, reflecting one of the many aspects of a voluntarist relationship between education, training and the state'.

The 1960s and 1970s saw a considerable expansion in the FE sector, not just within the area of vocational education but also in the development of professional and academic courses. Some of these were on a full-time basis, often for those students who were looking for an alternative to education provided in the school sixth form. In the late 1970s and early 1980s, world-wide economic recession led to a sharp rise in the number of young people in the UK who could not find jobs. The Labour and Conservative governments of the day sought to alleviate youth unemployment by introducing a series of youth training and work experience schemes (see Unwin, 1997). Parallel pro-grammes were also introduced for unemployed adults. Many colleges became involved in these schemes by providing off-the-job training and/or by acting as 'managing agents'.

The FE sector has always had a policy of 'inclusiveness' in its provision. That is, it has provided non-selective education for everyone over 16 who wished to benefit from extended education or vocational training. In many colleges this provision now includes everything from basic education to under-graduate and professional programmes. Colleges are multi-faceted organisations, on the one hand providing for the needs of their local commu-nity, as well as on the other hand, for a growing regional, national and, in some cases, international student clientele. At the start of their third century of existence, colleges are now opening their doors to young people between the ages of 14 and 16 who have been excluded from school and/or those who schools and colleges believe might progress more effectively in a college envi-ronment. In her 1997 seminal report on FE, Helena Kennedy declared that 'Defining further education exhaustively would be God's own challenge because it is such a large and fertile section of the education world' (Kennedy, 1997, p.1). Felstead and Unwin (2001, p.107) in an analysis of further edu-cation funding argued that colleges were trying to fulfil four key aims:

- Respond to the government's economic agenda to improve basic and inter-mediate skill levels of young people and adults and increase their participation in education and training;
- Fulfill their role as the main provider of sub-degree post-compulsory edu-cation and training at local level;
- Continue to provide a wide-ranging curriculum which bridges the voca-tional/non-vocational divide;
- Continue being a 'second-chance saloon' for young people and adults who want to return to learning.

In addition, many colleges are engaged in higher education (HE) provision, usually in partnership with local universities. How a college decides to tackle these aims will have profound consequences for its teachers, students and local community, as well as for rival education and training providers. The expansion of HE provision in FE colleges is particularly significant in this regard. In Scotland, 30 per cent of all HE students are actually based in FE colleges (Gallacher, Leahy and MacFarlane, 1997), and the majority of part-time HE provision in Scotland takes place in FE colleges (Osborne et al., 2000). In England, it is estimated that 10 per cent of all HE enrollments are in FE colleges (LSDA, 2002). In recent years, and as a result of the government's widening participation agenda, some colleges in England have merged with universities: for example, High Peak College in Buxton has merged with the University of Derby which is located 40 miles on the other side of Derbyshire. Prime Minister Tony Blair declared in 2001 that he wanted 50 per cent of 18–30 year olds to gain a university degree, and it is envisaged that FE will play a key part in helping the government reach this target. These developments pose interesting questions about the nature of student and staff identity, about the place of research in an FE teacher's portfolio, and, ultimately, about the extent to which the traditional status boundaries between FE and HE will dissolve. In its response to a recent HEFCE consultation on supply and demand in HE in England, the Learning and Skills Development Agency (LSDA) argued that 'There is a need for Government to articulate a clear role for FE colleges in relation to the delivery of HE as the basis for the strategic development of its capacity' (LSDA, 2002, p.2). LSDA also stressed that more research was required to gain a better understanding of learners' experience of HE in an FE setting and of the significance of critical mass in relation to the quality of HE delivered in FE.

Until April 1993, FE colleges were under the control of their local education authority (LEA) from whom they received the bulk of their funding, the rest coming from central government and other agencies. The 1988 Education Reform Act gave colleges and schools the power to manage their own budgets and thus began to loosen the control of the LEAs. In 1991, the White Paper, *Education and Training for the Twenty-first Century*, announced that colleges were to be given the 'freedom' they needed to play a 'central part in providing more high-quality opportunities' and to enable them to 'respond to the demand from students and employers for high-quality further education' (DES/ED/WO, 1991, p.58). In his foreword to the White Paper, the then Prime Minister, John Major, outlined his government's desire to 'knock down the barriers to opportunity', and for 'more choice' in order to 'give every one of Britain's young people the chance to make the most of his or her particular talents and to have the best possible start in life' (ibid., Foreword). Under the terms of the 1992 Further and Higher Education Act, which followed the White Paper, all colleges, including sixth form colleges, were removed from LEA control, just as polytechnics and higher education colleges had been in 1989. Colleges became independent self-governing corporations with responsibility for their own budgets, staffing, marketing, course planning and provision. Two new national funding bodies were established for England and Wales: the Further Education Funding Council (FEFC) in England; and the Welsh Funding Council. In Northern Ireland and Scotland, colleges were funded via the Northern Ireland Office and the

Scottish Office. In 1999, the Scottish Further Education Funding Council (SFEFC) was established.

The removal of colleges from LEA control was part of the Conservative government's attempts to reduce the power of local authorities following the Poll Tax debacle. Gleeson (1996, p.87) has argued that the 1988 and 1992 Acts and a further Education Act in 1994 led to post-16 policy being 'driven by market principles and deregulation' and a break with the 'municipal or public service view of school and further education which linked schools and colleges with LEAs within the spirit of the settlement which followed the 1944 Act'. Reference to the 1944 Education Act is important for it stated, for the first time, that it was a legal duty of LEAs to support FE provision and maintain colleges. The local political constraints on LEAs meant, however, that the funding available to colleges varied considerably from one part of the country to another.

Though free from LEA control, colleges in England soon found that the FEFC was to impose a strict funding methodology which would determine the nature of the courses and qualifications they could offer. Lucas (1999, p.54) has argued that 'few supporters of incorporation realised that a move away from the benign control of LEAs would mean so much FEFC regulation and downward pressure'. The creation of a national funding methodology was a central pillar of the FEFC's goal to forge FE into a coherent and more homogenised sector on a par with schools and higher education. What had often been referred to as the 'Cinderella' of the education sector was now expected, virtually overnight, to emerge from the shadows. The months and years following incorporation proved to be both an exhilarating and painful period for FE colleges. Taubman (2000, pp.82–3) records that following incorporation, 'further education had proportionally more days lost to strike action than any other sector of the British economy'. In their attempts to provide the 'choice' for students and employers laid out in the 1991 White Paper, and to maximise the funding on offer from the FEFC and other bodies, some colleges hit the media headlines for falsifying student numbers and other fraudulent practices (see Shattock, 2000, for a discussion of how this arose). Although it is fair to say that the vast majority of colleges managed incorporation without recourse to bad practice, the imposition by government of a market-driven approach across the public services in the mid-1990s encouraged educational institutions to compete in ways that did little to enhance the quality of education and training, nor to ensure that learners gained access to the most appropriate provision.

Just prior to the incorporation of colleges, the government had created a network of 100 Training and Enterprise Councils (TECs) in 1990 in England, Wales and Scotland (where they were called Local Enterprise Companies). The TECs (and LECs in Scotland) were established as employer-led companies whose objectives were to fund, organise and manage work-based training programmes for young people and adults, but also to stimulate enterprise in their local areas. As many colleges acted as managing agents for government-supported training schemes and also as off-the-job training providers for employers and other managing agents, they found themselves in a paradoxical relationship with the TECs and LECs. On the one hand, they depended on the TECs and LECs for some of their funding, whereas on the other hand they competed with them for customers. Every young person who accepted a place on a youth training scheme was also a potential full-time FE student (see Unwin, 1999).

In 1997, the new Labour government announced that one of its first priorities would be to carry out a major review of post-compulsory education and training structures in England. This led to a White Paper in 1999, *Learning to Succeed*, in which the government spelt out its dissatisfaction with the current arrangements for the funding and planning of post-16 education and training:

> There is too much duplication, confusion and bureaucracy in the current system. Too little money actually reaches learners and employers, too much is tied up in bureaucracy. There is an absence of effective co-ordination or strategic planning. The system has insufficient focus on skill and employer needs at national, regional and local levels. The system lacks innovation and flexibility, and there needs to be more collaboration and co-operation to ensure higher standards and the right range of choices . . . the current system falls short.
>
> (DfEE, 1999, p.21)

The White Paper proposed a massive restructuring of the landscape in England. Using very similar language to the 1991 Conservative White Paper discussed above, *Learning to Succeed* bases its reforms on the need for people to reach their potential by having access to as many learning opportunities as possible. Just as in a host of other policy documents dating back to 1976 when the then Prime Minister, James Callaghan, declared that the education system was failing the nation's economy, this new White Paper stressed the economic imperatives that should drive education and training provision. The FEFC would be abolished and replaced by a Learning and Skills Council (LSC) for England to oversee what is now called the 'learning and skills sector'. The TECs (though not LECs) would be abolished and replaced by 47 local LSCs. The abolition of the FEFC, which had inspected colleges as well as funding them, meant that new inspection procedures were required. The White Paper proposed, therefore, that Ofsted (Office for Standards in Education) would extend its remit from just inspecting schools to inspecting college-based provision for 16–19 year olds, and that a new Adult Learning Inspectorate (ALI) would be created for work-based provision for 16–19 year olds as well as all college-based post-19 provision. ALI replaced the Training Standards Council (TSC) which had been inspecting government-funded work-based training in colleges and other training providers. Finally, a new approach to careers advice and guidance was to be introduced. The White Paper announced that the existing Careers Services and organisations responsible for supporting young people more generally (e.g. Youth Service and Probation Service) would work together under the umbrella of local agencies to be called, *Connexions*. This latter reform had been recommended in a parallel report from the government's Social Exclusion Unit (see SEU, 1999).

THE NEW LANDSCAPE

In April 2001 the changes proposed in *Learning to Succeed* came into operation. In June 2001, the Labour government was re-elected and some further reforms, all of which will have some effect on FE colleges, were added. The DfEE was renamed the Department for Education and Skills (DfES). The significance of this is that responsibility for the Employment Service, which managed the New Deal programmes for unemployed people over the age of 18, passed to another new department, the Department for Work and Pensions (see Chapter 3 for details of New Deal in colleges). The Regional Development Agencies (RDAs), which have a central role in analysing labour market and skills-related information and fund some research and development in colleges, remained under the remit of the Department for Trade and Industry (DTI). The Cabinet Office established the Performance and Innovation Unit (PIU) responsible for researching and policymaking in the area of workforce development and skills. The Cabinet Office also appointed an E-Envoy with responsibility for pushing forward Labour's policy to promote e-commerce and the use of new technologies, while the DTI appointed a new Minister for e-Commerce and Competitiveness. The important point here is that colleges in England, with their wide-ranging interests, have to relate to all the government departments that have influence over some aspect of PCET provision. As we can see, that influence is not confined to the DfES.

The TECs and the FEFC have been replaced in Wales by the National Council for Education and Training in Wales (known as ELWa which stands for Education and Learning Wales). ELWa is responsible for all post-16 education and training for that country and incorporates both the Further and Higher Education Funding Councils for Wales. Unlike in England, ELWa will not be supported by local councils but will act as a national body with some local offices. ELWa is a public body sponsored by the National Assembly for Wales. The Scottish Executive, which was established as the devolved government for Scotland in 1999, has given responsibility for FE to its Enterprise and Lifelong Learning Department (ELLD). ELLD also looks after higher education, skills and lifelong learning, economic and industrial development, and tourism. ELLD funds FE through the SFEFC. The LECs remain in Scotland as does Scottish Enterprise and Highlands and Islands Enterprise, the two agencies which manage work-based programmes such as the Modern Apprenticeship. Scotland has retained its 17 Careers Service companies and 17

Adult Guidance Networks. In Northern Ireland, the Department for Employment and Learning (Delni) is responsible for FE, whereas the Training and Employment Agency looks after government funded work-based provision. The Northern Ireland Assembly has a Minister of Higher and Further Education, Training and Employment.

Following the move to devolved government for Scotland, Wales and Northern Ireland, these countries are developing their own distinctive strategies for FE and lifelong learning policies more generally. For example, Wales and Scotland have rejected the *Connexions* model for careers education and guidance and are developing provision aimed at adults as well as young people. A radical difference between England and Wales concerns the latter country's planned development of a post-16 framework for credit accumulation and transfer encompassing all qualifications up to and including postgraduate and professional. For the moment, however, the similarities in the practice of teaching and learning in FE colleges in these three countries and those in England far outweigh their differences.

FE FUNDING

The way in which educational institutions are funded has a major impact on their character. As we saw above, the establishment of the funding councils in 1992 was designed to rationalise a system of funding that was highly localised. In 1993, the Audit Commission and Ofsted produced a highly critical report on drop-out rates for 16–19-year-olds on full-time courses in English colleges. Titled, *Unfinished Business,* the report highlighted, for the first time, the large numbers of students who were leaving courses before completing (30–40 per cent) and condemned this as a huge waste of public money as well as a waste of students' time and effort (Audit Commission/Ofsted, 1993). The new funding councils were, therefore, charged with designing a more efficient funding regime which would improve retention and achievement rates.

Under this new funding methodology, every student enrolled at a college attracted funding units, the precise number of which depended on the course they were following, the progress they made and whether they achieved the intended outcome. This introduced the principle that funding should follow the learner. Each unit was worth an amount of money, known as the average level of funding (ALF). In 2000–01, the minimum ALF in England stood at £17.20. A college could earn additional units for pre-course guidance, for negotiating learning plans for each student, for providing extra support for students with learning difficulties or disabilities, and for waiving fees for younger students or adults on low incomes. In 1996, the average college received some 400,000 units compared to the smallest with 20,000 units, whereas the largest received 1.6 million units (FEFC, 1996a, p.15).

The FEFC also drew up a list of those qualifications it would fund (known as Schedule 2) and those it would not. Colleges could, of course, provide courses leading to non-Schedule 2 qualifications but it would have to charge students fees for these or get them funded from somewhere else. A further ploy was to repackage existing non-Schedule 2 provision to bring it within the Schedule 2 framework. As Unwin (1999a) discovered, this relied on the creativity of college lecturers and curriculum managers. For example, one college lecturer explained that 'flower arranging is off, but floristry is on because we can get that accredited', whereas another described how popular classes in interior design techniques such as stenciling were reclassified under the heading 'Decorative Paint Techniques' (ibid., p.79). For a qualification to be funded, it must be delivered for a minimum of 9 'guided learning hours'. A full-time student was defined in FEFC's terms as someone enrolled on a programme of at least 450 guided learning hours. Qualifications were divided into 7 bands according to the number of guided learning hours they took and each band was assigned a number of basic on-programme units. Qualifications in each band were also assessed against five cost-weighting factors (e.g. capital equipment costs) which further increased the number of funding units they would attract.

Colleges were awarded their funding allocation annually after submitting a strategic plan in which they set out a target number of units for that year (see Felstead and Unwin, 2001). To assist colleges with their funding plans, the funding councils introduced the Individualised Student Record (ISR).

Opinions differ as to the effectiveness of the FEFC funding methodology. McClure (2000) cites performance figures for 1993–8 in England, such as the rise in student numbers, improvements in quality of provision, and increased value for money for the public purse, to conclude that the new regime worked. On the other hand, Lucas (1999), while acknowledging some positive outcomes, argues that the FEFC model led colleges to put financial considerations above the quality of learning. Felstead and Unwin (2001) highlighted the way in which the need to amass funding units encouraged colleges to recruit full-time students to courses that were inexpensive to run. This, in turn, meant colleges were less concerned about local labour market needs.

We now turn to consider the remit of the new LSC in England. The LSC, which is based in the FEFC's old offices in Coventry, began life with a budget of £5.5 billion, and a mission 'to raise participation and attainment through high-quality education and training which puts learning first' so that, by 2010, 'young people and adults in England will have the knowledge and productive skills matching the best in the world' (see LSC website). The LSC's remit covers:

- funding FE and sixth form colleges;
- funding school sixth forms;
- funding government-supported training;
- developing arrangements for adult and community learning (with LEAs);
- workforce development;

Key objectives	2004 Targets	2000 targets
1. Extend **participation** in education, learning and training	80 per cent of 16–18 year olds in structured learning. Set baselines and targets for adults in next year's Plan.	75 per cent
2. Increase engagement of **employers**	Develop a measure of employer engagement, in next year's Plan	
3. Raise achievement of **young people**	85 per cent at level 2 by age 19; 55 per cent at level 3 by age 19	75 per cent 51 per cent
4. Raise achievement of **adults**	Improve literacy and numeracy skills of 750,000 adults.	Up to 7 million adults having difficulties.
	% of adults at level 2: set targets in next year's Plan. 52 per cent of adults at level 3	47 per cent
5. Raise **quality** and **effectiveness** of education and training	Set baselines and targets (inspection grades and structured feedback) in next year's Corporate Plan	

Figure 1.1 National learning targets to 2004

- providing information, advice and guidance to adults;
- advising government on the National Learning Targets;
- education–business links.

The establishment of the LSC means that FE colleges are now part of what the government calls the 'learning and skills sector'. They will be expected to play their part in helping the government achieve its newly revised national learning targets (see Figure 1.1).

David Blunkett, then Secretary of State for Education and Employment, announced on October 16th, 2001, the names of the 15 people who will comprise the national council of the LSC and claimed:

As we promised . . . leading figures from the business community will play a key role in the Council. They will ensure that Post-16 learning is consumer driven and that the LSC will find solutions to the education and learning problems business faces today and in the future. The LSC's National Council will play a crucial role in setting the vision and agenda for learning and skills and in bringing together the current range of Post-16

learning opportunities for individual learning and workforce development
into a single coherent system . . .

(DfEE, 2000a, Press Release 442/00, 16th October)

Here we see the same faith placed in people from the 'business community'
and in the merits of consumerism that has characterised education and training policy since the late 1970s. Yet, ironically, the LSC and its local network
are to replace the business-led TECs which were judged to have failed. Ainley
(2000) has pointed out that although it is not inevitable that local LSCs will
take over local education authorities (LEAs), it is 'structurally feasible' for
them to do so. The responsibility and leadership of PCET have been over-
whelmingly centralised, and delivery of programmes and services will be
through agencies which are contracted to the State (see Ainley and Vickerstaff,
1993, for an earlier discussion on the 'Contract State').

The LSC's aim is that, by 2004/5, it will preside over a common funding
approach for what it calls the 'four learning sectors': work-based learning;
further education; school sixth forms; and adult and community learning. For
2002/3, the LSC will introduce a national funding formula with the following five elements:

1 *National base rate* – reflecting the length of the programme of study and the
  basic cost of providing the programme;
2 *Programme weighting* – reflecting that some programmes of a similar length
  or leading to an equivalent qualification are more costly to deliver than
  others;
3 *Achievement* – a part (10 per cent for FE and 20 per cent for work-based
  learning) of the weighted national base rate, uplifted where appropriate,
  which is paid if the learner achieves in accordance with the Council's funding guidance;
4 *Disadvantage* – an uplift applied to the above elements that supports the
  policy intention of widening participation, reflects the costs of this and
  recognises that some learners come from backgrounds which have disadvantaged them;
5 *Area costs* – an uplift applied to the total rate payable which reflects the significantly higher costs of delivering provision in London and related areas.
  (LSC, 2001b, p.5)

The key change, according to the LSC, between the FEFC and the LSC
model is that the funding unit has been replaced by a 'learning aim' which will
attract a 'cash rate'. The LSC explains that, 'Each learning aim will have a
national rate, quoted in cash terms, which will either be a specific listed value
or reflect the number of guided learning hours involved in delivering the
learning aim' (ibid, p.32). Programmes will continue to be weighted according to how much they cost to deliver, but there will be no on-entry payment.

The percentage of the funding allocated to achievement has been raised from the FEFC's 7 per cent to 10 per cent. It is too early to say whether these changes in terminology mean that the funding of colleges will be significantly different and how they will impact on college managers, teachers and learners. Colleges would do well, however, to reflect on the words of the LSC's first Chairman, Bryan Sanderson, who, in a controversial lecture to the Royal Society of Arts in April 2001, said:

> Customers can be disaffected, there can be a high drop-out rate, there may be a mis-match between what the customer wants and what they get, there may be continuous rethinks on policy but none of those things seems ever to really matter because there's probably a belief that the money will come anyway. To be brutal, we in the Learning and Skills Council need to inject a little discomfort into this scenario – fear of the revenue streams suddenly drying up.
>
> (Sanderson, 2001, p.23)

Colleges will be required to submit an annual strategic plan with projected student numbers and general funding requirements to the national LSC, having consulted their local LSCs and other 'partners' such as regional development agencies (RDAs). Although this is desirable in order to plan and deliver a coherent system of education and training, there is always an uncertainty for colleges about 'who will turn up on the day'. This tends to make the so-called 'FE market' volatile and it is not simply a matter of predicting demand and matching supply to it. The sector was previously criticised for being too much dominated by the supply side (Audit Commission, 1985) and much has been done to adjust the balance but the problems are not easily resolved. Since funding is dependent on enrolments and outputs there are serious resource implications if demand and supply are not reasonably well aligned.

Colleges also draw funding from a number of other sources, for example, the European Union and 'full-cost' paying customers. Where there are undergraduate and postgraduate students following programmes in FE colleges, these will be funded through the Higher Education Funding Councils. From April, 1999, colleges in England have been able to bid for monies from the Standards Fund to help them target weaknesses identified during FEFC inspections. Another source of funding is available to colleges who provide services to LearnDirect (the trading name of the University for Industry). The following vignette presents details of how a typical college of further education in England is funded:

South-east Derbyshire College is a general tertiary FE college based in the small town of Ilkeston and covering the semi-rural districts of Amber Valley and Erewash. The first table shows the number of staff employed by the college. Colleges calculate their staff numbers using a formula known as 'full-time equivalents' (FTE).

Group	Full-time	Part-time	Total
Teaching Departments (including technicians)	152	40	192
Teaching support services (libraries)	8	4	12
Other support services (welfare, admissions and careers)	19	2	21
Administration and Central services	51	10	61
Premises	20	17	37
Other (research)	1	0	1
Total (FTE)	**251**	**73**	**324**

The second table shows the numbers of students enrolled at the college. The part-time column includes people who come to the college for off-the-job training as part of a government-supported work-based learning programme such as Modern Apprenticeship.

Student numbers

Group	Full-time	Part-time
14–19	1,350	300
19+	100	8,000
Total	**1,450**	**8,300**

The college offers courses across a wide range of subject areas as the next table shows:

Figure 1.2 South-east Derbyshire College

Subject areas

Social sciences;
physical sciences;
humanities;
languages;
art and design, media and music;
engineering (light), motor vehicle and electronics;
construction trades;
care, social care and early years studies;
art, design, media and music;
information and communication technology (ICT).

Courses for full-time students lead to qualifications including Advanced Level (AS/A2) in 30 subjects, and vocational qualifications from Foundation to Level 3 in 20 subjects. The college also runs an 'Enrichment' curriculum for 16–19-year-old full-time students. Courses for part-time students lead to National Vocational Qualifications (NVQs) in 20 subjects, and Higher National Certificates and Diplomas in engineering and business studies. Taster courses for progression to NVQs and Advanced Level qualifications are also offered to adults. The college also runs a vocational education programme for 14–16-year-olds who have been excluded from local schools.

Funding streams

In the fiscal year 2000–2001, the college received funding from the following sources:

- LSC participation grant for learning (£6.5m)
- LSC standards grant [objective specific] (£0.2m)
- Tuition fees collected from learners and employers (£0.3m)
- European Social Funds [social inclusion work] (£0.2m)
- Single Regeneration Budget (SRB) and similar grants [social inclusion in deprived communities] (£0.1m)
- Work-based learning payments (£0.5m)
- Work-based training levy from Construction Industry Training Board and JTL (electrical) (£0.2m)
- HEFCE (via University franchise arrangement) (£0.1m)
- Local Education Authority Year 11 contract (£10,000)

Given the complexity of these funding streams, colleges have to employ financial managers who are alert to the different sources of funding and who can make the most of the opportunities on offer.

Figure 1.2 (Cont) South-east Derbyshire College

COLLEGES AS RESPONSIVE ORGANISATIONS

In July 2001, the Secretary of State for Education and Skills, Estelle Morris, announced that 16 colleges in England had been declared Centres of Vocational Excellence (CVEs) in the first phase of a £100 million strategy devised by the previous Secretary of State, David Blunkett, for all colleges to have at least one CVE by 2004/5 (see LSC, 2001c). Each CVE is recognised for a particular specialism: for example, construction at Accrington and Rossendale College; childcare at South Birmingham College; printing at Leeds College of Technology; and media technology at South East Essex College. CVEs are intended to: '. . . develop new, and enhance existing, excellent vocational provision that will be focused on meeting the skills needs of employers, locally, regionally, nationally and sectorally. They will seek to give a greater number of individuals from all backgrounds access to the high quality vocational training that they need to succeed in a modern economy' (ibid., p.1).

This development marks an attempt to raise the profile of the FE sector and also recognises that, amidst the great diversity of provision within one institution, there will be a core subject area for which it is particularly well known. At the same time, the government seems to be saying that it wants FE colleges to be clearly seen as providers of 'vocational' programmes. As we noted at the start of this chapter, the first FE colleges were established to meet the needs of industry and commerce, but they have expanded to embrace education in the liberal arts, humanities and social sciences. The rhetoric surrounding the CVE initiative will no doubt give many staff in the FE sector a sense of deja-vu as they will have spent many years being responsive to the needs of employers and learners.

For some students FE represents a 'second-chance' education. This may mean that they are retaking examinations in which they were previously unsuccessful or embarking on new courses. For other students the 'second chance' may have come relatively late in life and may represent a return to learning after a substantial break. There are a wide range of courses available for adults wishing to return to education to update their skills or to learn new skills. The changing nature and patterns of employment mean that there will be a continued demand for vocational training and retraining, a demand for which FE colleges are well placed to provide. There are also those for whom secondary education has been a negative experience and who have completed compulsory education with few or no formal qualifications. Their basic literacy and numeracy skills may be poorly developed. The FE sector is able to provide for such students in a non-threatening environment and is being increasingly funded to do so. Some of this provision will be made away from main campus sites, in 'outreach' facilities. This work may be funded by the local LSC or through the ESF. Examples of such programmes are the courses for women returners.

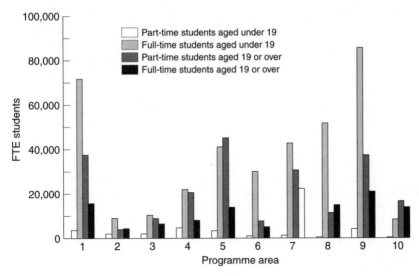

Source: Individualised student record (ISR14)

© The Learning and Skills Council (LSC)

Figure 1.3 FEFC-funded full-time equivalent (FTE) students in sector colleges by mode of attendance, age band and programme area, 1998–99

In the final report of the FEFC's (2001) Chief Inspector, ten main programme areas are listed, 'covering the full breadth of the further education curriculum' (see Figure 1.3). As Figure 1.3 shows, these areas vary greatly in terms of their student numbers, student age range and mode of attendance. They also differ in terms of qualification aims, levels of attainment and employment opportunities. The extent to which any one college offers provision in these curriculum areas will depend on the location of the college and the labour market which it serves. Changes in local labour markets will affect college provision; for example, those colleges which previously provided training for the mining industry have had to diversify or face closure. Figure 1.3 shows that engineering and construction, which once featured strongly in colleges, now account for far fewer students than the humanities, whereas the growing service sectors of the economy, such as business and health and community care have grown in size. This was previously the raison d'être of many FE colleges.

The expansion of HE students within FE colleges is another demonstration of the sector's responsiveness. In their study of HE students in FE, Scott and Bocock found that these students tend to be 'mature, mainly local and have non-standard entry qualifications' (Bocock, 1996, p.2). They reported:

Colleges made a real effort to acknowledge the life experiences such students bring wherever possible within the curriculum. This also meant the boundaries between academic and other forms of discourse became blurred. Also the staff were accessible in ways no longer possible in much of mainstream higher education because of expansion. Cumulatively these features provided a system of learning support that helped many students to succeed and gain confidence in their return to study.

(ibid.)

Colleges can mount 'full-cost' courses where learners, or their employers, are prepared to pay the real cost of a course. These include company-specific training programmes, short courses for business, seminars and workshops. Often these are provided by a separate business or enterprise unit within a college. The following extracts from an FEFC report on college responsiveness indicate the ways in which colleges are devising strategies to reach out into their communities:

A college in one area has been successful in promoting courses for the Sikh community at a local community centre, the local hospital and an Asian women's group. As part of this programme, the college offers open learning workshops and a home-study service. The provision was effectively marketed in the local Punjabi-speaking community as a result of a bilingual advertising campaign on local radio. The proportion of students from minority ethnic backgrounds attending the college is actually higher than represented in the local population.

(FEFC, 1996b, p.15)

One agricultural college conducted market research and held interviews with 12 local poultry producers in preparation for developing poultry provision. The research identified a range of training needs, including management, marketing and personnel skills as well as stockmanship. Poultry provision began in 1991 with six part-time students. Good links with industry enabled the college to use practical facilities owned by major companies. However, the lack of such facilities on-site was a limiting factor, and the college corporation decided to build a specialist poultry unit using industrial sponsorship. Over the next three years, a total of 45 industrial sponsors provided cash or equipment, allowing the college to build a modern facility costing £45,000. The unit . . . is run as a business partnership with industry, and now provides central training for large poultry firms.

(ibid., p.13)

Most FE colleges provide for students with learning difficulties, and much of this provision may be integrated into mainstream courses, but there may well be special courses for some of these students. For those students with multiple or complex learning needs, specialist independent institutions are available. The Beattie Committee in Scotland reported that: 'The current situation is therefore one of change. Students will experience a variety of provision from segregated special needs courses to fully integrated supported provision; some students might even be in colleges that have adopted the philosophy of "inclusive learning" where the individual needs of all students are considered paramount.'

COLLEGE STAFF

From the above description of the nature and scope of FE, it is clear that the staff who work in colleges are faced with many competing demands on their time and energies. Those who manage the system are responsible for multi-million-pound businesses. They are accountable to different funding bodies, to local and national employers and to the external inspectorates for the quality of education and training provision. These pressures may appear contradictory at times: for example, the need to provide excellence in vocational education and training at the same time as driving down costs and increasing student numbers. As one Midlands FE lecturer put it: 'it is impossible to put a financial value on people's learning needs and achievements.'

Employment patterns within the sector have changed in recent years with an increase in part-time staff, more flexible contracts, and the introduction of non-traditional teaching hours, for example, during weekends. The FEFC (2001, p.4) found that in 1999–2000, 26 per cent of the teaching staff in English colleges were employed on a part-time basis and that in 19 colleges, the figure was 40 per cent or more. In terms of quality of teaching, part-time teachers were judged to be weaker than their full-time colleagues (ibid.). The FEFC urged that 'more should be done to support part-time teachers and improve their teaching skills' and that colleges should ensure that all staff should 'take full advantage of development opportunities and support services' (ibid.).

New contracts issued by colleges outline very different terms and conditions of service from what one might expect for a teacher in a primary or secondary school. Edwards has suggested that 'the trends towards multi-skilling and flexibility elsewhere in the economy are also to be found in institutions of post-compulsory education and training' (Edwards, 1993, p.48). Hill (2000) reminds us, however, that the 'flexible firm' model has characterised the FE sector for many years due to the need for colleges to supplement their core staff with part-timers as they respond to the changing student market and to government initiatives. The following extract from a 2001 employment contract of a main grade lecturer in one of the largest FE colleges in England illustrates the extraordinary range of duties she will be expected to undertake:

> Formal schedule teaching, tutorials, student assessment, management of learning programmes and curriculum development, student admissions,

educational guidance, counselling, preparation of learning materials and student assignments, marking student work, marking examinations, management and supervision of student visit programmes, research and other forms of scholarly activity, marketing activities, consultancy, leadership, supervisory, administration and personal professional development.

The reference to 'research and other forms of scholarly activity' signals an interesting extension to the workload of FE teachers and one that is discussed in detail in Chapter 7.

Staff are being required to take on new roles so that in addition to a teaching and tutorial role they may have significant administrative duties (see Avis, Bathmaker and Parsons, 2001). Some FE lecturers may also have responsibility for promoting and marketing their courses. They may be expected to counsel students. Many staff have budgets to manage as well as their course teams. The introduction of distance and open learning systems has required some staff to take on the role of authors as well as develop new techniques for working with open learning students.

Edwards refers to the blurring of roles between 'lecturers and tutors, administrators and technical staff' (Edwards, 1993, p.48). There are hybrid support tutors who, rather than acting as traditional teachers, provide self-study support to students and are responsible for recording prior learning or achievement. A new or established teacher in the FE sector may be working on a number of part-time contracts in different institutions. The future workforce could comprise freelance professionals moving between colleges in response to demand for their expertise. This unpredictability in employment reflects the way in which the organisation of work in the wider society is being restructured, but the FE sector has been particularly affected by uncertainty since the mid-1990s. The General Secretary of the lecturers' trade union, NATFHE, told a Parliamentary Select Committee in October 2001 that 'a fifth to a quarter of colleges were in financial difficulty, with staff still seeing themselves as working in a neglected sector largely ignored by the media' (NATFHE, 2001). He added that the relatively low levels of FE teachers' pay compared with school teachers was a particular problem and that many colleges were suffering serious staff retention problems.

Avis (1999, p.251), building on the work of a number of commentators (e.g. Elliott, 1996; Hodkinson, 1997; Randle and Brady, 1997; and Ainley and Bailey, 1997) on the increasing problems faced by FE staff as a result of marketisation and managerialism, highlights the following areas for concern:

- Loss of control;
- intensification of labour;
- increase in administration;
- perceived marginalisation of teaching;
- stress on measurable performance indicators.

Gleeson and Shain (1999, p.558), however, argue that 'the influence of markets and managerialism is as much a contested as a controlling one', and that, 'While there is evidence of deprofessionalisation and casualisation in FE . . . there also exists competing forms of resistance and response from lecturers and senior managers which challenge the hegemony of managerialism at college level.' As in any other profession, FE teachers are subject to the controlling tendencies of managers and to the restrictions placed on their actions by external agencies. The extent to which FE teachers are able to exert their professional identities will differ from college to college and will also be influenced by the status of their subject area, their level of confidence in their ability, and the degree of support they receive from colleagues and managers. It is worth remembering that the FE teachers still spend much of their time with students and, as Bloomer (1997) argues, 'it is an individual matter as to how far teachers decide to exert agency and thus take control of their work situation.'

In their study of staff satisfaction in 80 colleges in England, Davies and Owen (2001, p.8) found that staff were much more likely to feel valued within a college that had 'an embedded culture of continuous improvement – rather than one of blame – which encouraged bottom-up initiatives within a clearly understood framework'. Such colleges might be said to have embraced the concept of the 'learning organisation', which has been much promoted since its emergence in the late 1980s (see Jones and Hendry, 1994). Within such organisations, work is organised along flatter as opposed to hierarchical lines in order to devolve responsibility and encourage greater sharing of knowledge and skills. Employees, at all levels, are encouraged to continually learn and develop. A key test of whether a workplace can be said to have the characteristics of a learning organisation is the way in which it treats newcomers. Lave and Wenger (1991) conceptualise workplaces as 'communities of practice' in which skills and knowledge are passed on from one generation to the next, thus ensuring that the community continues to thrive. Trainees or apprentices begin as ' legitimate peripheral participants' who, under the guidance of more experienced workers, gradually progress to become full participants in the community. The use of the term 'legitimate' is significant because it recognises the importance of a trainee's peripheral status. In other words, trainees need time to develop their skills and should not be expected to function as productive workers until they are ready.

The staff in FE colleges come from a diverse set of backgrounds. There will be some with academic qualifications and others with professional qualifications who have perhaps become teachers after a substantial career in business or industry. There will be those who have qualified through a craft or technician route, who have spent a considerable time on the shopfloor or training apprentices. In addition there is a range of support staff: kitchen assistants, laboratory technicians, audio-visual technicians. There will also be clerical and administrative staff and those responsible for student services. Robson (1998, p.588) argues that 'the very diversity of entry routes into FE teaching . . .

creates, in sociological terms, a weak professional boundary' and, thus, weakens the profession's overall standing. She adds that most FE teachers, who deliver technical and vocational subjects, retain strong allegiances to their first occupational identity (as formed in industry or commerce). Moving into a college can, therefore, be a stressful experience if those pre-formed occupational identities are threatened or disregarded.

One project (DfEE/FEDA, 1995) which attempted to create a map of the type of staff employed in FE colleges reported its findings under the following headings:

- Learning management (e.g. director of studies, head of department, curriculum manager, etc.)
- Co-ordination (e.g. course co-ordinator, college careers co-ordinator, etc.)
- Liaison (e.g. school liaison manager, employer liaison manager, etc.)
- Lecturing/teaching (e.g. senior lecturer, lecturer, tutor, community education officer, etc.)
- Learning resources (e.g. open learning staff, learning resource centre staff, etc.)
- Libraries
- Technical learning support (e.g. technicians, workshop managers, etc.)
- Assisting learning (e.g. instructors, demonstrators, language assistant, etc.)
- Governing (members of governing body)
- College management (e.g. principal/chief executive and deputies)
- Student guidance
- Human resources management (e.g. personnel director, staff development staff, etc.)
- Facilities management and support (e.g. campus manager, building and estates staff, etc.)
- Marketing and development
- Information and finance management and support

The job titles below are taken from newspaper advertisements for college vacancies. We have deliberately chosen them, rather than the standard advertisements for lecturers in specific subjects as they illustrate the complexity of teaching and learning in contemporary FE.

- Widening Participation and Basic Skills Manager
- Team Leader – Employers and Marketing
- Head of Enterprise Services
- Lecturers for Additional Learning Support
- Curriculum Co-ordinator for Essential Skills
- E-learning Manager
- Manager, Open Learning Centre
- Chief Executive
- Lecturer – Employability Programmes

The growth in staff with responsibility for 'learning support' reflects the increasing emphasis in colleges on flexible and student-centred learning and the need to improve retention and attainment levels. It has been estimated that the number of learning support staff in UK colleges could be as much as 13 per cent of the workforce (FENTO, 2001). The Further Education National Training Organisation (FENTO) defines a support role as 'one which directly supports teaching or learning, but for which teaching is not the main purpose', though they recognise that, in smaller colleges, the need to multi-task 'creates job roles which may overlap teaching, support and administrative roles' (ibid., pp.9–10).

From September 2001, all new teachers employed to teach in an FE college in England and Wales have had to possess a recognised teaching qualification delivered by a university and based on standards issued by FENTO. If they do not possess such a qualification, then they can be employed but must work towards a qualification within two years. Up until 2001, all staff responsible for the assessment and verification of National Vocational Qualifications (NVQs) and General National Vocational Qualifications (GNVQs) were also required to achieve assessor and verifier awards derived from standards issued by the Training and Development Lead Body (TDLB). Awarding bodies such as City Guilds administered TDLB units such as D32 and D33 for assessors, D34 and D35 for internal verifiers, and D36 for Advisors in the Accreditation of Prior Learning (APL). From the mid-1990s onwards, the imposition of the 'D' units, as they were commonly known, introduced a competence-based approach to college staff development and paved the way for the FENTO standards. These awards, now called 'L' units and administered by the Employment National Training Organisation, still exist but are no longer mandatory for NVQ and GNVQ teachers in FE as assessment skills are covered by the FENTO standards and, therefore, the new teacher training qualifications. At the time of writing, the government had signalled its intention that all new Principals of colleges will also be expected to gain a national professional qualification and that a new 'Leadership College' for the FE sector was to be established. In Scotland, national standards for FE teachers have been developed by the General Teaching Council in consultation with colleges and these underpin the Teaching Qualification (Further Education), known as the TQFE. The Scottish FENTO Advisory Group provides the link between FENTO, which has a UK-wide remit, and the Scottish teacher training agencies. A similar situation exists in Northern Ireland where colleges and universities providing teacher training qualifications for FE are being encouraged to adopt the FENTO standards. Teacher training qualifications are examined in more detail in Chapter 8, which also explores professional development for FE staff.

IN THE PUBLIC EYE

As we have seen, the FE sector has undergone a period of rapid and continuous change in the decade since the incorporation of colleges in 1993. The sector is having to face pressures on its funding, accommodation and resources in a climate of increased student enrolments and output-related performance indicators. The extension of vocational education to 14-year-olds and the increasing presence of this age group in colleges means that Ofsted and ALI will extend their remit, though, at the time of writing, the DfES is still consulting as to how that remit might be articulated. In Scotland, colleges are inspected by Her Majesty's Inspectorate of Education (HMI) on behalf of the SFEFC. In Wales, HMI (known there as Estyn) inspects colleges on behalf of Elwa, and in Northern Ireland, HMI inspects colleges on behalf of the Department of Education.

As well as publishing information on completion rates for all courses, since 1996 colleges have been required to publish the actual destinations (e.g. further/higher education, employment, training scheme, etc.) of all their students who achieved qualifications in the previous teaching year. Colleges are encouraged to use these destination data to spot patterns and trends and as a basis for evaluating student experience through the following types of questions:

- Why is the proportion of early leavers from some courses higher than others?
- Why are the percentages of students progressing from foundation to intermediate and from intermediate to advanced level courses within the college higher in some vocational areas than others?
- Why do the percentages of students progressing to higher education from advanced vocational courses vary significantly from one vocational area to another?
- How strong is the correlation between the subjects studied within GCE A level programmes and the degree courses to which students subsequently progress, and what are the implications of this for careers education and guidance?
- Why are there significant differences between the numbers of male and female students progressing to higher education from the same or similar courses?
- Are the trends in destinations of students on particular courses in step with changes made to the structures of those courses?
- Are enough students gaining jobs in those industries where the labour market is expanding?
- Does the number of unemployed students emerging from particular courses suggest that related labour markets are saturated?

(FEFC, 1996c, pp. 17–18)

In England, Ofsted and ALI inspect colleges every four years under the

Common Inspection Framework. This uses a seven-point grading scale to assess the quality of learning sessions, and a five-point scale to assess the quality of provision vis-à-vis curriculum and occupational areas and the quality of leadership and management. The key question which any inspection seeks to answer is: How effective and efficient is the provision of education and training in meeting the needs of learners, and why? (ALI/Ofsted, 2001) The grades are as follows:

Quality of learning

Grade 1	excellent
Grade 2	very good
Grade 3	good
Grade 4	satisfactory
Grade 5	unsatisfactory
Grade 6	poor
Grade 7	very poor

Quality of provision/leadership/management

Grade 1	outstanding
Grade 2	good
Grade 3	satisfactory
Grade 4	unsatisfactory
Grade 5	very weak

The colleges receive individual grades for: leadership and management; equality of opportunity; quality assurance; and their occupational/curriculum areas. Where an inspection results in a third or more of curriculum or occupational areas and/or leadership and management being graded 4 or 5, the entire provision will be deemed to be inadequate and will be reinspected. Where less than a third of the curriculum or occupational areas offered by a provider are graded 4 or 5, then only these areas will be reinspected. All reinspections are normally carried out within two years of the original inspection. Colleges are also required to produce an annual self-assessment report about their performance, identifying strengths, weaknesses and other improvements needed. In Scotland, Wales and Northern Ireland, HMI uses a much simpler grading system which judges provision and management to be *Very Good, Fair* or *Unsatisfactory.*

The following brief extracts from English college inspection reports for the period 1997–2001 give a flavour of the way in which inspectors articulate their findings. The extracts are presented anonymously, but all inspection reports for colleges in the UK can be found on the web sites of the inspection agencies (see p.196 for a list of web addresses).

Much of the teaching is of high quality and lessons are well-planned. Aspects of business are illustrated by appropriate case studies and students' own experiences of employment. Sometimes teachers do not check sufficiently on students' understanding within lessons. A few students are allowed to dominate discussions to the exclusion of others.

(Curriculum Area: Business, Grade 3)

Group work is well planned and managed. Students enjoy this participative method of learning and work confidently. Teachers are skilful in using questioning techniques to further students' knowledge and understanding. Good use is made of students' work experiences to provide integration with theoretical topics. In a small minority of lessons, insufficient time was spent introducing the topic and relating it to previous learning.

(Curriculum Area: Childcare, Grade 1)

The college has strong links with local construction employers and with the community . . . All full-time construction teachers are paired with local companies with whom they maintain regular contact.

(Curriculum Area: Construction, Grade 2)

Students work steadily through assignments and results are carefully recorded. However, the work is not checked against an initial assessment of each student's capability and, in some lessons, teaching is not varied enough to cater for individual students' requirements . . . Teachers often introduce assignments without explaining how the skills practised can be applied. The attendance in some groups is low.

(Curriculum Area: Basic Skills, Grade 4)

The new management structure is well understood and is welcomed by staff. Lines of responsibility are clear, and there is greater involvement in the management of the college by staff at all levels. For example, 65 per cent of the staff are members of cross-college committees. Staff have a shared vision for the college and are committed to its success.

(Cross-college Provision, Grade 2)

In 1992, when the Conservative government took colleges out of LEA control and made them corporate bodies, it meant that 'Governing bodies and college principals were required to change their modus operandi almost overnight' as they switched from a 'service philosophy' to 'one akin to entrepreneurialism' (Shattock, 2000, p.89). Colleges were now required to recruit the majority of members of their governing bodies from the private sector, as these people were expected 'to impose a proactive market orientation on colleges that had previously been reactive and bureaucratic' (ibid., p.91). This policy has since been questioned following a series of financial and mismanagement scandals which were widely reported in the national media from the mid-1990s onward. In 1999, the Labour government changed the regulations on college governance to create governing bodies which had a better balance of representation from business and the community. Gleeson and Shain (1999, p.553), however, note that college governing bodies in FE 'remain largely self-selecting organisations accountable only to the Secretary of State, and not to the communities they serve'. The Chief Inspector of colleges in England reported in his 2001 annual report that, whilst 'most governing bodies conduct their business effectively', in a 'significant minority' of colleges, that is 14 per cent, governance was found to be unsatisfactory or poor (FEFC, 2001, p.41). As Gleeson and Shain (1999) argue, it is impossible to separate the problems of FE governance from wider debates about democracy, inclusive management styles, deregulation and, crucially, the role of FE itself. For the FE teachers, however, the nature and style of their college's governing body will affect their professional life, and having some knowledge and understanding of the way in which their college is governed could be helpful.

This chapter has stressed that FE colleges are large, complex and heterogeneous organisations. They are busy, dynamic places of learning with shifting populations of students of all ages. In the following chapters, we examine the implications of this complexity for teaching and learning.

Chapter 2

The student body

Who will I teach?

DIVERSE STUDENT BODY

One of the distinguishing features of the FE sector has always been the diversity of its student population. Since FE is essentially 'education for all', this is reflected in its student body in terms of age, gender, ability, attainment levels, economic, social and cultural background and differing learning needs. Teaching in FE presents a set of challenges that are quite different from those presented in primary or secondary education.

The following vignettes illustrate the diversity of the student body in FE:

College 1 (city based with 3 main sites and 6 High Street information technology centres)
33,422 students (50 per cent ethnic minority) mainly from city and neighbouring boroughs. Courses in all programme areas apart from agriculture and at all levels from basic skills to higher education. Significant proportion of provision is below level 2. Twelve per cent of students under 19, and 16 per cent of all students study full-time. College is open seven days a week all year.
(Source: FEFC Inspection Report, 2000/01)

College 2 (set in 190 hectares of farmland)
5011 students drawn from surrounding county and region, with some from elsewhere in UK and overseas. Courses in agriculture, horticulture, countryside management, veterinary nursing, animal care, equine studies, floristry, engineering, outdoor recreation management and business management. Twenty-two per cent of students under 19 and 18 per cent of all students study full-time.
(Source: FEFC Inspection Report, 2000/01)

College 3 (city based with 3 sites)
10,000 students (12.5 per cent ethnic minority) from city and surrounding area. Courses in all programme areas and all levels from basic skills to higher education. Nineteen per cent of students under 19 and 16 per cent of all students study full-time. College has invested in a training and enterprise park and is strengthening its international links.
(Source: FEFC Inspection Report, 1998/99)

Most teachers in FE will be expected to teach across a wide range of programmes that could include basic skills programmes at one end of the
spectrum and undergraduate or even postgraduate work, at the other.
Similarly the students may range from 14 to 65 and beyond in age. At the
time of writing one London college has some 90-year-olds amongst its student
population as well as some pre-16-year-old pupils from a local school. These
different age ranges are not confined to particular programmes of study. An A
level group, for example, will not necessarily include only those of 16–18 year-
olds as would be the case within a school sixth form.

Students in FE represent an enormous range of different circumstances and
any one class or group of students will be heterogeneous in nature. In this
sense, the work is real mixed-ability teaching. It is not only the ability of the
students which differs, however, but also their motivation, prior experience,
expectations and the way in which they are funded. They may also have very
different social and cultural backgrounds and their domestic circumstances
may be widely different. Some of the students may be returning to learning
after a long break, others may be continuing their education but in a different
environment. Others will be attempting to combine full-time employment
with part-time study or juggling the competing demands of family commitments and study requirements. Some students may have physical disabilities;
others may have emotional and behavioural difficulties. The teacher in FE has
to be sensitive to this diversity in the planning, preparation and delivery of
programmes.

The patterns of attendance will vary between full-time and part-time, day
or evening, employment release, block release or attendance at individually
designed short courses. An increasing number of students are registering as distance learners or open learners. Some students may be attending a college
solely to have prior learning accredited for the purpose of acquiring an NVQ.
Others may never attend the college but will be taught by college staff at their
place of employment.

Since August 1998 in England and Wales, there have also been increasing
numbers of students of compulsory school age attending colleges for part of
their week. Under Section 363 of the 1996 Education Act schools were
allowed to set aside aspects of the National Curriculum at key stage 4 for some
pupils in order to offer them wider opportunities for work-related learning.
Such opportunities include: attendance at college in order to pursue vocational
programmes; extended work placements on employers' premises; and other
forms of vocational provision. Some colleges now have significant numbers of
14, 15 and 16-year old school pupils attending specially designed vocational
taster programmes or participating in existing courses. This trend is likely to
increase given the current interest in increased flexibility at key stage 4 and the
planned introduction of vocational GCSEs from September 2002 (see
Chapter Three). The move towards coherent provision for the 14–19 age
group, currently under review, will undoubtedly impact on the FE sector.

The 2001 White Paper, *Schools – Achieving Success*, outlined a scenario in which schools might cease to be the dominant locus of learning for 14–19 year-olds:

> Supported by the effective use of ICT, young people's learning from the age of 14 will increasingly take place across a range of institutions and in the workplace, complemented by extra-curricular activities such as sport, the arts and voluntary work . . . for the first time there will also be the opportunity of a predominantly vocational programme for those with the aptitude, beginning at 14 and going right through to degree level.
>
> (DfES, 2001a, Chapter 4)

It is likely that new partnerships between schools, colleges, training providers, businesses and their local Learning and Skills Councils will be forged. For staff in FE, teaching these 'new kids on the block' has proved challenging. For the young people it has often provided the introduction to further education and/or training, which they may not have considered while in school.

The attempts to develop more flexible provision for 14–16 year olds is partly a response to the so-called 'status zero' problem. The 'status zero' group of young people, as identified by Istance and Williamson (1996), are those who disappear each year from official statistics at both local and national level (see also Pearce and Hillman, 1998). They have variously been labelled: 'disaffected'; 'non-participants'; 'hard to reach'; 'socially excluded'; and 'at risk'. The current term, which has all the hallmarks of a public relations makeover, is 'not settled'. In September 1999, Education Maintenance Allowances (EMAs) (up to £40 per week) were introduced in 15 English LEAs to encourage disadvantaged young people aged 16–19 to stay in full-time education. Other initiatives at local level do not, however, seem to have had much effect on the 'not settled' who can amount to as much as 10 per cent of the 16–19 cohort in some areas of the country. The *Time off for Study* legislation, introduced in 1998 to give 16–18 year olds entitlement to a day off per week for part-time study, has been less than successful. This is not surprising for it puts the onus on the young person rather than the employer. The government has at least acknowledged the naivety of this approach, stating in its recent evaluation that the following barriers are preventing young people from approaching their employers: they may be apprehensive; many employers disregard the need for training; and careers services do not have the resources to support young people (DfEE, 2000b).

As we saw in Chapter 1, there are now more opportunities to enter HE via the FE route through the introduction of access programmes and 'two plus two' degrees. This has introduced a cohort of undergraduates to some FE colleges' student population. On the other hand, there are now more programmes aimed at encouraging people of all ages to improve their basic literacy and numeracy skills and some of them will be enrolled on government-funded schemes.

The need for FE colleges to market their services more actively both at home and abroad has led to an increasing number of overseas students pursuing courses in British colleges. Some colleges have established overseas offices, or agents, to market their courses and to attract overseas students; others send staff abroad to teach on college programmes. Many colleges are involved in vocational education and training research and development programmes sponsored by the European Commission or by the British Council. These may involve student or staff exchanges and study tours. Overseas students may be studying courses to improve their English language competence; others will be pursuing vocational qualifications.

Colleges now have to cope with a much wider range of student abilities, including those students with learning difficulties. The 1996 report of the Tomlinson Committee's review of FE's provision for students with learning difficulties and disabilities, *Inclusive Learning*, highlighted the need for the sector to make further improvements and to embrace the concept of inclusive learning (Tomlinson, 1996). As Dee (1999, p.141) explains, Tomlinson sought to reject the stereotyping of people with learning difficulties and/or physical disabilities. The Beattie Committee in Scotland was established to: 'review the range of needs among young people who require additional support to participate in post school education, training and employment; the assessment of need; and the quality and effectiveness of provision in improving skills and employability'. In 1998, the FEFC allocated £2million to support the inclusive learning quality initiative (FEFC, 1999). This was complemented by the provision made to implement the recommendations of the Kennedy Report (Kennedy, 1997), *Learning Works*, which highlighted the need for colleges to widen participation to include those under-represented groups in their communities. In his 2000/01 report, the FEFC's Chief Inspector noted that the development of an inclusive approach to learning was 'increasingly significant within the sector' but that staff were still not being given 'the training or time they need to put college intentions into practice' (FEFC, 2001, p.57). Dee (1999, p.142) argues that inclusion is a 'process and not an absolute state' and that colleges need to work towards inclusion (see also Bradley, Dee and Wilenius, 1994). An example of how colleges are trying to be more inclusive is illustrated by the following list of groups of people found in one English college's student magazine and who are encouraged to join courses: homeless; ex-offenders; people with mental health difficulties; people from ethnic minority communities; full-time carers; women in refuge; travellers; care leavers; single parents on low incomes; long-term unemployed; and those overcoming drug or alcohol dependency. Riddell, Wilson and Baron (1999), however, have analysed the position of people with learning difficulties within the 'education market' and the 'social care market' and argue that there is still a long way to go before their voice is properly heard and their needs met.

We are very aware that this brief discussion of the FE sector's response to the needs of people with learning difficulties and/or physical disabilities raises far more questions than can be dealt with here. Clough and Barton (1995, p.2) point out that people with what were once, and sometimes still, are called 'special needs' are the 'recipients of powerful professional categories' which 'envelop their identities'. There is also considerable debate about whether their needs are best met in specialist provision and the case for integration is by no means fully accepted. Corbett (1997, p.171) writing about young people, notes:

> The tensions within the inclusive ideology are evident. At one level, concepts of 'entitlement for all' and quality assurance measures suggest that the most vulnerable young people are no longer to be offered a second-rate education and training diet but are to be assessed and guided in a way that equates with the treatment given to their peers. At another level, they are no longer seen as 'special' or in need of additional protective care, which can open up opportunities for real progression into mainstream developments but can also mean that they become casualties of a market culture in which the weakest go to the wall. If they are included, this means inclusion into a harsh and uncaring economy where there are no favours given, only deals bargained for.

For further reading on the issue of inclusion see Chapter Ten.

Although funding for adult education and recreational programmes has been subject to governmental cut-backs, most FE colleges still offer some provision for adults wishing to pursue leisure or recreational programmes (see Unwin, 1999a). This adds another dimension to the work of colleges and to the student profile. Many of these students may be studying at outreach centres or in premises away from the main college site. It should also be remembered that there are eight residential adult education colleges in the UK: six in England, one in Wales and one in Scotland.

It is clear that the targets imposed for growth within the FE sector will mean that the student population is likely to become even more diverse. The FE teacher will be faced with more changes and challenges as colleges address the key priorities of widening participation, inclusion and raising standards. The inclusive college is one which caters for the widest possible student population with an enormous diversity of learning needs, where programmes may be delivered through a range of techniques. The inclusive college has to serve community needs as well as respond to a commercial market.

STUDENT NEEDS AND MOTIVATION

The motivations of such a diverse range of students will obviously be widely different, and the ways in which students learn will vary in pace and style. This requires a flexible teaching approach from FE teachers in order to provide for the needs of individual learners (see Chapter Five). The teacher will also have a central role to play in other aspects of learning support, for example through guidance and counselling, both on entry to a programme and throughout its duration. Returning learners may also need support not just in the subject being studied but in how to study it. These competing pressures on the FE teacher's time are not easy to balance when the substantial managerial and administrative loads which are inherent in most vocational programmes are added to them. How then is the new teacher in FE to prepare him or herself to be an effective practitioner?

Reflection

We now present a series of vignettes of typical students to be found in any college. We would like you to read each one and consider the following questions:

1 As a teacher what perceptions do you have of each of these students and of their learning needs?
2 How do you think each student feels about the learning situation and about you as a teacher?

Martin

Martin is 18 years old and is studying three A level subjects full time at his local college. His school experience was rather negative although he achieved four GCSE subjects with grades A*–C. His parents were not enthusiastic about his transfer to the local college at 16 and would have preferred him to have remained in the sixth form at school, as his sister had done. His school, however, had a sixth form entry requirement of five GCSEs. In addition one of the subjects which Martin wished to study at A level, psychology, was not available at school.

Since transferring to college, Martin has found A level courses particularly demanding and he has had to re-sit some of his modules. This means that he is often behind with his work. Nevertheless, he enjoys college and has taken an active part in drama productions and student affairs. He has enjoyed the freedom of being allowed to organise his own time although he has found it difficult to meet deadlines for handing in essays. Drama and music are now taking up more and more of his time and he has enquired about transferring to a Performing Arts programme.

His sister, now a medical student, has told him that 'the idea is ridiculous' and that he should not tell their parents about his loss of interest in his A level courses. She feels that he should just 'make the best of things and get on with it', adding that less time spent on drama productions and more time spent on writing coursework essays would be the sensible option.

Martin remains unconvinced, particularly since the drama tutor has said that he should think about auditions for drama school.

Trent

Trent is on a full-time GNVQ Intermediate programme in Leisure and Tourism. He left school last year with 4 GCSEs, grades D–E. He had no idea what he wanted to do and there was very little on offer at his school for those who had failed to achieve good GCSE grades. His mother insisted that he find some further course of study because she did not want him 'hanging around the house'. Because of his interest in football he thought that the course might be a reasonable way of spending the time. The course also provides an opportunity to gain a coaching certificate.

The course has proved to be a disappointment, mainly because it is not what he expected it would be. He enjoys the practical work, particularly playing football and spending time in the gymnasium. He dislikes the theoretical aspects of the course and finds the assignments very difficult. He cannot keep up with the volume of work and is constantly late in handing in assignments. He feels that he is falling further and further behind and is unable to manage his time to do anything about it.

He has two part-time jobs; one of them is in a sports retail outlet, the other in a local restaurant, usually washing-up and preparing vegetables. These are taking up more and more of his time, not just in the evenings and at weekends but sometimes on days when he is supposed to be at college.

Trent's mother was unaware that he was missing time from college. She is usually out of the house early in the morning before Trent leaves for college but one morning his tutor rang before she had left for work. The tutor was enquiring why Trent had not been at college for the last three days. As the conversation developed it became apparent that Trent's frequent absence was causing the tutor real concern. He was also seriously behind with his work. This came as a great surprise to Trent's mother who was hoping that the course would help Trent's re-engagement with education.

Margaret

Margaret is 42 and is a student in her second year of a 'two plus two' degree programme which is run jointly by her college and the local university. The first two years of the programme are delivered by the college and involve a social science foundation course followed by a first-year undergraduate programme in one area of the social sciences. Margaret has chosen to continue her studies in economics. Before starting the course Margaret had helped her husband in his building business; she had been responsible for the clerical and administrative side of the work and had dealt with the accounts and payment of salaries.

Although Margaret left school at 16 she had always pursued some form of part-time education through attendance at evening classes. She had gained qualifications in bookkeeping, typing and accounts, which had enabled her to help in the family business. However, when her two daughters started their secondary education, Margaret felt she would like to have the opportunity of pursuing a full-time course. She approached her local college about possible options and was surprised to find that she could enrol on the degree programme.

She approached the first year with trepidation and found the return to full-time education extremely unsettling. Although she found she could cope with the work she was always anxious about the expectations of staff and about the adequacy of her performance. She was particularly concerned about oral presentations and disliked having to give papers to other students and to lecturers who appeared to be about half her age.

She successfully completed the first year of the programme and achieved particularly high marks in the statistics examination. Now she is in the second year she feels more confident about the work and is doing well in her chosen specialization, economics. Nevertheless, she finds the work demanding and is anxious about the transfer to the university for the third and fourth years of the course. She fears that most of the students will be the age of her daughters. The college staff have assured her that she will be able to cope but she remains unconvinced.

Gary

Gary has been in college for six weeks on a craft diploma course in catering. He is 16 years old and left school with few formal qualifications. The catering course is essentially practical and provides the opportunity to acquire National Vocational Qualifications (NVQs) in catering and other related subjects such as food handling and hygiene. Basic numeracy and communication skills are also included in the course content.

Although keen at the beginning of term, Gary's enthusiasm began to wane after three weeks. He started to miss theory classes and by the fifth week he was turning up late for practical sessions. Staff noticed that he was not wearing correct kitchen uniform in spite of being repeatedly told about it. He appeared to resent any criticism from the staff.

The quality of his practical work is good when he is left on his own to complete a task. He is aggressive when asked to work with other students and takes extended breaks, which delay the completion of any joint activities. Other students have begun to resent this and have mentioned it to the lecturer in charge. The lecturer has discussed this with Gary who has given assurances about his future conduct. Gary has been told that he will not be allowed to participate in the work experience placement unless his behaviour improves.

During a practical session Gary became involved in an argument with another student who had suggested that Gary could not weigh or add up quantities correctly. Gary became abusive and threatened the student. He also used offensive language to the kitchen assistant who has lodged a formal complaint with the vice-principal. The catering lecturer has intervened and asked Gary to discuss the matter with him fully.

Arpinder

Arpinder works for a firm of accountants and attends his local college one day a week for an accountancy course. He is 32 and decided to study for accounting qualifications because he has friends who run a successful accountancy practice. He sees the course as the first step towards achieving full professional qualifications. He realises, however, that it will take a long time. Before starting his present job he worked for a retail chain as an assistant store manager, but he did not like the long and irregular hours of work.

The company for whom he works is reasonably supportive of Arpinder's attendance at college and allows him time off work to attend. However, they are not prepared to pay his fees. So far he has been able to meet the cost himself.

He is very keen to progress as quickly as possible and has found the course helpful, although he has been irritated by the repeated changes in the teaching staff. During a recent busy period his firm asked him to remain at work on college days with the promise of making up the time later when he needs some exam revision time. He cannot envisage the situation improving in the foreseeable future. In addition, his father has recently been seriously ill and he has had to spend a considerable amount of time supporting his family.

He is becoming anxious about the effect this is having on his course and the possible outcome for his examination result. He feels he has invested heavily in the course in terms of financial, personal and emotional commitment. He is becoming increasingly dispirited and depressed about the possibility of not meeting the goals which he has set for himself.

Grace

For three mornings a week Grace attends a basic skills programme run by the FE college at a local community hall. She is a single parent of 28 and has three children aged 6, 8 and 10. She had an extremely negative and disrupted school experience, having attended four different schools in a period of six years. She left school at the earliest possible opportunity without any formal qualifications. She did not expect, nor want, to have any further contact with the education system. On leaving school she took a series of low-paid, unskilled jobs none of which lasted for very long. She has had no paid employment since the birth of her first child.

When her children started school she began to take an interest in their work and in some of the activities in which the school sought parental involvement. She was interested in helping in a practical way but when approached about the possibility of 'listening to readers' she became very anxious. She was reluctant to become involved in case her own deficiencies were exposed.

When her husband left, Grace decided to try and find some part-time employment but soon realised that it was virtually impossible to find any work unless she improved her reading and writing skills. She also wanted to improve her basic arithmetical skills. She found that there were a series of classes being held in her local community hall, just ten minutes' walk from home. The FE college had been contracted to deliver them at a series of neighbourhood sites, as part of a European Social Fund (ESF) sponsored project. It was hoped that by making an initial contact with FE through an outreach activity students might be encouraged to continue their studies at the college itself.

Grace was extremely nervous about returning to study. For the first few weeks she attempted to disguise the nature of the course when talking to friends and neighbours. However, after a short time she began to gain confidence and discovered a new group of friends amongst the class members. The atmosphere was extremely supportive and the lecturers friendly. She began to look forward to the mornings spent improving her writing skills and started to enjoy reading. This new found confidence tended to spill over into other areas of her life. She was approached about standing as a parent governor at her daughter's school.

Grace now wants to continue her studies with the intention of gaining some qualifications. She has discovered that the next stage of the programme will be held in the college and not in the local hall. She is reluctant to travel the 5 miles (8 kilometres) to the college but she is even more reluctant to become a student there. The prospect of entering a formal educational institution is threatening; she is concerned about her ability to cope with the work.

George

At 35, George has been unemployed for the past 18 months. Prior to that he was employed as a storeman at a manufacturing company. The company was forced to close resulting in some 350 job losses. Some of the skilled workers eventually managed to find alternative employment but the large number of unskilled workers, like George, found it virtually impossible to find work.

George and several of his old workmates now attend college as part of the government's New Deal programme. This scheme is open to those who have been unemployed for more than six months. Funding for the programme is provided by the government through the Local Learning and Skills Council (LLSC). The LLSC is responsible for managing the programmes locally and may contract FE colleges to provide the off-the-job training element. All programmes must lead to the acquisition of NVQs. Trainees are paid a weekly rate, the receipt of which is dependent upon attendance at the programme. Colleges receive payment for the trainees, part of which is related to successful outcomes.

George is attending a painting and decorating training programme. He is hoping that even if he does not secure employment in a company, he may be able to become self-employed. In addition to the practical elements of the programme, sessions on how to complete job applications, interview techniques and presentation skills are provided by college staff. Having already suffered 18 months of unemployment, George is unsure about the value of some of the programme in helping him to secure a job.

Cass

Cass is a Year 11 pupil at a large, inner-city comprehensive school. She attends the local FE college one day a week as a part of a link programme which the college runs for a number of local secondary schools. The programme, entitled *Learning for Work*, is designed for those pupils who have been 'disapplied' from parts of the National Curriculum at key stage 4 in order to pursue a more vocationally-oriented curriculum. The programme includes some vocational 'taster' courses where students can choose particular modules, for example, catering or hairdressing, in which they might be interested for the future. It also includes an enterprise activity where students are expected to develop, promote and sell a product or service as part of a team building process. Students also work towards key skills in communications and information technology and there is a one-to-one personal target-setting tutorial with a tutor. She will be able to go on a placement at a well-known restaurant during the second term of the course.

Cass enjoys the day at the college and prefers the time she spends there to the time spent at school. She is particularly interested in the catering module and hopes to be able to continue with some form of catering course once she has completed year 11. She is not too happy about the enterprise project because she has been placed in a group with some pupils from another school who are very noisy and who want to disrupt the sessions as much as possible. She is afraid that their behaviour will reflect badly on her and that, as a result, the tutor may not recommend her for next year's catering course.

Sue

Saturday courses are a relatively recent development at Sue's local FE college and have received a fair amount of publicity in the local media. A wide range of courses are offered from recreational and leisure classes to courses leading to business and professional qualifications. Sue has enrolled on a ten-week short course within the Saturday college programme entitled: 'How to market your business'.

Sue has recently set up a small business providing household cleaning and ironing services, and employs five people on a part-time basis. The company has bought two vehicles and hired some office accommodation. This has involved some financial outlay and Sue is afraid that she may not be able to sustain the initial level of business growth. She realises that she needs to improve her marketing and promotional activity and, for this reason, has enrolled on the college course. The fees are quite expensive for her because the course is a 'full-cost' course. Nevertheless, she hopes that the outlay will be worthwhile and that business will improve.

She is not too happy about giving up her Saturdays for the course but realises that this is the only way she can attend. Sue is anxious to secure value for money for the investment which she has made in course fees, and hopes that the experienced college staff will be a useful resource on which she can draw.

Hussein

Hussein has recently arrived from the Middle East and has joined an intensive English language course at his local college before beginning a degree in engineering at a nearby university. He realises that he will have to work extremely hard in order to pass the English language competence test set by the university. This is a condition of entry on to the degree programme. He is concerned because there are 20 students on the English programme, from many different parts of the world and with a very wide range of English language competence. He is concerned that the weaker students will hold him back.

About half the students work as *au pairs* with English families and seem, as far as Hussein is concerned, to be using the classes as an opportunity to socialise. They do not hand in required pieces of homework and are reluctant to join in with some of the 'speaking' exercises. He feels that he is working hard and trying his best and finds the behaviour of the young *au pairs* a distraction and an irritation. He wonders if he should transfer to a small private language school where he knows the fees are higher but where, perhaps, he will receive more individual attention.

Phyllis
Phyllis is 50 and has recently joined an adult 'return to learn' programme at her local FE college. The timetable is arranged to suit individual needs and interests and it is possible to build a programme from a wide range of college courses. Phyllis has decided to concentrate on information technology and business administration. She is greatly enjoying the college environment and the opportunity it has provided for making new friends. There are times when she would prefer the course to be better organised, and has already spoken to the head of adult studies about it.

One aspect of the course particularly concerns her: the work experience placement. She will be expected to complete a period of work experience during the course and she feels that this is quite unnecessary for someone of her maturity. She is also concerned that she may be placed in a company with which she has contact on a personal basis. Her husband is a prominent solicitor in the town. She is hoping she may be able to gain exemption from this part of the programme although the lecturer in charge has said that it is an integral part of the course. Phyllis hopes she may be able to have a word with the vice-principal about it.

All of these students will have developed their own perspective on learning and will communicate that perspective through their behaviour in the classroom, workshop, tutorial, seminar group and so on. Their prior experience of education will have shaped their attitudes to learning, to teachers and to their fellow students. These issues are explored in detail in Chapter 5 and in Chapter 6, where we will return to these vignettes and consider which teaching and assessment strategies might be most appropriate for helping students such as these to learn most effectively.

Diverse curricula

What will I teach?

Just as the range of students in FE colleges is too wide to enable it to be described in tidy categorisations, to talk about an FE curriculum as if it were a homogeneous entity would be totally misleading. However, as the FEFC's chief inspector has pointed out, 'The qualifications available in further education colleges fall into one of four broad categories; that is, general education, general vocational education, job-related training, and non-vocational or leisure courses' (FEFC, 2001:71). Such divisions are not as simple as they might at first appear because even within these broad bands there is often a wide range of courses or programmes of study on offer. Figure 3.1 presents a categorisation of FE provision into 14 programme areas. As such, it extends the model presented in Figure 1.3 in Chapter 1. Colleges may also differ from each other in the curricula that they offer because of differences in their size, culture and location. Increasingly, colleges are talking about 'individualised learning programmes' for students. Such programmes imply that students should be able to access learning programmes as and when they wish and in whatever location, including perhaps from the comfort of their own homes via electronic means. However, the physical achievement of such flexibility is still a long way off and its appropriateness hotly contested. It should be remembered that many students value the opportunity of learning with others and of working co-operatively, and that learning within a community can challenge the prejudices and limited horizons of learners that can easily remain unchallenged when learning becomes an entirely individual affair.

It is not the purpose of this chapter to discuss the appropriateness, or inappropriateness, of particular curricular models or to embark upon curriculum design. Nor do we intend to describe what an optimum further education entitlement should be. These issues have been debated elsewhere (see, inter alia, Finegold et al., 1990; Richardson et al., 1993; Dearing, 1996; DfEE, 1997; Raffe et al., 1998; Young and Leney, 1999; Hodgson and Spours, 2001). The 16–19 phase of education has been, for example, particularly resistant to change, and the divide between vocational and academic routes has yet to be bridged. Young (1993, p.220) has categorised the English and Welsh 16–19 curriculum as representing 'divisive specialisation' with:

| Area 1
Sciences and Mathematics | Area 2
Land-based Provision | Area 3
Construction | Area 4
Engineering, Technology and Manufacturing | Area 5
Business Administration, Management and Professional | Area 6
Information and Communication Technology | Area 7
Retailing, Customer Service and Transportation |
|---|---|---|---|---|---|---|
| Mathematics and sciences, including physics, chemistry, biology and geology. Environmental and conservation studies. | Agriculture, horticulture, equine, animal care, gardening, fishing, environmental practice, chain-saw use and landscaping. | Construction trades and crafts, including electrical, mechanical and engineering services. Surveying and highways. DIY. | Marine/aero/ automotive, car/cycle maintenance, chemical, energy, electrical/electronic and mechanical engineering. Manufacturing, processing, coating, mining, quarrying and extraction. | All aspects of business, administration and management, legal, estate agency, accounts, economics, assessor/teacher/ trainer awards, marketing, quality assurance and personnel staff. | ICT users, engineers and technicians, programming/ software website design. Software use, DTP, CAD and keyboarding skills. | Merchandising/ distribution and packing, import and export, warehousing, call centres, fork-truck driving, air/marine/ road/rail and goods transportation. |

| Area 8
Hospitality, Sports Leisure and Travel | Area 9
Hairdressing and Beauty Therapy | Area 10
Health, Social Care and Public Services | Area 11
Visual and Performing Arts and Media | Area 12
Humanities | Area 13
English, Languages and Communications | Area 14
Foundation Programmes |
|---|---|---|---|---|---|---|
| Hotel/restaurant reception, food and beverages, catering, cooking. Travel and tourism, leisure services, sports coaching, exercise and fitness, outdoor activities, recreational sports and games. Travel agency. | Hairdressing, beauty therapy, massage, massage for sports, therapeutic techniques. | Care/health/dental, counselling, parenting, pre-retirement, bereavement, assertiveness, playwork, public/emergency services. | Art and design, crafts, ceramics, carving, dressmaking, embroidery, weaving, photography. Performing arts/theatre, music, dance. Journalism, media/video/radio/ printing, design and technology. Arts management. | General studies, history, genealogy, sociology, psychology, geography, law. Religious studies/ comparative religions, philosophy, classics, ancient languages. Access to HE. | English, communications, writing, French/ German/Italian/ Spanish, etc., community languages, EFL. | Employability programmes, foundation studies, life skills, basic skills, key skills, ESOL, citizenship, programmes for those with learning difficulties and disabilities. Return-to-work and vocational skills. |

Figure 3.1 Fourteen areas of learning

- sharp academic/vocational division;
- insulated subjects;
- absence of any concept of the curriculum as a whole.

In contrast to England, Scotland, which has always had its own separate education system, has been moving towards a more unified 16–19 curriculum since the mid-1980s and reached an important stage with the publication of *Higher Still* in 1994 (see Scottish Office, 1994). The Scottish vision is to establish a single ladder of academic and vocational modules, aimed at both older and younger learners. Since the establishment of the Welsh Assembly, Wales has signalled its desire to break away from England and develop a uni-tised framework of qualifications which, like the Scottish approach, allows for greater flexibility in mixing academic and vocational provision. Northern Ireland has the same qualification system as England, but, again, devolved powers to the Northern Ireland Assembly may result in a different pattern of educational reform. In 1996, just prior to winning the 1997 General Election, the Labour Party in England published *Aiming Higher*, which called for the broadening of A level programmes, improvements to vocational programmes, and the merger of all 16–19 qualifications within a single credit-based frame-work (see Hodgson and Spours, 1999). This drew on the 1996 Dearing Review which examined the complex system of regulation governing award-bearing courses for 16–19 year olds in England, Wales and Northern Ireland. Dearing's concern, probably shared by thousands of teachers and managers in the post-compulsory sector, was for greater coherence in the system. One outcome of the Dearing report was the reduction in the number of Awarding Bodies, mainly as a result of the merger of boards previously responsible for the award of vocational and academic qualifications. For example, BTEC merged with the University of London Examinations and Assessment Council (ULEAC) to form EdExcel. Once in government, Labour watered down its earlier proposals and published *Qualifying for Success* (DfEE, 1997). This caused Hodgson and Spours (1999, p.124) to conclude that 'New Labour's evolutionary approach to qualifications reform is practical but piecemeal and somewhat backward looking' and 'essentially reactive to the Conservative legacy', reflecting 'a historical preoccupation with academic learning'.

In September 2000, steps were taken along the road of reform in England with the introduction of vocational A levels (AVCEs), which replaced GNVQ Advanced, and the modularisation of A levels into groups of three and six units. This reform was intended to pave the way for greater flexibility post-16, thus affording students the opportunity of mixing vocational and academic qualifications.

These qualifications are now based on groups of three, six and twelve units, with the new Advanced Subsidiary (AS) level comprised of three units, the full Advanced (A) level six units, and AVCEs six units, or twelve units if the double award is taken. Assessment within the new AVCE is now graded in the same way as A level. The reforms, commonly referred to as *Curriculum 2000,* also introduced the opportunity for key skills (communication, application of number and information technology) to be available to all students, not just those pursuing a vocational programme. Before we continue with a discussion of Curriculum 2000, it is necessary to include some analysis of the development of key skills.

The idea that young people should develop generic skills that take priority sat above subject specific knowledge or practical skills has been debated by educationalists, employers and policymakers for at least 40 years in the UK (see Green, 1997). These so-called skills have been variously labelled 'generic', 'core', 'interpersonal', 'transferable' and 'life skills'. In 1979, the then Further Education Unit (FEU) published a landmark report, *A Basis for Choice,* which called for a 'core skills' curriculum, an idea that was forcibly promoted by the Confederation of British Industry (CBI) in its 1989 report, *Towards a Skills Revolution.* The basic idea is that there is a definable set of core or key skills, in, for example, communication and problem solving, and that are essential for employability, for transferring learning from one context to another, and for learning to learn. Over the years, various lists and categorisations of these skills have been produced. Most notoriously, the Manpower Services Commission (MSC) produced a list of 103 core skills to be acquired by trainees on the Youth Training Scheme in the 1980s. At the time of writing, QCA in England has specified six categories of what, since the 1996 Dearing Review of 16–19 Qualifications, have come to be labelled Key Skills:

- Communication;
- Application of Number;
- Information Technology;
- Improving Own Learning;
- Problem Solving;
- Working with Others.

According to the Learning and Skills Development Agency (LSDA) and the DfES, these skills are 'the generic and transferable skills that everyone needs to succeed in education and training, in work, and in life general' (LSDA, 2001a). Green (1997), however, argues that this fixation with key skills 'represents an impoverished form of general education' that has always been missing from the UK's approach to vocational education. There are complex philosophical and educational debates about whether such skills can be neatly categorised and whether they can be separated from the actual context of the subject that is being studied or, indeed, the workplace. The policymakers are certainly confused: one minute they advocate that key skills should be seen as embedded in subjects and contexts and so should be developed in an integrated fashion; the next minute they are saying it is possible to isolate key skills in order to set tests to assess them (see Unwin and Wellington, 2001, for a detailed discussion).

Under *Curriculum 2000*, a student could put together the following pro-gramme:

Year 1

AVCE Business	AS German	AS Maths	Key Skills
(Double award)	3 units	3 units	Communication level 3

Year 2

AVCE Business			
(Double award)	A2 Maths	Key Skills	
12 units	3 units	Information technology level 3	

A student might also wish to include some NVQ units if he or she had suffi-cient opportunities to demonstrate the skills required in a practical situation, for example through work experience or a part-time job. In the summer of 2001, widespread concern from teachers, students, teacher trade unions, pro-fessional associations, university admissions tutors and educational researchers about the new reforms led Estelle Morris, Secretary of State for Education and Skills, to announce a major review of *Curriculum 2000* by the Qualifications and Curriculum Authority (QCA 2001a, 2001b). Although teachers and stu-dents had welcomed certain aspects of the reforms (e.g. greater choice of subject in the first year of advanced study, and modularity), there were major problems caused by the rushed implementation (see Hodgson and Spours, 2001). As a result of QCA's review, the single key skills qualification was abandoned, although individual awards are available in each of the key skills. Further changes are also being considered including a reduction in the amount and timing of external assessment for AS level qualifications. It is clear that the debate around the 16–19 curriculum is set to run for some time yet. Also the focus of the academic/vocational debate has now shifted to the 14–16 phase with the proposed introduction from September 2002 of vocational GCSEs (General Certificate of Secondary Education).

Similarly, qualifications available for those in the work-based route have been the subject of reform over the past decade or more. Many young people attend college on a part-time basis in order to complement and accredit expe-rience gained in employment, or as part of a Modern Apprenticeship programme. National Vocational Qualifications (NVQs), were introduced in the early 1990s, following the establishment of the National Council for Vocational Qualifications (NCVQ) in 1986 (see Raggatt and Williams, 1999, for a detailed critique of the origins of NVQs). The Scottish equivalent of NVQs are called SVQs. NVQs are designed to confirm occupational compe-tence, put simply, that someone is qualified to carry out a specific job, for example, as a plumber or a chef. There has been a continuing debate since the introduction of NVQs about the appropriateness of these competence-based qualifications in terms of their underpinning rationale, their assessment

processes, their lack of specified content and their bureaucratic recording procedures (see, inter alia, Smithers, 1993; Hyland, 1994; Hodkinson and Issitt,
1995; Beaumont, 1996; Robinson, 1996). Since their introduction NVQs
have been continually revised and re-specified.

In addition to NVQs, there are thousands of vocational qualifications
that remain outside the National Qualifications Framework (see Fig. 3.2).
Such examples include BTEC National awards and those certificates offered
by trade and professional bodies. In 1998, the FEFC stated that 55 per cent
of qualifications funded by the Council could be described as 'other', that is,
qualifications that were not GCSE/A level, GNVQ, or NVQs (FEFC,
1998). Although attempts have been made to rein everything into a
common National Qualifications Framework by creating broad levels of
equivalence across different qualifications, the task is far from easy, since the
qualifications being compared are not the same and are often designed to
achieve different purposes. For example, an apprentice following a level 3
programme as part of his, or her, Modern Apprenticeship in Engineering
Manufacture will be taking units in hydraulics and pneumatics. The
approach may be quite different from that taken on an A level programme
in either maths or physics and yet both qualifications will be set at level 3 on
the framework.

A further part of the consolidation process seen as important in the development of the National Qualifications Framework was the merger in 1997 of
the NCVQ and the School Curriculum Assessment Authority (SCAA) to
form the Qualifications and Curriculum Authority (QCA). Within its remit
is the approval of awarding bodies, to ensure that, 'All qualifications comply
with rigorous standards of performance and quality assurance, and are provided by approved awarding bodies' (FEFC, 2000/01:72). In Scotland, the
Scottish Qualifications Authority (SQA) covers both the responsibilities of the
QCA and the awarding bodies in that it develops, accredits, assesses and cer-
tifies all qualifications other than university degrees. Scotland has its own
Scottish Credit and Qualifications Framework.

This brief introduction serves to highlight the complexity, and for the
new teacher perhaps confusion, that currently surrounds the notion of a
'curriculum for FE'. In reality there is no FE curriculum as its curricular traditions derive from a range of complex origins and prepare students for
different destinations. The purpose of this chapter is to familiarise the new
or intending FE teacher with the range and diversity of curricular offerings
within any one college, while, at the same time, reminding all teachers that
post-compulsory qualifications are subject to constant change. This is
inevitable since there are a large number of stakeholders in the post-compulsory curriculum. Squires (1987) has suggested that, 'It is at this point
that the "radical monopoly", to use Illich's phrase, of the education system
breaks down, and a plethora of institutions and interests become involved'
(Squires, 1987:96).

Level of qualification	General		Vocationally-related	Occupational
5	Higher-level qualifications			Level 5 NVQ
4				Level 4 NVQ
3 advanced level	A level	Free-standing mathematics units level 3	Vocational A level (Advanced GNVQ)	Level 3 NVQ
2 intermediate level	GCSE grade A*-C	Free-standing mathematics units level 2	Intermediate GNVQ	Level 2 NVQ
1 foundation level	GCSE grade D-G	Free-standing mathematics units level 1	Foundation GNVQ	Level 1 NVQ
Entry level	Certificate of (educational) achievement			

Figure 3.2 National qualifications framework

There are some compelling reasons for reform, not least among them the need to improve the quantity and quality of our vocational education and training in order to enhance the UK's competitiveness, particularly in relation to Germany, France, Japan and the USA (see, Green and Steadman, 1996; Brown, Lauder and Green, 2001). In addition the government has set ambitious targets for the FE sector, arguing that, 'Further education is a crucial part of the government's strategy to combat social exclusion, unemployment and skills shortages. Raising educational standards is critical to the government's social and economic agenda' (National Audit Office, 2001:1). Figure 3.3 is intended to indicate the large number of influences which may be impacting upon curriculum design. In addition, the balance of these influences will shift in response to changes in government policy, the numbers and types of students enrolling, the variations in funding mechanisms and so on. This raises

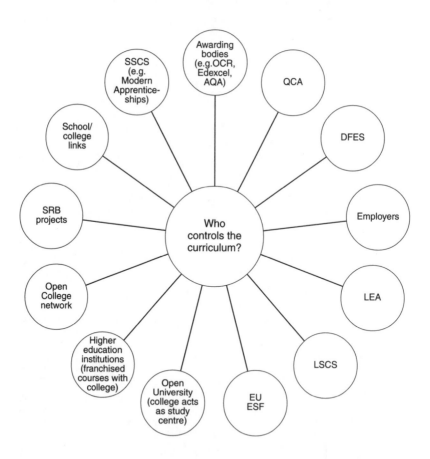

Figure 3.3 Influences on curriculum design

questions about the control of the curriculum. Are education professionals within the FE sector increasingly managers of the curriculum rather than curriculum designers since much of the curriculum is externally imposed? Bloomer (1997, p.188) has argued that:

> There has, during the 1980s and 1990s been a progressive narrowing of the curriculum. In policy, planning and, to some extent, practitioner circles it has come to mean little more than a prescription of 'content' coupled with a series of checks for its successful implementation. 'Objectives', 'outcomes' and 'quality assurance' now cover all, while 'delivery' is the metaphor to describe the process.

There are several reasons why FE curricula are so complex and diverse. A major reason is the shifting nature of the student population, a profile of which was provided in Chapter 2. Differing modes of attendance and patterns of learning may also determine what the curriculum looks like. Students who enter FE colleges do so at different ages and stages of their educational development. Achievement is not age-related, as it tends to be in the compulsory school sector, particularly in England and Wales where National Curriculum testing relates assessment to performance at key stages at the ages of 7, 11 and 14. In contrast in an FE college, a GCSE in history, for example, can be taken at 17 or 70, and students may be achieving basic numeracy at 35 or even older. This is likely to be increasingly the case given the government's commitment to raising the standard of adult basic literacy and numeracy following the publication of the Moser (1999) report, *A Fresh Start: Improving Literacy and Numeracy:* and the introduction of a national strategy for adult basic literacy and numeracy, *Skills for Life* (see DfES 2001b). If the concept of lifelong learning is to take hold this means that individuals could be moving in and out of colleges throughout their lifetime. In the future they may not even have to attend the college but will be able to access learning programmes by a range of routes, for example through computer-based learning.

The 1996 Higginson Report made recommendations for an £84 million investment in hi-tech initiatives for the FE sector in order to increase the use of new Information and Learning Technology (ILT) in FE (FEFC, 1996d). From 2001, the Joint Information Systems Committee (JISC) has been responsible for providing colleges in England with resources to improve their information technology facilities, including internet access, to enhance teaching and learning. In Scotland, the Beattie Resources for Inclusiveness in Technology and Education Initiative (BRITE) has allocated funds to create a virtual staffroom where staff in FE colleges can meet to discuss ILT-related issues. Andrew Duncan, Team Leader of the Social Inclusion and Learning Technologies Team at the DfES, has explained how ILT in colleges 'is now positioned as part of the wider strategy for lifelong learning, which encompasses e-learning in general and specific measures to close the digital divide' (Duncan, 2001, p.36). More and more people are using ILT facilities in their homes and at work, but as Duncan acknowledges, there is a significant divide between those who do have this access and those who do not. Some teachers in FE may find that their students have much more sophisticated ILT skills and equipment than they do.

Students, of course, need support in mastering the skills required to use the new learning technologies effectively. Thus, many colleges now have Learning Resources Centres. These are usually 'drop-in' centres where students can use the technology available in order to complete assignments or where they can access additional units to support other learning. This trend may increasingly lead to more individualised learning programmes with students being able to 'pick and mix' different units and elements of courses in order to meet their own needs. Although this individualism may open up the whole college curriculum provision to a much wider clientele than has previously been the case, there are implications for student guidance and counselling. Students need help in accessing the parts of the curriculum that meet their needs. They also need guidance in constructing a coherent and integrated programme of learning from the wide range of offerings available. In this situation the FE teacher becomes a facilitator of learning rather than a provider. The issues raised here will be further developed in Chapter 5 but the following extract from an ALI/Ofsted inspection report of a medium-sized English college in 2001 illustrates the strategies which colleges can employ to meet the needs of individual students:

> The induction process is not tied to a particular time of the year. Students starting courses at any time receive induction following the guidelines produced by the college . . . Students' additional learning needs are determined through an initial assessment during induction. Appropriate help is then offered within two weeks of assessment. There are clear documents describing the help available to students. Additional learning support staff are deployed effectively. . . All full-time students have a personal tutor.
>
> (ALI/Ofsted Inspection Report, 2001)

The promotion of e-learning and the use of new technologies in general has its critics. Some are concerned about the emphasis on the individualised nature of this type of learning. For example, Field (2000, p.55) points out that 'From the perspective of an older type of adult education – dedicated to enlightenment, social improvement and the support of social movements – this individualism represents an abandonment of social purpose'. Guile and Hayton (1999, p.123) raise concerns about a prevalent and very misguided belief that 'the individualised, technological approach to delivery is a cheap option.' In addition, they note that recent research in the UK and the United States 'is increasingly demonstrating that ILT is not, by itself, a vehicle for assisting people to become acquainted with new ideas or for enabling them to think in theoretically informed ways', but rather, 'that the effective use of ILT involved teachers rethinking the relationship between the process of learning and their role in supporting such learning' (ibid.).

The range of courses on offer will also be dependent upon the size of the institution and upon its location. Traditionally colleges have served their local communities and have been dependent upon local companies sending their employees on day-release programmes, usually at a craft apprentice or technician level. Notable examples were the colleges in parts of South Yorkshire and Nottinghamshire, which were almost entirely dependent on the local mining industry for their students. Pit closures have subsequently meant that these colleges have had to diversify to seek and exploit new markets. Similarly, many large engineering departments have contracted or closed down. Against this background, new courses catering for the burgeoning demands of the information technology industries and for the service industries have been developed. All of this will affect the curriculum offerings of a college. The following extract from a 1996 FEFC inspection report illustrates how a college in the South East of England is meeting the challenge of closer links with Europe:

> The college is a lively participant in European links. The European Business and Language Centre offers courses to companies. Clients have included the major ferry operators and Eurotunnel; a number of concerns with substantial export interests; and retailers such as Tesco and Marks & Spencer, whose staff need to be able to sell in at least two languages. The European Business and Language Centre now has funding from the Esme Fairbairn Foundation to develop open-learning materials; to link the college campuses electronically; and, with substantial further funding from the European Union, to introduce an audio-conferencing network with seven colleges in other European countries. There are a dozen exchange agreements with colleges in France, Germany, Denmark, Belgium and Sweden. These produce over 100 student exchanges each year, with financial support from the European Union. In addition, about 25 students cross the Channel in each direction for work experience. There are courses in the college, which have preparation for employment in Europe at their heart. These include a degree in European business and finance, a course for bilingual secretaries, and a Business and Technology Education Council (BTEC) national diploma in leisure studies which is jointly run with a private college in Arras.

In drawing up strategic plans for their institutions, college managers are supposed to pay attention to the needs of the local labour market and to reflect these in their provision. Funding is often tied to the ways in which courses meet the needs of the local community. However, this is sometimes a difficult task since local labour markets can be volatile and predicting future training requirements is not an exact science. There is also a further consideration in that the demand from students may not match the supply of jobs within the local, regional or even national labour market. Pressures for increased student numbers and, hence, increased funding may persuade colleges to offer those courses, which are popular irrespective of job opportunities. One of the first tasks of the Local Learning and Skills Councils (LLSCs) in England has been to undertake an audit of existing post-16 provision within their areas in order to identify both gaps and duplication.

Reflection

The diversity of curriculum provision is revealed in these titles from the classified pages of the educational press. What type of curriculum do you think is offered in these faculties/departments or divisions?

Faculty of the Built Environment
Department of Hospitality and Tourism
Department of Health and Social Care
School of Science
Division of Sport, Leisure and Tourism
Faculty of Business, Management and Humanities
Faculty of Visual Communication
Faculty of General Education and Student Services

You might also want to consider how these different aspects of a college's provision relate to each other.

We now turn to look in more detail at the differing types of curriculum provision found within FE colleges in England, Wales and Northern Ireland. The situation in Scotland is different. Building on the recommendations of *Higher Still* (Scottish Office, 1994), the SQA has broken down all national qualifications (academic and vocational) into Units which can be studied at five levels: Access; Intermediate 1; Intermediate 2; Higher; and Advanced Higher. Raffe (1997, p.185) explains that *Higher Still* was a response to the 'need for post-16 education to cater for the whole age group', addressing 'issues of differentiation and diversity'. Canning (1999, p.192) reminds us, however, that 'the "academic divide" cannot be simply legislated away . . . by creating new forms of qualifications based on a notional sense of equivalence.' As we have noted at the start of this chapter, there are clear signs that Wales may follow the Scottish approach, but for the moment, Welsh FE colleges provide the same curricula provision as their English counterparts.

GENERAL EDUCATION

Advanced level curriculum

Most of the provision within the general education category in England, Wales and Northern Ireland includes GCE A/AS level, AVCEs, and GCSEs. Statistics for 2000 show that 16 per cent of students in English FE colleges were studying A/AS levels (DfES, 2001e). The overall standard of passes is lower in colleges than schools but one should remember that FE colleges (not necessarily sixth form colleges) accept students with lower grades at GCSE than is the case in most school sixth forms.

The subject specifications are set by QCA; Awarding Bodies develop these specifications into awards, oversee assessment and set and mark examinations. They are subject to QCA's quality assurance procedures to ensure that specifications are complied with and that there is standardisation across the different Awarding Bodies. Students are free, subject to the capacity of the college, to choose which subjects they will study at A level. Although full-time students may take a programme of several A level subjects, there are other students who may study one A level on a part-time basis by evening attendance. Some may combine both academic and vocational A levels, as in the example above.

A levels were first introduced in 1951 and have, until very recently, been the only entry route into higher education. As Young and Leney (1997, p.53) note, 'A levels represent a highly insulated form of subject specialisation which directs learners' attention entirely to individual subjects treated separately.' During the past ten years or so there has been increasing criticism of the narrowness of A levels, particularly since young people were forced to make choices at 16 which would effectively limit their opportunities to pursue a broader based curriculum. In addition, Young and Leney (ibid.) remind us that, 'knowledge is more and more being produced at the interface of subjects and disciplines, not in subjects in isolation from each other.' For those of you with an interest in these issues, there is an extensive literature on the subject, which we do not have the space to consider fully here. (See, for example, DES/WO, 1988; Finegold et al., 1990; Nash, 1992; Dearing, 1996; Hodgson and Spours, 1997; Edwards et al., 1997; Raffe et al., 1998).

The new A level is divided into six units, each of which is assessed through examination and coursework. The first three units of the A level form the Advanced Subsidiary (AS) level. This is both a qualification in its own right and the first half of the full A level. To achieve a full A level candidates must complete a further three units, known as A2. Both AS levels and A levels are qualifications in their own right, the A2 units are not a qualification. A maximum of 30 per cent coursework is permitted in most A levels, with the exception of practical subjects where a higher percentage is permitted. Examinations may be re-sat, either at the unit level (once) or for the whole qualification. The new vocational A level, or AVCE, has replaced the former GNVQ (Advanced). This qualification has been substantially revised to make it more comparable with other A levels.

It could be argued that the advanced level curriculum is merely a collection of subjects, and only gains coherence at individual student level. In this model a teacher's attention is naturally focused upon achieving the desired number of student passes and at acceptable grades. There may be a danger of 'teaching to the test' rather than considering the development of the whole individual. This situation may be exacerbated by the fact that a proportion of students taking A levels in colleges may be re-sitting examinations in which they have previously been unsuccessful. Since entry to HE is normally dependent upon achieving specified grades at A level, there is pressure on students and teaching staff to concentrate on 'getting through'. As a teacher your lesson planning will be informed not only by the subject specifications but also by the content of past examination papers.

Every summer when the A level results are published, there is an outcry from certain sections of society who claim the exams must be getting easier as each year the pass rate improves. The elite universities (e.g. Oxford, Cambridge, London and Bristol) also complain that it is getting harder to distinguish between the best A level candidates. From 2003, students will have the chance to take yet another new qualification, the Advanced Extension Award (AEA). These awards will replace S level qualifications and may be used by some universities to get what Hodgson and Spours (2001, p.28) refer to as 'better differentiation at the "top end"'. In his analysis of academic A levels, Young and Leney (1997, p.52) reminds us that although they 'enable students to gain unrivalled access to bodies of specialised knowledge in a small number of knowledge areas and to the concepts that go with them . . . there is a price to pay for these advantages . . . the A level curriculum is both socially and intellectually selective.' The introduction of AEAs would seem to perpetuate these problems.

GCSE curriculum

The second major area of general education provision within the FE sector is that of courses leading to GCSE. There has been a long tradition in FE for students to enrol in order to re-sit GCSE examinations in which they were unsuccessful at school. These numbers are dropping as young people choose to make a fresh start by enrolling for a GNVQ programme (either at Foundation or Intermediate level) or other vocational education courses rather than retaking GCSEs. Some students, particularly adults, may be tackling GCSE subjects for the first time, perhaps combining one or two of these with other qualifications. As with the A level programmes, curriculum content will be determined by the subject criteria laid down by QCA. Examinations are externally set and marked by a range of awarding bodies.

There is also the opportunity for a limited amount of coursework assessment.

For those teaching on general education programmes that are accredited by awarding bodies, the content of the curriculum is, therefore, prescribed. The flexibility comes in the way in which teachers interpret the content and in the manner in which they seek to deliver it. The question of teaching style will be considered more fully in Chapter 6. You will, no doubt, wish to reflect upon the type of approach, or variety of approaches, that you might wish to adopt when teaching on general education programmes.

The starting point will be the specifications issued by the awarding body with whom your candidates are registered. It is from these that the teacher will need to plan a coherent scheme of work. This will then be broken down further into individual lesson plans. You may already have noticed that in this curricular tradition there is an emphasis on input, or knowledge to be imparted, to achieve a particular outcome; that is, success in the examination. However, as teachers you should always be mindful of your students' wider developmental needs as learners. These may include: help with study skills; additional or specific learning support; personal and inter-personal skills development. As (Dimbleby and Cooke, 2000:78) argue, 'A curriculum model based on developing the broad talents of each individual leads to a range of learning models.' Chapter 4 will help you to think about students' different learning preferences.

Vocational GCSEs and increased flexibility at key stage 4

From September 2002, new GCSEs in vocational subjects will be available at key stage 4 and post-16 (see Blunkett, 2001). These are intended to replace GNVQ Part One (see below) and to provide an introduction to a broad vocational area. They are intended to facilitate progression to further education, training or employment. The new GCSEs build upon the existing Part One GNVQ, which will gradually be phased out following their introduction. They are also intended to incorporate many of the features of GNVQ Part One and provide opportunities for links to the 'world of work', including extended work experience.

Eight subjects will be offered initially and each vocational GCSE will be the same size as two existing GCSEs. The titles will emphasise the applied nature of the award; for example, specifications will be available from 2002 in Applied Art and Design, Applied Business, Engineering, Health and Social Care, Applied ICT, Manufacturing, and Applied Science. The vocational GCSEs will consist of three common, compulsory units in each subject. The regulatory authorities will develop the subject criteria in consultation with Sector Skills Councils (which will replace National Training Organisations from 2002 onwards), subject associations and other interested parties. The awards will be available at 2 levels: level 1 (Foundation); and level 2 (Intermediate). This is the same as for other GCSEs. Assessment will combine both internal and external elements – an externally set and marked test and internal assessment of the candidate's portfolio.

These awards are intended to allow schools and colleges to provide a more flexible offering to students by creating opportunities for the integration of work placements, practical activities and visits, amongst other things, into the programmes. From the college perspective, the introduction of these awards is likely to create more partnerships between schools and colleges, since it is envisaged that school pupils may access some, or all, of these programmes at a local college. This could create some challenges for FE staff who may have had no training, or experience, of teaching younger students. However, as we noted in Chapter 1, many college staff have become accustomed to teaching younger pupils since the introduction of the 1996 Education Act, Section 363, made provision for the 'Disapplication of the National Curriculum at Key Stage 4 to permit a wider focus on work-related learning'. This legislation created opportunities for pupils to be 'disapplied' from parts of the National Curriculum in order to 'give schools more scope to use work-related learning opportunities to motivate pupils and encourage them to learn, and to offer courses that are not compatible with existing statutory requirements' (QCA, 1998, p.1).

One large London college has been running a very successful programme for pupils from five neighbouring schools, including a Pupil Referral Unit. The specially designed programme, entitled *Learning for Work*, involves small group vocational work, personal skills development, a work placement, IT, and an enterprise module in which students have to research, develop and sell a product, or service, to fellow students and friends. The evaluation of the programme points to the motivational aspects of the course and to high levels of student satisfaction (Huddleston, 2000a).

The new GCSEs are not intended for the less able, or for the disaffected, but they are presented as equal status alternatives to the existing GCSEs. Given the introduction of these new qualifications, it seems that the debate concerning the so-called academic/vocational divide is likely to embrace the 14–16 age range. At the same time, provision for the 14–19 age group is also being reviewed in order to achieve greater coherence and opportunities for progression across the whole phase. As an FE teacher you are likely to experience the impact of this review as new and different groups of students move into your college.

GENERAL VOCATIONAL EDUCATION

Let us now turn to the curriculum tradition of general vocational education. The FE sector has always been the main provider of general vocational education in the UK. During the 1980s there were some developments within schools in both pre-vocational and vocational education through initiatives such as the Certificate of Pre-Vocational Education (CPVE) and the Technical and Vocational Education Initiative (TVEI) (see Pring 1997 for a discussion).

However, since the introduction of GNVQs in 1993, which we discuss in more detail below, the involvement of schools in this area of work has increased considerably. In many parts of England and Wales, schools and colleges are in direct competition for GNVQ students. GNVQs are, however, just one of many types of vocational education programmes offered by colleges.

Vocational qualifications (not GNVQs or NVQs)

There are still programmes leading to National and Higher National awards, which are well respected by employers, popular with students, and which are neither GNVQs nor NVQs. In some cases you will still hear these referred to as BTEC awards, named after the original awarding body, even though BTEC ceased to exist as a separate awarding body in 1996. Often these programmes pioneered an integrated curricular approach:

> BTEC courses, in common with some other vocational programmes, require an integrated and multi-disciplinary approach in their core modules. The emphasis is on the application of knowledge to realistic business or working environments rather than purely on the understanding of theoretical concepts. The development of work related skills is an important feature of the programmes. Assessment, which is based on coursework assignments, may be developed in conjunction with employers.
>
> (Abbott and Huddleston, 1995, p.6)

Other awarding bodies, for example City and Guilds (C & G) and OCR, also offer vocational qualifications which stand outside the National Qualifications Framework. Professional bodies also award vocational qualifications. The banking sector, for example, has continued to use its own professional qualifications rather than embrace the NVQ model. In 2001, the National Audit Office (NAO) reported that benchmarking data collected by the FEFC categorised 60 per cent of qualifications as 'Other', marking a 10 per cent increase on figures collected in 1998. This is remarkable at a time when government policy has focused upon the inclusion of all qualifications within an overarching National Framework. The remaining qualification types amount to the following proportions: National Vocational Qualifications (11 per cent); Open College Network (9 per cent); General National Vocational Qualifications (8 per cent); A- and A/S levels (7 per cent); and General Certificate of Secondary Education (3 per cent) (National Audit Office, 2001, p.46).

One way in which general vocational qualifications may regain the prominence they had before the introduction of GNVQs and NVQs, is through the introduction of Technical Certificates. Concerns about the breadth of training on the Modern Apprenticeship had been raised in 1999 by the National Skills Task Force (NSTF), which recommended that all apprentices should complete what it called a Related Vocational Qualification (RVQ). The RVQ would 'attest to their (apprentices) technical knowledge and understanding as well as an

NVQ which attests to their competence' (NSTF, 1999, p.41). The NSTF also highlighted the fact that only 20 per cent of apprentices were on programmes that contained mandatory periods of off-the-job training (ibid., p.33). In response, the then Department for Education and Employment (DfEE) asked the QCA to develop a range of vocationally-related qualifications, to be called 'Technical Certificates'.

These Certificates would:

- deliver the underpinning knowledge and understanding relevant to the NVQ included in the particular Modern Apprenticeship framework;
- be delivered through a taught programme of off-the-job learning;
- permit a structured approach to the teaching and assessment of the underpinning knowledge and understanding of an NVQ (or a related suite of NVQs).

(QCA, 2001)

Between 2002 and 2005, all Advanced Modern Apprenticeship programmes, which currently require apprentices to gain an NVQ Level 3, will be required to incorporate a Technical Certificate, and this requirement may be extended to the Foundation Modern Apprenticeship, which currently leads to an NVQ Level 2. In occupational sectors such as engineering where apprentices have continued to study for a knowledge-based qualification alongside an NVQ/SVQ, existing qualifications, such as the BTEC National award in engineering, will be re-badged as Technical Certificates. In sectors which lack a tradition of vocational education, however, new qualifications will have to be designed.

The introduction of Technical Certificates forms part of a series of reforms to the Modern Apprenticeship (see DfES, 2001c). For example, the NTOs responsible for the Modern Apprenticeship frameworks have been asked to ensure that all apprentices cover the topic of Employment Rights and Responsibilities (ERR) which includes:

- the rights and responsibilities of workers;
- the organisation, discipline and representation structures of the industry;
- how employees are affected by public law and policies.

(QCA, 2002)

The QCA (ibid.) suggests that ERR can be covered in one of the following ways: through the NVQ; as part of the Technical Certificate; or through another aspect of the training programme such as induction.

It is too early to judge whether Technical Certificates will enable the Modern Apprenticeship to develop into the NSTF's vision of a programme that ensures apprentices in all sectors have access to substantive vocational education as well as competence-based training. These new qualifications do, however, provide a major opportunity for colleges to play a greater role in providing off-the-job vocational education for the Modern Apprenticeship than they have done to date. For a critique of the Modern Apprenticeship, see Unwin and Wellington (2001), Fuller and Unwin (2001a), and Ryan and Unwin (2001).

GNVQs

> GNVQs are becoming increasingly established as a qualification leading to higher education or to employment. Close on 450,000 students have now achieved full GNVQ awards in the seven years since the qualification was launched.
>
> (Baroness Blackstone, DfES Press Release 4.11.99)

The 1991 White Paper, *Education and Training for the 21st Century*, announced a proposal for the phased introduction of GNVQs into colleges and school sixth forms (DES/ED/WO, 1991). These new qualifications were intended to offer an alternative route for those remaining in full-time education beyond 16. They were to offer a broad preparation for employment or HE and were intended to develop the skills, knowledge and understanding required for the related occupations. In addition, the government announced that these qualifications were to have a parity of esteem with academic A levels. Indeed, the then Secretary of State for Education, John Patten, said they should be thought of as vocational A levels, a theme taken up by Sir Ron Dearing in his review of qualifications for 16–19 year olds. Sir Ron preferred the term 'Applied A level', which was suggested to him by the National Council for Industry Training Organisations (NCITO):

> The name, Applied A level, has the advantage of bringing home to everyone that the qualification matches A level as a distinctive approach to learning, based on the application of knowledge. To many the thought of studying something that is related to practical applications but is part of the A level family will be attractive. It would help to give parents a better understanding of the value society places on the GNVQ.
>
> (Dearing, 1996, p.71)

As we noted earlier, in September 2000 the Advanced GNVQ was renamed, and re-specified, as the Advanced Vocational Certificate of Education. Despite substantial take up of Advanced GNVQ, some teachers, students, parents, HE admissions tutors and employers remained unconvinced of its equivalence with A level. It remains to be seen how much re-branding and product enhancement will result in a change of heart.

In 1992, pilot GNVQs were introduced into 107 schools and colleges, involving 8,500 students in one or more of five broad vocational areas: health and social care; leisure and tourism; business; art and design; and manufacturing. Further vocational areas have since been developed, including: information technology; construction and the built environment; hospitality and catering; science; retail and distributive services; media communication and production; management studies; performing arts; engineering; land and environment; and leisure and recreation.

GNVQs now form a major part of 16–19 provision in schools and colleges. Spours (1995) has suggested that the GNVQ curriculum model has its roots in the different vocational initiatives that developed in the 1980s, namely:

1 The NVQ methodology for defining standards and assessment.
2 The BTEC First and National Diplomas, which are integrated group awards.
3 CPVE's promotion of active learning strategies and portfolio approaches to recording achievement.

The first of those initiatives, namely the development of NVQs within a competence- and outcome-based model of education and training, was the strongest influence on the nature and design of the GNVQ. These will be discussed in more detail later in this chapter. GNVQs, however, differ significantly from NVQs, most notably in that they are not competence-based. 'The award of a GNVQ does not imply that a student can perform competently in any occupation immediately on qualifying, but rather that she or he has a broad foundation of learning upon which to build' (NCVQ, June 1995, p.12).

Whereas NVQs span five levels, GNVQs, at the time of writing, are limited to the first three levels of the National Qualifications Framework:

Foundation GNVQ   NVQ Level 1
Intermediate GNVQ   NVQ Level 2
AVCE (formerly GNVQ Advanced)   NVQ Level 3

For a picture of how GNVQs fit within the overall qualification framework see Figure 3.1, p.40. The defining features of GNVQs are as follows:

• They are vocationally specific qualifications relating to broad vocational areas.
• Assessment is carried out through a series of coursework assignments and through externally set and marked tests.
• Evidence of achievement is collected throughout the programme to form an individual student portfolio.
• Each GNVQ is made up of a number of units.
• Opportunities for key skills development are signposted within every unit.
• They place emphasis on practical application of skills, knowledge and understanding within a broad vocational area.

The Foundation and Intermediate GNVQ programmes are normally intended to take one year's full-time study and the AVCE normally two years' full-time study. From September 1995, 14–16 year olds have been able to follow specified units in order to complete just over half a GNVQ programme, known as the Part One GNVQ. The Part One is currently available at both Foundation and Intermediate levels. As we saw in the previous section GNVQ, Part One is to be phased out following the introduction of the new vocational

GCSEs in September 2002. It is also intended that both the Foundation GNVQ and the Intermediate GNVQ (full awards) will be gradually phased out. This has caused some concern amongst FE providers and practitioners since GNVQ Foundation and Intermediate programmes have been attractive options for students who do not wish to re-take GCSEs in which they have previously been unsuccessful. For many of these students moving on to college and taking a new and different programme of study from those followed at school proved motivational (Huddleston, 2000b). At the time of writing, it is anticipated that the last opportunity for students to register on either a Foundation or Intermediate GNVQ programme will be September 2003, for the two year course, and September 2004, for a one year course.

GNVQs are unit-based qualifications. There are two types of GNVQ unit available: mandatory and optional: mandatory units are the same for all awards, irrespective of the awarding body; optional units are specific to a particular awarding body. A candidate may also take additional units to enhance the award at all levels but does not need to complete such units in order to achieve the award satisfactorily.

The introduction of such radical changes to the nature and structure of general vocational awards, followed by their subsequent review and revision, has been a cause of major upheaval in colleges, and in schools. It is not surprising that a new teacher may feel bewildered by the seeming complexity of the structure, pedagogy and assessment procedures involved in such a system. In terms of structure the position may be summarised as follows:

AVCE	<u>6 units in total</u> 3–4 mandatory units (dependent on the vocational area) 2–3 optional units (dependent upon the vocational area) <u>12 units in total</u> (double award) 6–8 mandatory (dependent on the vocational area) 4–6 optional (dependent on the vocational area) <u>3 units in total</u> (a limited number of 3 unit awards are currently available) 3 mandatory units
GNVQ Intermediate	<u>6 units in total</u> 4 mandatory units 2 optional units
GNVQ Foundation	<u>6 units in total</u> 3 mandatory units 3 optional units

Any additional units which students take will be recognised in the student's record of achievement (see Chapter 6). The award will be granted when all the mandatory and optional units for that level of award have been satisfactorily completed.

Before moving on to discuss the implications for teaching on such programmes, it is necessary to understand a little more about their structure. It has been noted that GNVQs are unit-based qualifications; the unit being the smallest part of a GNVQ qualification that can be accredited by an awarding body. Here is an example of a current specification for an Intermediate GNVQ programme.

STRUCTURE OF INTERMEDIATE GNVQ IN BUSINESS

SUMMARY OF MANDATORY UNITS

Unit 1   Investigating how businesses work
Unit 2   How businesses develop
Unit 3   Business finance
Unit 6   People in business

SUMMARY OF OPTIONAL UNITS

Unit 4   Personal finance
Unit 5   Customer service
Unit 7   Promotion
Unit 8   Preparing for self employment
Unit 9   Communication and administration
Unit 10   Enterprise activities
Unit 11   Introduction to retail and distributive services
Unit 12   Merchandising and display
Unit 13   Introduction to international markets

(Source: OCR, 2000)

You will probably be perplexed as to how this might be transformed into a scheme of work, or into individual classes, especially if your own experience has been on academic programmes. The subject specifications provided by the awarding bodies are your starting points. These have recently been re-designed to be more user friendly and student focused. Each specification is addressed to the student and comprises a number of sections:

About this unit: this provides some contextual information about the topic to be covered, outlines the knowledge and skills to be developed, makes links to other units and indicates how the unit will be assessed, either by external test or portfolio;

What you need to learn: this section looks much like what you may recognise as a syllabus. It lists the subject content to be covered, it indicates the knowledge and understanding to be developed during the programme and on which students will be assessed.

Assessment evidence: this states exactly what students have to do for their assessment task, for example, 'produce a portfolio based on your investigation of two contrasting businesses, including information selected from your own work and materials you have collected' (Source: OCR, 2000). The guidance goes on to state precisely what the portfolio should include and indicates the criteria for a pass, merit or distinction grade. You should note that grading for Foundation and Intermediate GNVQ is based on pass, merit and distinction, whereas for AVCE the grading has been changed, as part of Curriculum 2000, in order to align it with A level grades, namely A–E.

Opportunities for key skills development are signposted within the unit specifications. For example, when candidates are presenting findings on business performance they may be able to compare data from their selected case study businesses and compare them with national data, thus fulfilling some of the criteria for numeracy key skill. Similarly, they will be able to present data in the form of charts and tables and so complete some of the IT key skill criteria. The inclusion of key skills, through an integrated approach, is part of the curricular design, although in practice this integration has been difficult to achieve. Even where integration has been achieved it has still met with criticism (see, for example, FEU, IOE and Nuffield Foundation, 1994; Capey, 1995; CEI 2001).

Reflection

You might wish to consider the ways in which you could incorporate opportunities for key skills development in some of the following vocational assignments. Remember, the key skills are: communication, application of number and information technology. The so-called wider key skills are: improving own learning and performance, working with others and problem solving.

Prepare a plan of the layout of the workshop indicating options for optimising use of space, remember to consider the health and safety implications of your choices. (Engineering)

Provide a monthly breakdown of the numbers of customers using the college restaurant, the most popular choices from the menu, the average spend per customer, the percentage of waste. (Hotel and Catering)

Together with other members of your assignment group, prepare a presentation for the steering committee on the feasibility of offering access to the college's sports facilities to local residents on a paying basis. (Leisure and Recreation).

Spours (1995, p.38) has indicated some curricular strengths in the GNVQ design, namely:

- their organisation around assessed units could be the basis for encouraging a step-by-step approach to achievement and a flexible approach to credit transfer between qualifications;
- strong formative assessment, an active approach to learning and the compilation of coursework portfolios encourage students to manage their own study and acquire the habit of lifelong learning;
- GNVQs include a wide range of vocational areas and key skills which have not previously been associated with nationally recognised qualifications.

You will already have recognised that teaching and learning on GNVQ programmes are different from those encountered on traditional academic programmes. In GNVQ programmes, the emphasis is on developing the skills of the learner, to enable him or her to become more self-reliant. The responsibility has to shift from the teacher to the learner but these are skills that have to be cultivated. It may be difficult for teachers who have been accustomed to 'leading from the front' to change to a more student-centred approach. Equally, it may be difficult for students to come to terms with a more flexible approach.

Here are some responses to group work from different students in the same GNVQ Intermediate programme:

I really enjoyed this, we could get on in our own way and help each other if we liked. There should be more classes like this.

The teacher should give us more idea what to do, like what will get us the best marks and things. He didn't tell us what this was all about. I don't like working in groups because I don't get on with other people and I've had some trouble with that.

The last three years have witnessed an enormous degree of change in the pattern of provision of general vocational qualifications in our FE colleges. The range of GNVQ courses and the numbers of students have increased dramatically. Such rapid change has obviously brought in its wake a number of issues still requiring resolution. As a teacher you will want to keep up to date with these new developments in qualifications, particularly for the 14–19 age group. There are a range of support programmes and activities available to you, including websites, helplines and in-house consultancy services. You should refer to the websites of such bodies as QCA, SQA, Elwa, Deni, the Learning and Skills Development Agency (LSDA), the Scottish Further Education Unit (SFEU), DfES and the Key Skills Support Programme (KSSP) for the latest information. Your awarding body should also be able to provide you with up to date information.

NVQ/SVQs and job-specific training

FE has a long tradition of providing job-specific training for both young people and adults covering a wide range of occupational sectors. The provision of vocational training was the *raison d'être* of many early technical colleges and much of this provision was on a day-release basis. Employers generally funded this training and were sometimes represented on college advisory boards. In the main, however, employers would have to place employees on courses that were available at colleges and had very little influence over what would be provided or when or how this would be achieved. In this sense, provision was supplier led; that is, colleges offered a range of courses structured around a traditional 36-week college year and it was anticipated that demand would follow supply.

In addition to day-release provision, colleges have always provided evening classes for those wishing to pursue job-related qualifications in their own time. Many of those achieving vocational qualifications in the past have done so by attending evening classes for anything up to five years or more.

According to DfES (2001), since their introduction in 1987 just under 3.2 million NVQs/SVQs had been awarded to the end of September 2000. Take up of NVQ/SVQs varies by age, gender, economic activity and level of award taken. For example, in 1999/2000 44 per cent of awards were made to people aged 25 and over, 15% to people aged 21–24, and 41 per cent to people aged 20 and under. Over 52 per cent of all awards were made to females, with just under a half of them falling into the over-25 age group. Males were predominant in the under 20 age group. Level 2 is still the most common NVQ/SVQ awarded although the growth in numbers of awards at this level has slowed down as Level 3 awards have increased. The number of awards at Level 1 has also begun to decrease. The overwhelming majority of those gaining awards are economically active (89 per cent) reflecting the work-based nature of the assessment. About 9 per cent of those on government supported training and employment programmes were reported to be studying towards an NVQ/SVQ.

Of course, not all these qualifications are awarded through FE colleges. Assessment of candidates for the award of an NVQ/SVQ must be done through a recognised centre. Such a centre can be a workplace, a college or a training provider. Assessment through a college does not imply that the training took place at the college but that assessment was carried out through the college. This often involves college staff, who are qualified assessors, assessing candidates in their workplaces. For example, one college located within a popular tourist town offers local guesthouses the opportunity of NVQ/SVQ assessment for their staff within the workplace. It is clear, however, that FE still remains the major provider of vocationally specific training both for NVQ/SVQs and for traditional vocational awards.

The next section will focus specifically on the impact of NVQ/SVQs on college provision since this has introduced a significant change in the way in which teaching and learning takes place. It is important to recognise that an NVQ/SVQ is not a course of study and it is not necessary to undertake a specific training course before competences are demonstrated. NVQ/SVQs confirm that the holder possesses the competences required to carry out a specific job.

The majority of these awards are available within the FE sector although some are delivered within companies to their own employees. The reluctance of some employers to become involved with the delivery of NVQ/SVQs has meant that FE colleges have been at the forefront of development and implementation. The barriers to implementation perceived by companies have been highlighted in a number of reports (see IES, 1994; KPMG Peat Marwick, 1994; CBI, 1994; IES, 1995; Beaumont, 1996).

NVQ/SVQs are unit based qualifications, the number of units required for each qualification are set out within the specifications and will vary according to the occupation and level. A unit is the smallest part of an NVQ/SVQ for which a candidate may be awarded a certificate. In order to gain the full award, however, all the mandatory and optional units required for the award must be achieved. NVQ/SVQs are available at five levels (see Figure 3.2 page 45). EMTA Awards Limited, an awarding body for the engineering sector, describes these levels in the following way:

Level 1: Foundation or basic level employees
Level 2: Operators or semi-skilled employees
Level 3: Technicians, craft, skilled and supervisory employees
Level 4: Technical and junior management positions
Level 5: Professional engineers and senior management positions.
          (Source: EAL NVQ/SVQ Engineering Maintenance Level 2 and 3
                                                         EMTA, 2000)

Let us now look at the structure of an NVQ/SVQ. In order to gain a full NVQ/SVQ, candidates must complete all the units necessary for the award. Each NVQ/SVQ is comprised of a number of *mandatory* and *optional* units. Each unit is further divided into a number of elements. Here is an example taken from the Engineering Design specification at level 3.

A candidate must complete all THREE mandatory units and FOUR optional units in order to gain the award. The *mandatory* units are:

- Identify and assess factors impacting on engineering requirements;
- contribute to the effectiveness of work activities;
- design engineering products.

There are fourteen *optional* units available from which a candidate must select and complete four.
    These units are:

- Provide detailed drawings for engineering activities;
- provide technical information for engineering activities;

- determine requirements to achieve engineering objectives;
- establish objectives and methods for engineering design and development projects;
- identify and evaluate development options for engineering products/assets;
- establish customer technical requirements;
- plan engineering activities;
- develop technical engineering specifications;
- support technical sales transactions;
- provide technical information and advisory services;
- co-ordinate activities with others;
- diagnose faults in engineering products/assets;
- contribute to improving the organisation's working practices and procedures;
- control and monitor the use of allocated resources.

If we now look at one of the Engineering Maintenance units at level 2 we can see that it is further sub-divided into a number of elements, all of which have to be achieved in order to complete the unit.

Unit title: Maintain the condition of engineering assets
Elements: Maintain equipment
                   Adjust equipment

The assessor, who may be an engineering lecturer in a college, has to confirm evidence that the candidate can carry out such tasks either in a real, or simulated, workshop. He, or she, may draw upon evidence, for example, witness statements provided by workplace supervisors. Other forms of evidence may also be permissible for inclusion in a candidate's portfolio, for example, artefacts, design drawings, photographs, depending upon the nature of the award being sought. Early critics of the qualification (Ashworth and Saxton, 1990; Smithers, 1993; Hyland, 1994; Richardson et al., 1995; Bates et al., 1995) argued that the lack of underpinning knowledge and skills rendered the qualification deficient. The FEFC (1994) suggested that 'The contribution of NVQs to vocational education and training would be enhanced if NCVQ insisted on greater clarification of the knowledge, understanding and core skills elements of each NVQ before qualifications are accredited' (FEFC, 1994, p.6). Following a number of reviews of the qualification (for example, Beaumont, 1996; QCA 1999a, 1999b) some changes have been incorporated into their design in order to improve assessment and to specify more clearly the necessary underpinning knowledge and skills required.

Although NVQ/SVQs were designed as essentially work-based qualifications, many of which would be taken by adults already in employment, a large proportion of uptake has been by young people in initial training. It is estimated that in 1999/2000 nearly 44 per cent of NVQs were awarded to people of 25 and over and 41 per cent to people aged 20 and under (DfES, 2001a). This is not surprising since with the introduction of Modern Apprenticeships in 1994, NVQ/SVQs were incorporated as the mandatory qualification outcome into the training frameworks developed by the relevant National Training Organisation (NTO) for each sector offering an apprenticeship. To secure funding, an apprenticeship programme had to include NVQ/SVQs to levels 2 and 3 (see Fuller and Unwin, 2001a).

Assessment methods for NVQ/SVQs include workplace observation of performance, skills tests, practical projects, assignments, written and oral questioning. Because of the need for candidates to demonstrate competence in the workplace, colleges have had to find suitable work placements for full-time students and unemployed students on NVQ/SVQ programmes. This has not always been easy for colleges particularly since there are so many competing demands on employers to provide work placements. Some colleges have been able to provide realistic learning environments, for example in college restaurants, or hairdressing salons. For other colleges it has been much more difficult to provide a simulated work environment. The FEFC (2001b, p.19) has indicated that in engineering this may be more difficult since 'the quality of accommodation and equipment across the sector is very mixed. In some cases, the facilities are modern and the equipment good. In other cases, accommodation is less satisfactory and/or machinery and equipment are out of date. This applies to both computer-aided engineering and basic engineering.' Some employers are also doubtful about the validity of assessment undertaken in a simulated environment.

NVQ/SVQs are not dependent upon any particular mode, duration or location of study. This is one of several significant changes which colleges have had to face in reorganising their provision for those wishing to acquire NVQ/SVQs. Candidates may claim credit for competence previously acquired providing that they can furnish sufficient evidence to demonstrate such competence. This process is known as the accreditation of prior learning (APL). Colleges show enormous diversity in their capacities to handle APL effectively.

The development of competence-based curricula in FE colleges has highlighted the need for some significant changes of approach in course delivery. These may be summarised as follows:

- The need for more flexible and responsive provision which can accommodate individual student needs;
- the development of learning support materials and learning resource centres which students can access individually according to their own needs, with or without the help of a lecturer;
- the modularisation of curricula, although this is by no means universal, to enable students to 'pick and mix' units which they require in order to complete an NVQ/SVQ, rather than having to follow a complete programme;

- the development of partnerships with employers in order to ensure an adequate supply of work placements for students;
- the design of simulated work environments within colleges, for example, college restaurants, hairdressing salons, vehicle maintenance workshops, to allow students to demonstrate competence under the same conditions and pressures as they would in employment;
- the need to develop adequate systems of guidance, advice and counselling to enable students to access the appropriate parts of the curriculum;
- the incorporation of support structures to enable students to build portfolios of evidence and to identify learning opportunities within the workplace and within the college.

These may be seen as pre-conditions for the so-called flexible college. However, while the curricular offerings are so diverse, lecturers may find themselves moving between programmes during the course of a working week.

Reflection

How does the teacher juggle these possibly competing demands?
How can the potential learners seek impartial and informed advice?
How does modularisation of the curriculum affect the teaching timetable?
What are the implications for teachers of a modularised curriculum?
If students are allowed to 'pick and mix' units, how can they build a coherent programme of study?

The fact that such questions, and many more, are raised by the introduction of competence-based approaches suggests that there are, and have been, some significant challenges to colleges in introducing the new qualifications. Perhaps the most significant impact lies in the fact that because NVQ/SVQs are specified in terms of outcomes rather than inputs and can be assessed in any context where competence can be appropriately demonstrated, colleges do not have the monopoly in job-specific training. Colleges are in competition with private training providers and with companies' 'in-house' training programmes. Cost may be an important factor when employers or LLSCs decide where to place their training contracts. In an on-going climate of competition, colleges are competing not only with companies and private training providers but also with each other and with school sixth forms.

A more detailed examination of such issues lies outside the scope of this book. However, as a teacher in the sector you will naturally be concerned about the curriculum offerings available to students and how best to accommodate their learning needs.

The following example of an innovative scheme for engineering trainees (recruited through the Modern Apprenticeship) in a major motor manufacturing company outlines the ways in which the post-16 curriculum might become more flexible. Here a curriculum has been designed to suit the specific training needs of both the trainees and the company. The design has been realised by selecting those elements of different curricular models which meet the requirements for a flexible, skilled labour force. In Chapter Four, we explore learning in the workplace in more detail.

Learning on the Modern Apprenticeship
Apprentices are combining the Intermediate GNVQ and AVCEs with NVQ Level 2 and 3 as appropriate. The key skills units provide breadth and flexibility to the training that it might not have if it were purely an NVQ programme. Some of the key skills units are achieved through a week's 'outward-bound' style of residential programme which involves all the apprentices and some of the college staff and company personnel. This takes place at the beginning of the programme. At this time students are also introduced to the concept of portfolio building and shown how to collect evidence to meet both GNVQ/AVCE and NVQ requirements.

On completion of the GNVQ and NVQ the apprentices will then move on to either an HNC, a Foundation Degree or a full degree programme. The strength of the scheme is that it allows flexibility between and across different routes and the apprentice is not artificially restricted from moving from what was formerly a 'craft' route into a 'technician' route. The introduction of the scheme has caused colleges and company training personnel to work closely together and fundamentally to change the curriculum model.

The model recognises that learning takes place both in the college and in the workplace. The assignments which apprentices complete as part of the GNVQ/AVCE are work-based assignments. That is, they have been identified from the work placements which students undertake in the company. This requires both workplace supervisors and college staff to identify jointly the learning opportunities within the workplace. Once these have been identified, and there is no reason to believe that there would be any shortage of such opportunities, assignments are designed that will enable the apprentices to reflect upon the learning experience and to demonstrate what they have learned.

In this model the assignment is at the heart of the learning process rather than being something that is added on at the end of a period of instruction. The specifications for the NVQ and GNVQ/AVCE indicate what has to be achieved; the assignment is a means of achieving them. Perhaps more importantly it links the learning with workplace experience and ensures that what is being learned is both realistic and relevant. In the past employers have sometimes complained that college practice did not mirror current workplace practice. As one head of department put it: 'When I came here a few years ago, students were still hammering lumps of metal.' No account had been taken of the changes in manufacturing processes and the developments in computer-aided design and manufacture (CAD/CAM). He went on to say: 'That has all changed here now; this programme has been developed with our partners in the company and reflects current practice. Teaching can be carried out by both company and college staff on either college or company premises; the whole thing is much more flexible.' The college staff even wear company overalls.

In this model the apprentices have to take responsibility for their own learning.

The objectives of the programme are stated at the outset, and the unit specifications clearly demonstrate what has to be achieved. The apprentices have to decide how, when and where they will achieve them. There is, of course, support from both college and company staff and each apprentice is provided with a company mentor to support him or her through the programme. There are deadlines to be met and the apprentice has to decide how best to meet them. In this curricular model a great deal of the 'ownership' of the programme has been devolved to the apprentice.

(Updated from: Huddleston, P., 1996)

HIGHER EDUCATION (HE) AND ADVANCED STUDIES

Higher education generally refers to those advanced courses usually, though not exclusively, provided by a university or by its constituent or associated institutions. Advanced in these contexts refers to courses which are deemed to be beyond A level, or equivalent, standard. Although some FE colleges have always provided a certain amount of advanced work, for example through Higher National Diploma (HND) and Higher National Certificate (HNC) programmes, the provision of degree-level courses is relatively recent. Nevertheless, some colleges have expanded their provision rapidly in this area through franchising arrangements with universities. In 1999/2000, the FEFC in England funded 72,000 students on courses of further education, which fall under schedule 2 of the Further and Higher Education Act, 1992 provided at universities and colleges in the higher education sector (FEFC, 2001).

It is not the purpose of this book to debate the nature and form of the HE curriculum; this has been considered elsewhere and there is an established literature on the subject. The intention is to highlight the developments that have occurred within the FE sector in its relationship with HE institutions.

Squires (1987) suggests that 'the pattern of undergraduate studies in the UK depends on two things: where one studies and what one studies' (Squires, 1987, p.130). He then goes on to explore some of the features of academic and professional courses and draws attention to developments in the modularisation of some undergraduate programmes. In those universities where modularisation has been whole-heartedly embraced, the course unit or module becomes the essential element of the programme. In its most extreme form students may 'pick and mix' across a very wide range of units to build a whole programme. Each unit may be assessed and accredited on completion until a full degree has been built up. There are obviously various stages along the continuum from what Squires (ibid.) has described as a 'holistic' to an 'aggregative' curriculum.

One of the reasons for drawing attention to these developments is to suggest that once the curriculum has been unitised in this way then the place in which it is studied becomes less important provided there is adequate quality control. The Open University allows students to study through a variety of means and in widely dispersed locations. The unifying factor is, of course, the content of programmes, which is centrally regulated. By devolving delivery in this way, universities can reduce their costs, or rather not incur further costs, while increasing student numbers.

The delivery of some parts of undergraduate programmes in colleges has enabled students to access the HE curriculum locally. Relationships between colleges and HE institutions may vary. In some cases colleges are delivering the first two years of a degree programme, with the third and fourth years being delivered in the university. In other cases, colleges may deliver the whole of an undergraduate programme. There may be franchising arrangements in place or colleges may have their own programmes accredited by an HE institution. Sometimes the HE institution may not be local to the college. There are further examples where colleges may be running whole or part of degree programmes from several different HE institutions.

Where FE colleges are delivering programmes through franchising arrangements then curriculum content will be prescribed by the HE institution. There will also be control over the staffing of programmes and other resource issues. Standards of assessment will be monitored and verified, examinations will be set by the university. Those involved in teaching such programmes in colleges may be located within a separate department or unit specialising in HE courses. This will not always be the case, though. HE courses may fall within the remit of a Department of General Education or within a curriculum area, for example, Business and Management.

Students on HE programmes may have come through special access courses which the college offers, and many of them will be mature entrants. As teachers you will need to consider these factors in developing your teaching strategy. If you return to Margaret, the HE student described in Chapter 2, you will see that she has particular learning needs as an HE student, some of which derive from a lack of confidence.

There is a continuing debate concerning the role of FE in HE provision. Some FE practitioners argue that colleges should concentrate on the delivery of high-quality vocational education and training and that they should 'not turn themselves into universities' (TES, 9 February 1996). Nevertheless, it seems likely that much of this growth will have to come via the FE rather than the HE route given the government's commitment to raising participation in higher education and its associated National Learning Target: by December 2002, 28 per cent of adults to have achieved a Level 4 qualification. The recent introduction of Foundation Degrees is also likely to impact on FE provision.

Foundation Degrees were introduced in 2001 to provide people with knowledge and skills required for jobs at associate professional and higher technician levels and are awarded by universities and higher education colleges. They can be studied on a full-time or part-time basis, and are classed as Level 4 in the

National Qualifications Framework. Many Foundation Degrees are being delivered in FE colleges working in partnership with a local HE institution. Having completed a Foundation Degree, which might take up to two years, students can then progress to a full honours degree. There are already around 70 courses available covering subjects such as: aircraft engineering; classroom assistance; commercial music; fashion design technology; hospitality; retail technology and logistics; and sports science. It will be interesting to see how successful these courses are and to what extent they supplant the existing Level 4 vocational qualifications such as HNDs and HNCs which have long enjoyed the respect of employers and students alike.

ADULT EDUCATION

The term 'adult' as applied to education is not easy to define. For some it has connotations of anything beyond the phase of compulsory schooling, whereas for others it may be regarded as post initial education, that is the period beyond initial HE. Some institutions may use age 25 to distinguish between ordinary and mature students, whereas for funding purposes 19 is frequently regarded as the difference between youth and adult status.

The scope of adult education has always been, and is, extremely wide. There are some institutions which exist primarily to teach adults, for example, the Workers' Educational Association (WEA), the Open University and adult education services, where they still exist, provided by local authorities. (For a more detailed discussion of the history of adult education provision see Fieldhouse and Associates, 1996). Adult education may also be engaged in through a whole range of informal mechanisms, including, for example, church groups and voluntary organisations. In its widest sense adult education may be described as any form of education or training in which adults engage. The current interest in the fostering and development of lifelong learning will focus attention on the ways in which, and the means by which, adults engage in continuing education and personal and professional development. It is worth noting that many universities across the UK have begun to rename their adult education and continuing education departments as Institutes of Lifelong Learning.

The concept of lifelong learning came to public attention in 1994 when it formed a major part of Jacques Delors' European Commission (EC) paper on competitiveness and economic growth (CEC, 1994) and the EC declared 1996 the European Year of Lifelong learning. Since then, governments around the world have urged their citizens to become lifelong learners. Field (2000, pp.viii-ix), in a detailed critique of lifelong learning, bemoans the way in which 'lifelong learning has been used by policymakers as little more than a modish repackaging of rather conventional policies for post-16 education and training, with little that is new or innovative.' He continues, 'This tendency to wrap up existing practice in a more colourful phrase can also be seen in the rush by providers to claim their adherence to lifelong learning: and even professorial titles have all been subjected to this rebranding. The educational result is a kind of linguistic hyperinflation, in which the term is constantly devalued' (ibid.). Field goes on to argue that although politicians have largely promoted lifelong learning as being essential for economic prosperity, the 'silent explosion in informal and self-directed learning' has 'only partly been driven by economic changes' and has equally as much to do with 'transformations in people's lives and identities' (ibid.). (See also Coffield, 1999 and Johnston, 1999 for critiques of lifelong learning.)

One way in which the Labour government has responded to the lifelong learning agenda is through the creation of Learndirect which is the operating name of the University for Industry (UfI). In 1998, the then DfEE published its prospectus for UfI, which it saw as a UK-wide network of learning centres, many of which would be based in colleges, public libraries, schools and other existing sites of learning (DfEE, 1998). A pilot version of UfI was established in Tyne and Wear in the North-east of England where 35 learning centres were linked to a central database which could be accessed through a call centre and a web site. The initiative attracted criticism for: a) using the name 'university'; b) using the term 'industry' which suggested its function was purely economic; and c) for setting up yet another quango which would take money away from existing providers. An example of the media reaction to the UfI name is the following extract from an editorial column in the *Times Higher Education Supplement* in April 1998:

> The first obvious thing about it is that it is no university. It is designed to trawl the highways and byways, using all the modern means of public persuasion, to draw in those who have learned little and like it less. Only very much second and later is it to help people who are already skilled but seek retreading . . . Tackling educational failure and skill shortages is admirable, but calling the project a university risks debasing the currency which the government has said it wishes to defend.
>
> (THES, 1998, p.11)

The tone of the THES's comments does, of course, say a great deal about the academic vocational divide in the UK and social class. In response to criticisms about the name, the government re-launched UfI as Learndirect. An example of a Learndirect centre is Optimum, based in a residential suburb of Derby and linked to Derby Tertiary College. Optimum is open seven days a week, including four evenings, and has full disabled access including facilities for the visually and hearing impaired.

Other notable government responses to lifelong learning have been the introduction of Individual Learning Accounts (ILAs) and the Union Learning Fund. Like Learndirect, ILAs and the Union Learning Fund represent a human capital approach to education and training by placing responsibility on the individual to improve their skills and knowledge. This approach has been criticised for failing to address the deep structural, social and cultural problems which prevent people from participating in formalised education and training (see Coffield, 1999). They also reflect a view held by UK governments since the late 1980s, that individuals will be encouraged to engage in more learning if they can operate as 'customers' in an education and training marketplace. An earlier example of a policy which attempted this was the failed Training Credits initiative aimed at 16–19 year olds (see Unwin, 1993, and Hodkinson et al., 1996, for critiques). ILAs were introduced in September 2000. To open an ILA, an individual over the age of 19 had to register with Capita, the company contracted by the DfES, the Scottish Executive and the Northern Ireland Office to run the scheme across the UK. Individuals placed £25 of their own money into the ILA, which then gave them access to a further £150 to spend on courses with education and training providers. Although open to any individual, ILAs were particularly targeted at 19–30 year olds with few or no qualifications, non-teaching school staff, labour market returners and the self-employed. In November, 2001, the BBC Radio 4 programme, *File on 4*, broadcast a damning expose of financial mismanagement at the heart of the ILA infrastructure. It was found that some providers had taken advantage of the system, causing the DfES to immediately suspend ILAs, while the police were brought in to investigate allegations of fraudulent practice. This debacle highlights the dangers inherent in presenting learning as just another commodity. Sadly, many of the learners whom ILAs were supposed to help may be even less persuaded to join the lifelong learning bandwagon than ever.

The Union Learning Fund has a much more positive history than ILAs. Established in 1998 by then the DfEE, the fund has enabled trade unions to train learning representatives who provide advice and guidance to potential learners in the workplace, and to develop a range of collaborative projects to stimulate participation in education and training. The Union of Textile Workers, for example, has used funds to develop an on-site learning resource centre in a Staffordshire manufacturing company, working in partnership with a local FE college, the Open College Network, and other related agencies. Trade Unions have, of course, a long history of providing educational opportunities for their members. A recent example is the Return to Learn programme launched by the public sector union, UNISON, in 1989 (see Munroe et al., 1997).

For the purposes of this book we are focusing on the provision for adults in the FE sector where, as we have seen in Chapter 1, the majority of students are over the age of 19. Although most courses will not be specifically targeted at a particular age group, some will naturally be more appealing to younger rather than older students and vice versa. There are, however, some programmes, which are definitely targeted at adults, for example, those involving government schemes for the long-term adult unemployed, such as New Deal. New Deal 25 Plus aims to help people aged 25 and over find work after a long period of unemployment. There are also programmes, often funded by the

European Social Fund (ESF), which are designed to meet the needs of those adults wishing to return to work, particularly women.

A proportion of adult provision will cover basic education. These programmes tend to focus on the achievement of basic literacy and numeracy skills and will often include the development of a range of interpersonal and social skills. Topics such as applying for jobs and interview techniques may be covered. Some adult programmes will also include an introduction to specific vocational areas.

A West Midlands college which currently offers NVQs in hairdressing for adult returners provides an example of this type of programme. The lecturer in charge of hairdressing reported that the skills development and confidence building inherent in the course design had enabled some of his students to gain employment before the end of the programme and in areas other than hairdressing, for example, reception work.

Although this is a very significant outcome for the adult student, it does not help the hairdressing lecturer in achieving the targets for his department. The department's funding will depend not only upon students enrolled but also upon course completion and outcomes, that is NVQs achieved. This calls into question a funding methodology which is based upon a 'payment by results' principle. In terms of the adults involved, eventual employment is a significant outcome.

Squires has suggested that 'the older meaning of adult education confined it to two or three headings: liberal, recreational and basic' (1987, p.177). More recent definitions, and indeed those adopted by the DfES, the National Institute for Adult Continuing Education (NIACE) and the Basic Skills Agency tend to regard adult education as continuous and ongoing, in fact, any form of education, training or development in which adults engage. Informal settings may be just as significant as formal areas in this context. There is a sense in which nothing may be discounted.

Recreational classes for adults have always been provided by FE colleges. The funding for such programmes comes from the local community, not from the local Learning and Skills Councils. These programmes have been seriously curtailed during recent years. In some areas they have been retained because adults have been able to pay a full rather than a subsidised cost. In other areas the programmes have been redesigned to lead to NVQs, or units towards them, and they have, therefore, been able to attract funding (see Unwin, 1999a).

There is also an increasing interest in continuous professional development amongst employed adults. In certain professions it is a requirement in order to continue practising, or to be allowed continued membership of professional organisations. The introduction of appraisal processes in the workplace may also highlight areas for professional and personal development. Colleges are now looking at ways of meeting some of these individual and company developmental needs.

Recent figures from a survey conducted by the National Institute for Adult and Continuing Education (Aldridge and Tuckett, 2001) indicate an increase in the number of adult learners compared to 1996. Although the growth has been greatest for those who are in full-time employment, are already well qualified and are in social classes AB, increases in participation have occurred across all social classes. Learning has been interpreted very widely in the survey and not all the learning takes place within formal settings such as FE colleges, nevertheless, adults represent a large market for colleges.

It will be clear from this diverse picture that the adult education curriculum is 'more diverse in terms of aims, content and form than anything that precedes it' (Squires, 1987, p.207). It is quite impossible to talk about an adult education curriculum. It is perhaps more useful to think about the ways in which adults learn and the strategies that we as teachers might develop in order to help them learn more effectively. These themes are returned to in Chapters 5 and 6.

This chapter has attempted to outline the range and diversity of the curriculum post-16. As a teacher you will be constantly re-examining your position in relation to these differing curricular models. It is not only you as a teacher – your students too may be exposed to a range of curricular models.

Reflection

If you return to the students in Chapter 2, you will see that several of them are following a mixed curricular model. This means that their experiences, as learners, may be quite different in different parts of the programme. This is not just because they may be taught by different staff but because the content and, more importantly, the pedagogy of the separate elements may be different. For example, Margaret is an HE student, but she is also a mature student. Gary is following a general vocational education programme with some job-specific elements. You might like to consider the programmes being followed by the other students. To what extent are they having a mixed curricular experience?

Part II

Teaching and learning

Chapter 4

Approaches to learning

When adults teach and learn in one another's company, they find themselves engaging in a challenging, passionate, and creative activity. The acts of teaching and learning – the creation and alteration of our beliefs, values, actions, relationships, and social forms that result from this – are ways in which we realise our humanity.

(Brookfield, 1986, p.1)

The constructs a learner brings to the learning environment are interwoven with personal meaning and value, are frequently implicit and deeply embedded. Any acquisition of new knowledge will entail adjustments to this system and if personal horizons of understanding are to be extended, new learning must be assimilated with what is already known.

(Harkin, Turner and Dawn, 2001, p.37)

In order to meet the challenge of teaching in the FE sector, it is essential to have some knowledge of the different theories that explain how people learn. As we discussed in Chapter 2, you could be teaching students whose ages range from as young as 14 to those in advanced old age, all of whom will have spent some years being taught in other educational institutions and learning in informal settings, and possibly in their places of work. You will, therefore, be confronted with people who have a great deal of experience as learners, and that experience will be of a particularly personal nature. For some of your students, their learning experiences may have been entirely pleasurable, whereas for others learning may be equated with anxiety and even pain. You will meet students who lack confidence as learners and many who find it difficult to know how to learn for themselves without being totally dependent on a teacher. The nature of a person's prior learning experience has a profound effect on their approach and attitude to further learning activity. As such, teachers do not start with a clean sheet. It may seem unnecessary to point out that people, whether they be teenagers or adults, learn in different ways, but it is a truism whose implications can be lost in the hectic whirl of the average teaching day.

Just as your students will approach their learning in different ways, you too will have developed your own strategies for acquiring knowledge and understanding and for learning new tasks. That very personal approach to learning will influence your approach to and style of teaching.

Reflection

Give some thought to the following questions and try to answer them as honestly as possible. You could also try them out on a friend, partner or member of your family.

1 What was the last thing you learned?
2 Do you attend a regular class of any kind, for example, keep-fit, camera club, local history? If you do, why do you attend and how did you get started?
3 Do you enjoy learning? Do you, for example, enjoy learning from books, listening to lectures, watching experts, finding out answers for yourself?
4 Do you consider yourself to be a good learner? How would you define a good learner?
5 Given your answer to question 4, were you a good learner at school? Have you improved as a learner since leaving school?
6 Is there anything which prevents you from learning?

In answering the questions above, you may have revealed aspects of your persona as an adult learner that even you find surprising. The last question, for example, may have brought forward a certain personal barrier to learning that you have not articulated before.

Your answers may also reveal something about your own personal definition of what learning means. You might, for example, agree with the 'behaviourists' who say that, in order to claim learning has taken place, a person's behaviour has to change (see Skinner, 1968). The 'behaviourist' school of thought was pre-eminent in the 1950s and 1960s, particularly in the USA through the work of B.F. Skinner, and had a great influence on workplace training and the programmed learning approach adopted in correspondence courses. Indeed, the competence-based approach (discussed in Chapters 3 and 6) has been criticised as being a return to the techniques of behaviourism. What the 'behaviourists' overlooked, and as a result are now seen to be the 'bad guys' of learning theory, is the contribution and consciousness of the learner.

Kolb, whose work has been influential in adult education and workplace training, defines learning as 'the process whereby knowledge is created through the transformation of experience' (Kolb, 1984, p.41). His 'learning cycle' claims that learners progress through four stages – observation and reflection; generalisation and abstract conceptualisation; active experimentation; and concrete experience – each of which can be entered first, on their learning journey. Although praised for its contribution to the development of learning theory, Kolb's model has also been criticised for being too simplistic. For example, Jarvis (1987) has pointed out:

> consider the situation where a person is reading a complex mathematical tome and is involved in abstract conceptualisation from the outset: the next stage of the learning process might be reflection rather than active experimentation and so the arrows would need to point in both directions. In addition, Schon (1983, pp.49–69) discusses the idea of reflection-in-action in which they occur almost simultaneously. Hence there may be stages of Kolb's cycle that are not sequential.
>
> (Jarvis, 1987, p.18)

Despite the flaws in his model, however, Kolb's key contribution is his emphasis on the central importance to learning of experience. There is a general consensus among adult learning theorists that the experiences that adults have gained during their lives play an important part in any learning activity on which they embark. Those experiences can have both a positive and negative effect. They can help adults contextualise and conceptualise new information, but experience can also hinder learning by reminding adults of past failures. The recognition that adults learn in different ways and that each adult comes to learning with a unique set of experiences has contributed to the development of the theory of 'experiential learning', echoes of which are to be found in the work of Piaget and the American educationalist, John Dewey. (See Piaget, 1970 and Dewey, 1938.) In its simplest form, experiential learning recognises that adults approach any learning activity with some preconceived idea about what it is they are about to try and learn. This is because of the wide range of experience they already have, so they do not approach learning with a totally blank mind. A great deal of teaching, in all sectors of education, undervalues this prior experience in learners and tends to follow what the Brazilian adult educator, Paulo Freire, called the 'banking' concept of education. 'Education thus becomes an act of depositing, in which the students are the depositories and the teacher is the depositer. Instead of communicating, the teacher issues the communiques and makes deposits which the students patiently receive, memorise, and repeat (Freire, 1974, p.58).

Although the role of the teacher in FE may be constrained by the prescriptive nature of much of the curriculum and, particularly, by the emphasis on the assessment of predetermined outcomes, a recognition that learning is a highly personalised activity should guide the teaching and learning process. Indeed, it could be argued that many of the developments in the FE world, such as modularisation of courses, competence-based qualifications, open and flexible learning, and the redefinition of the student as a 'consumer' of learning, necessitate teaching styles that are largely learner-centred and experiential in emphasis. The danger in treating students as consumers, however, is that the 'product' (e.g. a module or a qualification) they are 'buying' becomes more important than the learning process. Whether they are learning on their own or in groups, students should not be seen as, or even allowed to be, simply passive participants.

For some FE teachers, the promotion and advocacy of learner-centred and flexible approaches to teaching and learning by management are to be viewed with suspicion and even cynicism as Wilmot and McLean found when they evaluated one college's attempts to introduce flexible learning:

> The thread that runs through teachers' discussion about flexible learning is that it is being promoted for non-educational reasons. Several teachers feel that flexible learning is an educational justification for an economic measure. An important observation among teachers is that encouraging students to become self-motivated is not a cheap option. The economic pressure for larger class sizes and shorter class contact time militates against workshop style delivery – and not for it. Likewise economic pressures leading to less contact time with students may reduce opportunity for supervised discovery methods of learning, which take more time – as one teacher observed: 'Nothing can be done more quickly than telling students all the answers' . . . They (teachers) are not opposed to flexible methods which enhance the process of guiding the students to more independence, but there are two sources of tension between teachers and managers. First, teachers are anxious that management's priority of cost-effectiveness will mean that flexible learning is interpreted in ways that are not educationally desirable. Secondly, teachers point out that management do not directly observe student responses to flexible learning styles and, at times, evince unwillingness to accept that some independent learning strategies do not result in positive outcomes for students.
>
> (Wilmot and McLean, 1994, p.103)

A QUESTION OF AGE: THE CONCEPT OF ADULTHOOD

You may be surprised by the references to adult learners and adult learning when we began this chapter by acknowledging the fact that you could be teaching people as young as 14. If you were teaching in a school, you might regard all students up to the age of 18 as children and would probably, therefore, turn to theories of how children learn for some insight before preparing to teach. People mature differently and there are some 12-year-olds who demonstrate greater sophistication as learners than many twice or even three times as old. Colleges of FE have always seen themselves as being different to schools in a number of ways, but a key difference is in their attitude to students. The vast majority of students in colleges have left the compulsory stage of education and entered the non-compulsory world in which they will be required to take responsibility for their own learning. Although, in reality, significant numbers of students in the 16–19 age bracket may have been persuaded to attend college by their parents, from the college's point of view they have chosen to attend as opposed to being obliged to attend by the state. The following quotations from college prospectuses illustrate this:

> We treat our students as adults who want to take responsibility for their own lives and who will thrive in the supportive and lively atmosphere of the college.
>
> (Sixth Form College)

> The college prides itself on creating an adult atmosphere in which all students are treated with respect and seen as individuals with individual needs and aspirations. In return, we ask our students to behave responsibly and make the most of their opportunities at college.
>
> (College of Art and Technology)

That colleges actively promote themselves as being 'adult oriented' reflects their appreciation of the fact that young people in the 16–19 age bracket, who could continue their post-16 education in schools, are attracted to FE colleges precisely because they want to get away from the 'child-oriented' ethos of their secondary education. As they enter the second half of their teenage years, these young people will be developing a sense of self which, according to Rory Kidd (an influential writer on adult learning), 'is essential to all learning' (Kidd, 1973, p.127). Attending college offers young people the chance to develop this sense of self within a context which allows social interaction with people of all ages. It is not surprising, then, that colleges devote considerable resources to ensuring that the social and student support facilities they provide are of a high enough standard to encourage social interaction in addition to that which takes place in the formal learning situation. For the more mature students in a college, development of a sense of self may also be a central feature of their college experience, particularly if they are returning to learning and studying for the first time in a number of years. In their research with American women mature students in HE, Belenky et al. (1986) asked these women to try and describe how they saw themselves. One woman said, 'I don't know . . . No one has told me yet what they thought of me' (p.31).

Reflection

It might be useful at this point to revisit the vignettes in Chapter 2 and consider the ways in which the development of a sense of self applies to those students. Consider these questions:

1 How might Martin's parents affect his personal development?
2 Can Clive develop a sense of self within his current peer group?
3 How might Margaret overcome her self-consciousness about her age?
4 How could Grace be helped to transfer with confidence to the college?
5 Will Cass's experiences at college affect her attitudes towards school?

In Chinese culture, there is a tradition which says that people cannot be classed as adults until they are married. In the UK, the legal system has a curiously confused approach to adulthood. For example, a 16-year-old can marry but cannot vote, drive a car or be served with alcohol in a public place. Employers, too, often display somewhat illogical attitudes to age in their recruitment strategies. For example, some employers advertise for experienced and skilled people yet only consider applicants under the age of 35, whereas others categorise all 16 to 19 year olds as lacking enough maturity. Given the spread of student age in an FE college, you could find you are teaching people a great deal older than yourself one day, followed by a day when your students are very close to your own age or the same age as your children.

YOUNGER LEARNERS

As we explained in Chapter 1, colleges in England are now having to make provision for students as young as 14. There are dangers in separating out 'young learners' for special attention. As Griffin (1993, p.23) explains, 'Youth/adolescence remains a powerful cultural and ideological category through which adult society constructs a specific age stage as simultaneously strange and familiar.' Adults criticise young people for behaving badly while, at the same time, reminding themselves that they probably behaved in the same way when they were teenagers. In the 1950s and 1960s, radical forces in society including the civil rights movement in America, the student riots in Paris, the huge growth in youth consumerism, and the close links between music and drug taking led to young people being defined as a social problem (see Furlong and Cartmel, 1997, for a detailed discussion). Economic prosperity gave young people the financial means to indulge their interests and greater leisure time than had been enjoyed by their parents. Although the economic crisis of the late 1970s and early 1980s put a stop to the relatively smooth transition from school to work that teenagers had been enjoying in the previous two decades, the importance of identifying oneself as part of a youth culture had been firmly established. We see this continuing today with the importance young people place on having the right make of mobile phone and designer clothes, and the means to go clubbing, even if that means getting into serious financial debt. Furlong and Cartmel (1997, p.61) explain that, 'In late modernity, the visual styles adopted by young people through the consumption of clothing are regarded as having become increasingly central to the establishment of identity and to peer relations.' They stress, however, that although this consumerism is evident across all social classes, not everyone has the financial means to keep up with the latest fashions, resulting in a pattern of both financial and cultural exclusion.

The way in which many teenage students in full-time education service their consumer needs is by working on a part-time basis, sometimes as much as 20 hours per week. We know from research that the majority of 16–19 year olds work part-time (see, inter alia, Lucas and Lammont 1998), and many have some work experience from the age of 14, so that 'earning and learning' has become the common experience for young people (Hodgson and Spours, 2001, p.386). The massive growth of the service sector in the UK has benefited from a willing army of young, part-time workers whose identity shifts, often on a daily basis, between student, employee and consumer. Service sector employers can offer flexible hours, the possibility of working long shifts to earn extra money, and employment close to home. And employers will often demand little in the way of prior experience or qualifications (see Lipsig-Mumme, 1997). For teenagers concerned to earn just enough money to cover their social life and mobile phone bills, such jobs are very attractive. The implications of this shift in meaning of the term 'full-time student' are considerable. Teachers in schools and colleges alike are finding that they cannot assume that young people will devote their time outside the classroom to homework or that they will be alert enough to pay attention in class. Some teachers are trying to solve these problems by making use of their students' work experience in, for example, the development of key skills, or as the basis for assignment work. What is clear is that where once colleges relied on young people using their 'free' periods to continue their studies in a self-directed manner, they now have to acknowledge that this time is more likely to be spent on the till in the local supermarket.

The nature and scope of young people's life chances are largely dependent on their family background, current level of educational attainment, gender, ethnicity and geographical location. As the work of Furlong and Cartmel (1997) and Hodkinson, Sparkes and Hodkinson (1996) has shown, young people's lives do not generally follow the neat linear pattern envisaged by policymakers (see also Hodkinson, 1996, 1998 and Unwin, 1999b). Their 'horizons for action', to use Hodkinson et al.'s term, may expand or constrict, sometimes through their choice and sometimes because of circumstances beyond their control. And as Evans (1998, p.20) points out, 'Young adults may be caught in disjunctions and contradictions of policies which do not recognise the interplay of the private and public domains and are based on invalid assumptions about common characteristics and needs of age ranges.' For the FE teacher, it is worth remembering that, as Furlong and Cartmel (1997, p.41) explain, youth is a 'period of semi-dependency which forms a bridge between the total dependence of childhood and the independence of adulthood.' It is a time of great experimentation and indulgence, but it can also be a time of great anxiety. Teenagers can find themselves homeless as a result of family breakdown, they may be coming to terms with having suffered sexual and/or physical abuse, they may be single parents, and they may be responsible for the care of a parent or sibling. As Harkin et al. (2001, p.59) point out, 'we know that educational achievement is likely to be as much the product of environmental factors as of any innate tendency to a particular learning style or type of intelligence.' The instabilities of modern life can catapult teenagers into a more adult role than they would wish or are capable of performing.

As we highlighted in Chapter 3, developments in ILT mean that many young people are used to using the Internet as a means to acquire information, and are skilled in word processing. Such assumptions can, however, be misleading for teachers who may find that a significant proportion of their young students have only really used computers to play games. In addition, the reliance on the Internet that some young people have developed for gathering information may have had a restricting influence on their ability to think critically or to study subjects in-depth. Although the use of ILT has to be handled with care, these new technologies also offer considerable potential for aiding learner autonomy, for delivering on-going feedback, and, through the use of email and web-based chat rooms, for more creative types of group interaction. Young people will expect ILT to play a considerable part in their learning experience at college.

In their research into young people's experiences in FE, Bloomer and Hodkinson (1997, p.61) developed the concept of the 'learning career' which they define as 'the development of a student's dispositions to learning over time'. These 'dispositions' are affected by experience both within and outside college, but Bloomer and Hodkinson (ibid.) found that the vast majority of the young people they studied were surprised at just how much their dispositions changed during their time in FE. Although, for some young people, the extent and type of transformation they experience as learners will be influenced by their previous life history, in the main the pattern of one's learning career was not wholly predictable. Some of the many factors which Bloomer and Hodkinson (ibid.) found contributed to changing dispositions to learning were: examination results; new teachers; fellow students in a class; course content; course assessment; learning activities; college resources; course availability; course status; financial circumstances; job opportunities; and access to advice. Bloomer and Hodkinson (ibid., p.79) conclude that 'For those entering FE from school, it is a period of maturation, of unfolding and developing personal identity, of transition, transformation and change.'

Teenagers and young adults can find that being a student does not sit well with their life outside college. There are a number of difficult issues with which young people may have to grapple:

- personal identity and life goals;
- sexuality;
- the generation gap with their parents;
- their status in society;
- personal finances;
- balancing part-time work with their studies;
- relationship with siblings;
- relationship with peer group;
- coping with living apart from their family.

In addition to any personal problems they may have, young people are aware of the fragile nature of the labour market and recognise that they may have to be prepared to change career several times during their working lives. Indeed, the problems faced by young people have been of concern throughout the European Union for some time, as this CEDEFOP report highlighted:

> The youth phase has become more extended in duration; established and normative sequences of transitions are breaking up into much more variable and individually less predictable patterns; many young people's material circumstances have deteriorated in absolute or relative terms; lifestyles and values are also shifting and becoming more pluralised. At the same time, of course, macrosocial and economic change in Europe is producing new structures of opportunity and demand in the labour market; and systematic social inequalities have by no means declined, but have rather intensified and become more complex.
>
> (CEDEFOP, 1994, p.6)

It would be ridiculous to give the impression that all young people are suffering from stress or experiencing significant hardship, but many of them do encounter problems that will have an impact on their ability and motivation to learn.

Research carried out in Cheshire, by one of the authors of this book, sought the views of 16–19 year old FE students as to where and when they encountered barriers to learning (see Unwin, 1995). They identified seven areas of concern:

1 Teaching and learning styles
2 Curriculum issues
3 Progression between courses and institutions

4 Peer group relationships
5 Financial worries
6 Level of family support
7 Labour market pull

The young people who were interviewed were studying full time for either A levels or GNVQs. They came from different social backgrounds, some lived in rural areas, others in urban settings, and they were all part way through a two-year course. As they talked about their experiences at college, they reflected on their schooldays and compared being a student then to now. The following quotations have been selected to show how the learning of young people is affected by the actions of others and also by their own perceptions of their personal ability and situation:

Learning styles (notably study skills and transition from one style of teaching/learning to another):

At school you were made to work and you had the teacher telling you what to do . . . college is different: I like it but I have to do it on my own now . . . it's hard.

I wasn't used to all this taking notes, they seem to want to cram as much in as possible. I don't think I'm enjoying it as much as I thought but perhaps it's because I'm worried about how I'm going to get through all this stuff.

We seem to get a load of assignments to do all at once, six or seven just before Christmas but none for ages. Why can't they be more consistent?

It would help if we had the books we need, the library is useless.

My friend helps, she's good at using her notes and she can write the assignments – I wish they would show you early on how to do what they want. I feel as though I'm a little kid again, as if I haven't been to school before; it feels stupid but I want to get through.

It depends on the lessons, some are really good. Organisation, they need to be more organised so that we can plan our time better.

My mate left because he couldn't get his stuff in on time. There's another lad who will leave too, he's had enough. They should spend some time at the start making sure you know what you're doing.

Curriculum and timetable (nature of chosen course may not meet expectations, prove to be too difficult, be too far removed from their previous experience, too much freedom):

I've made the wrong choice – my fault. I didn't really know what I wanted to do and now I'm stuck with it.

I chose the course [A level] because it followed on from my best subjects at GCSE but it's nothing like the same. I'm amazed at this; they should have told us it was nothing like the GCSE.

I wanted a job really but my parents said stay at school. The courses go together, I suppose, but I'm not interested as I don't want to go to university.

Being at college is much better than school but we do waste time – like when we have, say, three hours in the middle of the day free we go into town and so there's not much point going back for an hour at 4 pm. School made you turn up; here it's a lot easier to miss lessons.

Progression (level of difficulty may be far higher than the recognised feeder course prepared them for)

The BTEC First was dead easy and we did lots of projects together. Now [the National] it's all taking notes and learning tons of subjects. You're not as involved as a student as last year.

The GCSE science course I did was totally simple. A levels are something else. I've had to spend ages trying to cram because of the difference. We just weren't prepared.

It must get the teachers down that we find the course too hard but we were told we could come on it because we'd passed last year. I might leave. I'm a bit fed up with not doing well, gets you down.

Peer group (relating to a new group of people can cause problems, yet the need for group support is vital):

In my group we're all glad we're not in the other group – they mess about and seem weird.

We all help each other. The residential at the start of the year was brilliant. I didn't know anyone when I came here as my friends had gone to another college, but I've got a great set of friends now. I wouldn't like to be left out.

Our group gets on my nerves . . . the teachers don't like the group but nothing gets done.

Some people in the group can't do the work so the teacher has to spend ages with them . . . why do they let these people on the courses?

Financial (issues here range from actual poverty to peer pressure related to dress and possessions):

The costs of this course [BTEC art and design] are incredible, I've just spent another £12 on paint and next week we've got to have some thick card that costs a fortune. I reckon I spend about £5 a week on materials and sometimes it's a lot more.

You can't survive without a job.

My course expects you to go abroad on a trip and we had a residential weekend to pay for.

Family support (domestic difficulties cause pressure at home; some students leave home to live independently):

There's nowhere to work at home.

My dad is out of work . . . he's really down so I just moan at college . . . I've got to moan somewhere.

I've got a room now but I won't be able to afford it so I'll have to leave and get a job. The college helped, gave me some money, but it's no use.

Labour market pull (temporary jobs, albeit low paid, are available in all areas):

There's a German supermarket opening in Crewe soon . . . jobs at £6.00 an hour. Lots of my friends are going to go down there and see what it's like.

This agency lets you ring up when you've got some free time and gives you part-time jobs, so when I've got a day off college or I've not got any assignments due in I ring up. It's better than having a regular job like my mates . . . I can fit my college work in better.

We all know we should finish our course but if there was a job some of us would go for it . . . I know this lad who's earning £150 a week.

The financial difficulties experienced by young people deserve comment. The majority of those interviewed explained that they required money for equipment related to their courses, for food and clothes. There was some evidence of peer pressure as regards fashion and appearance but, in general, young people were struggling to find enough money to meet their everyday expenses. (For a review of literature on young people's attitudes to education, employment and training, see Morris et al., 1999.)

Mature adults can face many of the problems identified by the younger students above, particularly if those problems are introduced by their teachers and the college in which they are studying, or if they are created by external pressures. In addition, mature students are more likely to face health problems and have the general burden of the responsibility for managing households.

For many mature women, their barriers to learning are wrapped up in the very fact of being female. Their lives tend to be more disrupted than men's as they take time out of education and careers to raise children or to support partners. The following comment from a 30-year-old mother of three captures the battle which some women have to gain lost ground:

I'm just getting to the point where everybody else starts. Do you understand what that means? Most people, when they leave home or graduate from high school, already have an idea of what they are worth. An idea that they go out and conquer the world. I'm just getting to where everybody else is at.

(Belenky et al., 1986, p.53)

In order to support women who are returning to learn and who may feel threatened or ill at ease in the company of male students and tutors, some colleges run women-only courses. Maggie Coats, who advocates such courses, found from her own research (Coats, 1994, p.118) that there are both advantages and disadvantages for the women who attend:

Advantages

- allows women to gain confidence from shared experiences and group support in a non-threatening environment;
- encourages women to locate their own personal experiences in a wider social context and thus understand those experiences;
- provides a secure base from which to go out into wider society and to which women can return for further support and encouragement.

Disadvantages

- the experience of women-only provision can only be transitional and women will lose the support of the group when they progress to further education, training or employment;
- the relevant practical support needed may not be available in other provision.

Although many would argue against separating men and women for educational or training purposes, the issues which concern the advocates of women-only courses apply to the central issue of the impact of gender on learning.

Reflection
Consider to what extent your own gender might influence the way in which you will teach and relate to your students. For example, if you are a young man, how will you relate to mature women or to young teenage girls? If you are a young woman, how will you cope with teaching a class full of 18-year-old male apprentices or a room full of aspiring managers from the private sector? How will your students see you? (See Further reading).

HOW DO PEOPLE LEARN?

Stephen Brookfield, whose quotation opened this chapter, has said:

> To specify generic principles of learning is an activity full of intellectual pit-falls. Even if we leave aside the variables of physiology, personality, and cultural background, we still have to consider the implications of those developmental theories that hold that adults function in very different ways when responding to the societal and personal imperatives required of them in young adulthood, midlife, and old age. This suggests that the generic concept of adulthood is so broad and oversimplified as to be of limited use as a research construct.
>
> (Brookfield, 1986, p.26)

Brookfield goes on to recognise, however, that a number of people have contributed since the late 1950s to the creation of a theory of adult learning, which has proved to be important to both learners and teachers:

- Gibb (1960) – adult learning must be problem and experience-centred, provide feedback, and have learner-set goals.
- Miller (1964) advocated cognitive models of learning above behaviourist models.
- Kidd (1973) placed importance on lifespan, role changes, egalitarian relationship between teacher and student, self-directedness of adults, meaning of time and the prospect of death.
- Knox (1977) – adults learn continually and informally, achievements modified by individual characteristics, learning is affected by physical, social and personal characteristics, and by content and pace. Adults underestimate their ability and allow school experience to dominate, prior experience can both hinder and advance capacity to learn.
- Brundage and Mackeracher (1980) identified 36 learning principles including: adults learn throughout their lifetimes, they construct meaning through experience, they learn best in situations which value the status of the learner and when they are in good health and stress-free, they need clear goals to learn new skills, they enjoy a combination of individual and group activity.
- Smith (1982 adults have four key characteristics: multiple roles and responsibilities, many accumulated life experiences, experience of a number of development phases (physical, psychological and social), and anxiety and ambivalence about their learning activity.

The theorists cited by Brookfield all recognise the significance of internal and external pressures that impact on any adult's capacity for learning. One study of adult learning, carried out in Canada by Allen Tough and reported in 1971, was particularly influential in seeking to identify the ways in which adults differed in their learning from children. Tough observed the ways in which adults plan and organise their own learning and how they set about acquiring knowledge and understanding. His key finding was that adults are 'self-directed' in their learning for which 'more than half of the person's total motivation is to gain and retain certain fairly clear knowledge and skill or to produce some lasting change in himself' (Tough, 1971, p.6). Tough's findings built on earlier work in the USA by Johnstone and Rivera who found that a huge number of adults were engaged in learning outside the formal adult education system, which they termed 'independent self-study' (Johnstone and Rivera, 1965). This and later studies of adult participation in learning showed how the amount of adult learning could be wildly underestimated if the only measure was the numbers attending formal classes in institutions. By recognising the determination of adults to further their learning and that this motivation made them much more self-directed than children, the need for the development of distinctive models of adult learning theory was advanced.

One of the most distinctive theories has been put forward by Malcolm Knowles (1978) who developed the concept of 'andragogy' (from the Greek aner (stem andra), which means 'man') which stresses that children and adults approach learning in different ways and that this should be taken into consideration by those who help adults learn. Knowles noted the following differences between adults and children:

1 Children see themselves as dependent – adults see themselves as independent.
2 Adults bring experience to learning and value that experience.
3 Adults are ready to learn for specific reasons as their development is linked to the evolution of their social role – children's development is physiological and mental.
4 Children see much of their learning as being for the future – adults learn as a response to the here and now.

Although much of this work has a common-sense ring to it, there is a danger that the individual learner becomes lost in a sea of generalisations. The vignettes in Chapter 2 show how dangerous it is to generalise. Take, for example, the case of Clive whose behaviour as a learner seems to have more in common with the characteristics of children as identified by Knowles above, rather than with those of self-directed adult learners. There is a sense, too, with Grace that she may still be at a dependent stage as a learner owing to a lack of confidence, despite her age and experience.

Reflection

Given below is a list of instructions based on the Japanese art of Origami for making a salt cellar. (When made up, some of you may recognise the object as one which was, and may still be, popular at school for playing a game of choices.) In order to learn how to make this object, you could do one of the following:

1 Go through the instructions step by step as you would an instructional manual.
2 Ask a partner to assist you – one reading, one folding the paper.
3 Ask a partner to make the object first and then demonstrate to you as in a typical class in which, for example, the teacher demonstrates how to ice a cake or set up a chemistry experiment.

Using one of the above methods, have a go at making the object and record your experiences. When reflecting on your performance, try to consider the following questions:

1 Do you learn best by yourself or do you like/need the support of someone else?
2 Do you follow instructions to the letter or do you improvise?
3 Would you have worked better from a picture?
4 Do you prefer to be shown how to do something?

If you have the time and/or the opportunity, ask a fellow adult and a child (under the age of 13) to attempt the same exercise and compare their learning experience with your own.

Paper folding instructions

1 TAKE AN A4 SHEET OF PAPER
2 PLACE PAPER PORTRAIT WAY UP
3 FOLD BOTTOM RIGHT HAND CORNER AT 45° UNTIL IT MEETS LEFT HAND EDGE
4 TAKE SCISSORS AND CUT OFF RECTANGULAR UNFOLDED SECTION OF PAPER, AND DISCARD
5 UNFOLD SQUARE PAPER
6 MAKE ANOTHER DIAGONAL FOLD, SO THAT THERE ARE NOW TWO DIAGONAL FOLDS THAT CROSS IN THE CENTRE OF THE PAPER
7 UNFOLD
8 TAKE THE LEFT EDGE OF PAPER AND FOLD OVER TO MEET RIGHT EDGE
9 UNFOLD
10 TAKE BOTTOM EDGE OF PAPER AND FOLD OVER TO MEET TOP EDGE
11 UNFOLD

12 YOU SHOULD NOW HAVE A SQUARE PIECE OF PAPER WITH TWO
    DIAGONAL FOLDS AND TWO SQUARE FOLDS THAT CROSS IN
    THE CENTRE OF THE PAPER
13 FOLD ALL FOUR CORNERS, ONE AT A TIME TO MEET THE
    CENTRE POINT
14 TURN WORK OVER
15 FOLD ALL FOUR CORNERS, ONE AT A TIME, TO MEET THE
    CENTRE POINT
16 TURN WORK OVER
17 PUSH DIAGONAL FOLDS TOGETHER AND OPEN OUT THE
    POCKETS IN EACH OF THE CORNERS TO PRODUCE A 'SALT
    CELLAR'

When you analysed your approach to and experience of the paper folding
exercise, you may have found yourself engaged in Kolb's learning cycle. You
might also recognise some of your experience in the following eight-stage model
of learning which has been advocated by Gagne, an educational psychologist
who developed and extended some of the early work on behaviourism. We
have summarised and adapted Gagne's model and suggest that the term 'learning' be seen as encompassing knowledge, skills and understanding:

Stage one   *Motivation*
(Student's motives and expectations identified
and brought in line with teaching objectives)

Stage two   *Apprehending*
(Teacher gains student's attention by various means)

Stage three   *Acquisition*
(Knowledge, skills and understanding acquired
by the student in a form in which they are ready
to be lodged in the memory)

Stage four   *Retention*
(Student is helped to memorise and assimilate new
learning)

Stage five   *Recall*
(Student encouraged to retrieve learning ready for
application)

Stage six   *Generalisation*
(Student transfers learning to range of situations)

Stage seven   *Performance*
(Student tries out newly acquired learning)

Stage eight   *Feedback*
(Student is helped to judge performance and reflect)

As with all models, this one has a simplicity which can be misleading – teaching and learning can often be a messy business and individuals do not, necessarily, want to have their learning confined within a chronological framework. Clearly, the stages shown above can be fused and their order might be rearranged or disrupted in order to reflect particular circumstances. It is, however, a useful model for teachers to keep at the back of their mind when they are planning teaching sessions and it can be used during sessions as an evaluation tool if a teacher feels the right amount of progress is not being made. We will return to this model in the next chapter when we examine teaching strategies.

You will have seen that Stage one in Gagne's model is 'motivation', a word which will figure highly in most teachers' everyday discourse, whether they are thinking about their own levels of motivation or that of their students. Just like the weather, motivation can change from one hour to the next and it is a difficult concept to unpack. Rogers (1994, p.61) explains that motivation can be said to be dependent on either 'intrinsic' or 'extrinsic' factors:

> Extrinsic factors consist of those external incentives or pressures, such as attendance requirements, external rewards and/or punishments or examinations, to which many students are subjected. These, if internalized, create an intention to engage in the learning process. Intrinsic factors consist of that series of inner pressures and/or rational decisions which create a desire for learning changes.

It is clear that even this differentiation is problematic. Rogers (ibid., p.62) acknowledges that within intrinsic motivation there is a hierarchy of motives. He gives this example: 'a desire to please some other person or loyalty to the adult group that keeps the student attending even when bored with the subject is seen as an intrinsic motive of a lower order than a desire to complete a particular task'.

A key theorist of motivation was Maslow (1968) who devised what he called a 'hierarchy of needs', pictured as follows:

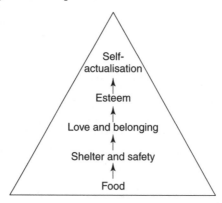

Figure 4.1 Maslow's hierarchy of needs

In this rising model of motivation, Maslow asserts that adults and children move up the layers as their need in each one is satisfied. Despite its limitations, this model has proved useful to teachers in pointing to the need to remember that their students are individuals with emotional, intellectual and physical needs. Harkin et al. (2001, p.62) have adapted Maslow's model by filling in some useful detail: they convert Food into guidelines for making the learning environment pleasant, including adequate refreshment breaks; Shelter and safety refer to non-threatening classrooms, ground rules and induction pro-grammes; Love and belonging covers openness of communication, recognition of different learning styles and valuing learners' life histories; Esteem relates to setting achievable tasks, giving positive feedback and support for learner autonomy; and Self-actualisation is concerned with supporting progression and transfer of learning.

Another theorist whose work offers useful insights for understanding how people learn is Bloom who distinguished between learning that takes place in the cognitive domain and that in the affective domain (see Bloom, 1965). For Bloom, cognitive learning runs in parallel with affective learning so that at the same time as a learner develops knowledge, his or her behaviour as a learner is also developing. The affective side to learning can be seen as a way to intro-duce some kind of value system to the learning process so that as one acquires knowledge, one also learns to appreciate the role that knowledge plays which, in turn, encourages the learner to be committed to the process.

A particularly powerful view of the way in which people learn is that pro-vided by Jean Lave and Etienne Wenger (1991) who developed the concept of 'communities of practice', which stresses that learning is as much a collective as an individual activity. This is a social theory of learning, which sees learn-ing as 'an aspect of participation in socially situated practices' (Lave, 1995, p.2). What is important here is that knowledge and skills are seen as not belonging solely to an individual but things which are to be shared and devel-oped collectively. In addition, it is the social, political, economic and cultural dimensions of any community of practice and the nature of the interactions between members that determine how much learning occurs. Eraut et al. (1998), for example, have drawn on Lave and Wenger's ideas to show how people learn from each other in contemporary workplaces, whereas Fuller and Unwin (2001b) have argued that the quality of learning on the Modern Apprenticeship is very dependent on the way in which a company's existing community of practice sees apprentices as primarily learners or productive workers.

The concept of a community of practice, which has tended to be used pri-marily by researchers into workplace learning, can be applied to a college, a classroom or group of students working together on a project. It can provide a useful device for teachers to examine the social context in which they expect their students to learn. In addition, by examining their own community of practice, whether as members of a department, a course team or at the level of the whole college, teachers can also reflect on how those communities facilitate or impede their professional development and sense of worth.

Lave and Wenger's work forms part of a growing body of research in the USA and Europe centred around socio-cultural activity theory which builds on the work of the Russian psychologist Lev Vygotsky (see Cole et al., 1978; Cole, 1985). As Guile and Young (1999, p.113) explain, Vygotsky was concerned with 'the progress that students make with their studies as they relate their "everyday" concepts – the understanding that emerges spontaneously from interaction with other people and in different situations – to the "scientific" concepts that they experience through textbooks and the formal curriculum'. He developed the concept of the 'zone of proximal development' which he defined as: '. . . the distance between the actual development level as determined by independent problem solving and the level of potential development as determined through problem solving under adult guidance or in collaboration with more able peers' (Vygotsky, 1978, p.85).

Where Vygotsky was concerned with child development, researchers such as Lave and Wenger and the Finnish activity theorist Yrjo Engestrom have extended his ideas to adults and to learning outside formal classrooms, including the workplace. Guile and Young (1999) have argued that social-cultural activity theory could provide a way of linking work-based and school-college-based learning. In Chapter 5, we discuss the concept of 'scaffolding', a teaching and learning strategy that was stimulated by Vygotsky's work.

BARRIERS TO LEARNING

There are an infinite number of barriers to prevent people from learning, some of which are external in nature, perhaps caused by domestic or financial difficulties, and some of which are internal, arising from psychological or physiological problems. In addition, teachers can, of course, create barriers for their students. These barriers might be created as a result of the following:

- a teacher's personal behaviour towards a student;
- the choice of teaching technique;
- lack of attention to the teaching environment, for example too much noise, room too hot or too cold, not enough light, etc.

Reflection
Consider the ways in which you have been prevented from learning during your life and, in contrast, try to identify anything which has been a positive support to your learning. Make your notes in two lists:

List one: Barriers to Learning
List two: Support for Learning

In the lists you made, you may have identified your family or domestic relationships as a feature in one or perhaps both lists. Clearly, domestic life has a major impact on the way in which children and teenagers learn, but it can be forgotten that young and mature adults can be equally affected by their domestic environment. In his study of married, male, full-time university students in Canada, Lauzon makes the following comment:

> The decision to become a student and the subsequent changes in the student's personal identity will necessitate changes in family members and patterns of family interaction. One way of conceptualising these changes is to examine the student from a familial systematic perspective. This perspective views the family as the main unit of study; all family members are subsystems of the main family system. Any change experienced at the subsystem level will necessitate change at the system level. In the case of a family where one member experiences changes in social roles, responsibilities, beliefs and/or values, other members will be required to make changes in order to accommodate the change at the level of the system (Satir, 1983). Hence not only must the individual adapt but the family must also adapt. The decision of the adult to become a full-time student forces all family members to make some behavioural and emotional adjustment. The bulk of the adjustment, however, would appear to occur in the husband/wife relationship rather than the father/child relationship . . . Despite the obstacles and demands placed in front of, and on, the adult student, they continue to pursue their dreams. As one respondent put it: 'It's the dream that keeps me going. Knowing that something better is just over the horizon.' But sometimes the dream turns to a nightmare and the world of the adult student falls apart. A few months after this study was completed the researcher had the opportunity to talk to one of the respondents. He reported that he was currently engaged in a vicious divorce and custody battle and attributed the breakdown of his marriage to his being a student. Sometimes the dream just isn't enough; education for the adult can be costly.
>
> (Lauzon, 1989, pp.43–4)

Only a minority of adult learners end up in the regrettable position of the one quoted above, but Lauzon is right to draw attention to the stress and tensions that having a student in the family can create. Although his research was based on male, full-time university students, Lauzon's conclusions about the impact on family life and the adult learner would seem applicable to female as well as male students and to a wide range of learning situations.

Before writing this book, one of the authors was responsible for running a series of residential training courses for in-company trainers and supervisors. Many of the participants on these courses had not attended a course of study for several years and often not since they had left school. One of the most interesting aspects was to observe the changed behaviour of some of the women who attended the courses. These particular women had not stayed away from their partners and children before and came away worrying about how their families would cope without them. One woman related in detail how she had filled the freezer with meals and separately labelled packs of sandwiches for lunches and had arranged for a neighbour to be on stand-by to wash and iron items of clothing at a moment's notice. By the end of the third day of a one-week course, the women began to question their attitudes and by the end of the course they were threatening domestic revolution. The last thing the group facilitator wanted was to cause mayhem in families but the power of the learning situation, and particularly the chance to draw support and ideas from peers, was considerable for those women.

In her study of why mature students leave FE and HE courses before completion, McGiveney (1996) reminds us that whereas women students tend to cite family commitments as their main reason for withdrawing from courses, men tend to cite problems with the course, finance and employment-related issues. But McGiveney also points out that it would be unwise to stereotype adult learners as potential course 'drop-outs':

> several studies have found that mature students are currently slightly more likely than younger ones to complete courses. It has been suggested that this may be because students who remain in full-time education mainly because of the erosion of job prospects for school leavers are unlikely to be totally committed to study (Payne and Storran, 1995), whereas adults with work experience and those who have made considerable sacrifices in order to participate in further or higher education will be far more highly motivated.
>
> (McGiveney, 1996, p.111)

In their study in South Wales, Rees et al. (2000, p.186) found five key indicators of whether adults were more or less likely to participate in lifelong learning: time (older people felt they had had fewer opportunities when younger); place (the culture of where people are born and brought up); gender (men were more likely to participate than women; family (social class, educational history and family religion all had an impact on participation); and initial schooling (positive experience plus extended schooling both encourage participation).

Usher et al. (2002, p.79) have drawn attention to the 'negative imagery' of the concept of barriers to learning. They write, 'The learning process is characterized as one full of blockages and barriers, things that impede or hold back the self-as-learner from attaining various ends, such as efficacy, autonomy, self-realisation or emancipation.' Instead, they argue, that the 'postmodern story of the self' means that 'we tell stories about our experience' and that our subjectivity is always 'shifting and uncertain'. This is a complex debate, but the importance of Usher et al.'s analysis is that learners' identities are not fixed and, therefore, simplistic notions of what constitutes a barrier to learning might be very misleading when trying to understand learners' needs.

THE TEACHER–STUDENT RELATIONSHIP

At the beginning of this chapter, we explored some of the theories that might explain how individuals approach learning and stressed that a person's learning style will influence their approach to teaching. There is a long-running column in the TES in which well-known people from all walks of life recall the special characteristics of a teacher who, at some point in their lives, had a particular impact on them. Other newspapers and magazines often carry similar features, the common link between them being that individual teachers have the power to affect people's lives, sometimes in quite dramatic ways. The comedian and author, Ben Elton, who left school at 16 to do a drama and liberal arts course at an FE college in Warwickshire, has written about one of the college's drama teachers:

> He believed that drama was an essential part of life, that you shouldn't have to want to be an actor to enjoy it but that you should see drama as a way of learning, a way of understanding life and other people . . . He believes, passionately, that young people should be encouraged (with great vigour) not to shrug their shoulders and say 'Oh . . . it's all crap', not to be cynics but to get involved. He led by enthusiasm and I believe that the greatest gift a teacher can have is that ability to enthuse, to inspire with interest, to get people involved . . . He was a good teacher. He did the formal bit thoroughly and made it interesting . . . In setting up that course Gordon was a major, major influence on my life. He was a ball of energy. He enabled me to stay in education at the same time as sort of leaving it, and he did fundamentally affect my growing up.
>
> (TES2, 8 September 1995, p.20)

To be praised by an ex-student in this way would make any teacher feel proud and, of course, most teachers, at some point in their careers, receive thanks and best wishes from their students. Most of the time, however, as in the rest of life, any gratitude that students feel tends to go unspoken and teachers have to plough on in the hope that their work is appreciated. Just as teachers can have a very positive effect on their students, they can sometimes be a negative force and there are many people who would claim that their insecurities and blocks about learning stem from a certain teacher who made them feel inadequate. The teacher–student relationship is, therefore, a complex and dynamic one and, as such, needs to be treated with care.

The following table lists a number of labels which can be applied to someone in a 'teaching' role and to someone in a 'learning' role.

Teaching role	*Learning role*
Teacher	Student
Instructor	Trainee
Trainer	Learner
Tutor	Apprentice
Facilitator	Participant
Supervisor	Candidate
Mentor	Pupil
Demonstrator	
Coach	
Lecturer	

Each of these labels carries with it a great deal of terminological 'baggage' and much has been written about the power of labels in determining behaviour. For example, the term 'facilitator' is used widely in management training where it is regarded as being much more learner-centred than terms such as lecturer or teacher. On the other hand, teachers in FE colleges are usually referred to as 'lecturers' despite the fact that many of them spend very little time giving 'lectures'. From the point of view of learners, how they are described could denote how they might expect to be treated, the culture and ethos of the institution, and the context in which they are learning. Terms such as 'trainee' and 'apprentice', for example, are generally used in work-based settings, though the term 'trainee' might also be used in colleges for young people on youth training schemes. Labels can also change so that a 'student' might become a 'candidate' at the point when he or she is going to be assessed; a 'lecturer' becomes a 'tutor' when seeing a student for an individual tutorial meeting.

Teaching in a college will require you to switch between the different roles suggested by each of the labels listed above. Whatever your subject area, you might, in any one session, carry out the following functions:

- spend ten minutes giving a lecture;
- facilitate a group discussion;
- demonstrate how to use a piece of equipment or perform a certain task;
- spend a few minutes with individual students to give them specific tutoring;
- supervise small groups of students carrying out project work.

To be able to switch from one role to another certainly requires flexibility, but it also demands that the teacher is able to recognise which role is the most appropriate in a given circumstance. (Chapter 6 provides more detail on choosing and applying teaching strategies.) Rory Kidd (1973), building on earlier work by John Dewey, has described learning as a 'transaction' to which both the learner and the teacher have to bring something of value for both parties to feel the transaction has been effective and produced the desired outcomes. In order for this to happen, teachers and learners have to get to know each other and be prepared to change and adapt. This may take time but the process can be accelerated through the willingness of the teacher to create an atmosphere that encourages the following:

- enables students to articulate their learning needs;
- enables students to identify and discuss any barriers which might prevent them from learning;
- enables students to develop the confidence to share their own ideas and actively contribute to the learning situation;
- provides students with constructive criticism and praise so that they feel supported and, in turn, learn how to support each other;
- encourages all students to achieve at their own pace, regardless of ability;
- encourages both teacher and students to work together with a sense of community and shared purpose;
- promotes respect for individuals within the learning community.

As Ben Elton found with his drama teacher, the individual approach and personality of each teacher mark them out as being distinctive, and so teachers differ as much as their students. Indeed, it would be a very dull day for a student if all teachers were the same. In terms of maintaining order within the teaching situation, whether it be with one or a group of students, teachers will certainly behave in different ways and choose different methods for ensuring that both teacher and students concentrate on their joint purpose in coming together. As teachers gain in experience, keeping control of the proceedings becomes a subconscious activity, so that neither the teacher nor the students are aware that control is being exerted. Students, too, can be encouraged to develop self-discipline, to control their behaviour in respect of the community in which they are learning, and learn how to maintain order as a group. A useful model for sharing ideas about control and order is transactional analysis (TA) which was developed by the American psychologist, Eric Berne.

Berne calls TA a 'theory of social intercourse' and used it to help people understand and improve their behaviour towards others. He wrote:

Observation of spontaneous social activity, most productively carried out in certain kinds of psychotherapy groups, reveals that from time to time people show noticeable changes in posture, viewpoint, voice, vocabulary, and other aspects of behaviour. These behavioural changes are often accompanied by shifts in feeling. In a given individual, a certain set of behaviour patterns corresponds to one state of mind, while another set is related to a different psychic attitude, often inconsistent with the first. These changes and differences give rise to the idea of ego states.

(Berne, 1970, p.23)

Berne identified three ego states which, he believed, people move regularly in and out of during their daily lives:

Parental
Adult
Child

Of the three ego states, the Adult (demonstrated when a person is in control and displaying maturity) is thought to be present in everyone but often needs to be uncovered or activated. The Child state can be exhibited in two forms: the adapted Child, who modifies behaviour under the influence of a parent and the natural Child, who is freed from parental influence to be creative or to rebel. In this latter state, the Child can be petulant and difficult to handle. The Parental state also has two sides: first, it can be authoritarian ('Do as I say'); second, it can be nurturing ('Let me help you').

Berne's hypothesis is that problems occur when these ego states are at cross-purposes. For example, if someone who is in the natural Child state meets someone in an authoritarian Parental state, then they will have trouble communicating. Similarly, if students in the Adult state meets someone in the nurturing Parental state, they will feel frustrated or even patronised. The trick, as far as being a teacher is concerned, is to recognise both your own ego state and that of your students. You can also use TA as a model for handling colleagues and running meetings.

The teacher–student relationship will, of course, like any other interpersonal relationship, be constantly tested and there may be some occasions when it breaks down completely. In the main, however, the relationship will work because most of the people involved will realise that, if it is effective, then life for everyone will be happier.

Some of the pressure on the relationship will come from external forces that the teacher or students can do little about and that can have a positive or negative effect. The following model (Figure 4.2) illustrates how those external forces, as well as the internal feelings of teachers and students, can impact on the teacher–learner relationship. The model (adapted from Unwin and Edwards, 1990) is overlaid with three bands – class, gender and race – which exert influence throughout society and from which no relationship can be exempted.

Reflection

You might wish to make your version of the model to reflect the particular circumstances in which you are working. You may, for example, expand some of the bands so that you can include more variables. One way of creating your own version is to use coloured card. The model could also be used with students as a way of encouraging them to identify the variables which affect their relationship with you as a teacher and/or as a group of learners. This works well as a group activity so long as individuals are not forced into isolated positions.

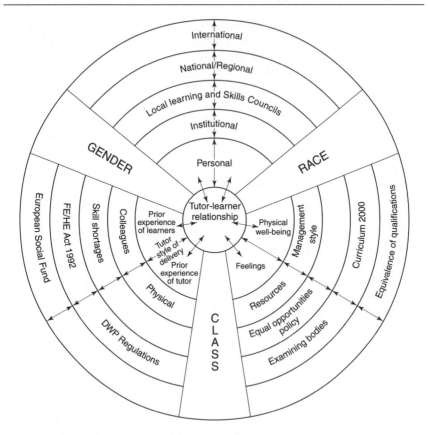

Figure 4.2 Teacher–learner relationship

GROUP LEARNING

Most of the teaching you will do in FE will be with groups of students. As in all sectors of education, pressure on resources demands that group teaching (and often in groups of considerable size) is the dominant mode. Despite the managerial reasons for favouring group-based learning, however, there are distinct benefits that students gain from learning together. We will look at specific strategies for achieving effective learning in groups in Chapter 6 but, for the moment, we will briefly explore the general benefits to be gained from group-based learning.

We have paid a great deal of attention in this chapter to the needs of individual students, and you saw in the student vignettes in Chapter 2 how different those needs can be. By bringing students together, they can begin to learn how their own needs compare and contrast to others and develop shared strategies for advancing their learning and for overcoming problems. Learning in groups can often be much more fun than singly and can facilitate the continuation of learning once the formal session has ended. Students may continue to discuss ideas outside the classroom or workshop and apply themselves creatively to group tasks.

Given the emphasis in FE on individualised learning, and the increasing use of ICT, there is a danger that learning in colleges may become too individualised. Although groups of students may be together in the same space, they might all be working completely separately on different tasks or units of competence. For Wildemeersch, such a scenario represents a 'farewell to dialogue and a welcome to individualised technicism' (Wildemeersch, 1989, p.68).

The collegiality created by group-based learning can act as an important locus of support for students who lack confidence, have problems outside college, or who gain extra motivation from the discipline of having to keep up with their peers. The teacher can capitalise on that collegiality to encourage the more able students to help others. Jaques (1992) has stated that groups operate at both a task and a socio-emotional level and within both intrinsic and extrinsic dimensions. (See Jaques' diagram in Figure 4.3.) He notes that there is a tendency to concentrate on the extrinsic dimension and explains:

> Teaching is often solution-orientated rather than problem-orientated and seems to take external requirements as its starting point rather than the needs and interests of the students. Moreover, a lack of attention to the socio-emotional dimension means that many of the task aims cannot be achieved. Without a climate of trust and co-operation, students will not feel like taking the risk of making mistakes and learning from them. To achieve this, the tutor would have to balance a concern for academic standards with a capacity to understand and deal with the workings of group processes as well as an attitude of generosity and praise for new solutions to old problems.
>
> (Jaques, 1992, p.72)

There are groups and groups, of course, and not all will provide the collegiality referred to above. Rory Kidd states that there are three characteristics which have to be present in a group if effective learning is to take place:

1 A realisation by the members of the group that genuine growth stems from the creative power within the individual, and that learning, finally, is an individual matter.
2 The acceptance as a group standard that each member has the right to be different and to disagree.
3 Establishment of a group atmosphere that is free from narrow judgements on the part of the teacher or group members.

(Kidd, 1973, p.80)

	Task	Socio-emotional
I N T R I N S I C	Expressing selves in subject	Greater sensitivity to others
	Judging ideas in relation to others	Judging self in relation to others
	Examining assumptions	Encouraging self-confidence
	Listening attentively	Personal development
	Tolerating ambiguity	Tolerating ambiguity
	Learning about groups	Awareness of others' strengths and weaknesses
E X T R I N S I C	Follow-up to lecture	Giving support
	Understanding text	Stimulating to further work
	Improving staff/ student relations	Evaluating student feelings about course
	Gauging student progress	Giving students identifiable groups to belong to
	Giving guidance	

Source: Jaques (1992) Reproduced with permission from Taylor & Francis Ltd

Figure 4.3 Types of aims and purposes in group teaching

SUPPORT SERVICES FOR STUDENTS

'The development of a better understanding of what it means to manage the process of learning for each and every student is central to the challenge facing college staff and governors. The sector is still in the early days of developing fully inclusive strategies to ensure that the particular needs of each learner are met' (FEFC 2001, p.3). One of the most important ways in which learners can be supported is to give them access to a range of support services. Such support can include advising them as to the most appropriate modules in a course, how to stagger their studies to fit in with professional demands, how to seek financial support for fees, and putting them in touch with professional counsellors if personal problems become too difficult to handle alone. A great deal of support can be provided by organisations and teachers by actually listening to students and interpreting their needs correctly.

A major issue here is the extent to which individual teachers accept that they have a role to play in supporting learners above and beyond putting across the actual subject matter of a particular course of study. In particular, the teacher can have a significant impact on a student's sense of well-being as McGiveney emphasises with this quote from an FE teacher talking about part-time students:

> The reality of formal part-time study is that individual tutors can make or break a learner's experience. The tutor is central to the creation of the essential, supportive social environment of the classroom which reduces drop-out. We can talk till the cows come home about the vital importance of guidance but we are seriously in error if we do not acknowledge the pivotal guidance role of the tutor for the part-timer. For many the teacher is the guidance system.
>
> (McGiveney, 1996, p.135)

Egan's (1975) three-stage model of the skilled helper originated in his work as a counsellor, but it can be usefully adopted by teachers as a basis for supporting individual students:

Stages	*Steps*
Stage 1	Exploration
	Focus on specific concerns
Stage 2	Developing new perspectives
	Setting specific goals
Stage 3	Exploring possible ways to act
	Choosing and working out a plan of action
	Implementing the plan
	Evaluation

Colleges arrange their student support services in recognition of the fact that students' support needs stretch from, for example, help with basic skills such as literacy and numeracy, to careers information, but also include the need for access to a confidential service to deal with very private matters. The following details from a college prospectus show how one college defines student support in the broadest terms. Its services combine, under the heading of support, to provide a lively environment in which students can feel they are cared for by the institution (see also Figure 4.4).

Figure 4.4 College guidance map.

	Entry	On-programme	Exit
Educational guidance	**Programme choice:** guidance officers **Specialist programme advice:** programme area advisors **Placement and referral:** admissions tutors **Self-assessment and specific learning needs:** assessment and support officers **External training and educational opportunities:** guidance officers and routeways counsellors **APL advice:** guidance officer	**Management of learning:** tutors **Support for tutorial planning and development:** guidance officers **Transfer and learning support advice:** guidance officers **Retention counselling [individual and group]:** guidance officers **Individual retention counselling:** careers service	**Progression planning and preparation:** tutors **HE choice and applicant support:** tutors and careers service
Personal and welfare guidance	**Learner support provision:** guidance officers **Financial planning to support study:** guidance officers **Transition counselling:** guidance officers	**Personal support:** tutors **Financial welfare, legal and learner support:** guidance officers **Personal counselling:** guidance officers **External referral to specialist agencies:** guidance officers **Crisis and emergency support:** guidance officers **Student representation and complaints:** guidance officers	**Examination stress:** guidance officers **Practical, financial and personal support for transition:** guidance officers
Vocational guidance	**Career and progression planning:** vocational guidance officer and careers services [16–19] **Post-results guidance [GCSE and A level]:** careers service and guidance officers **First-language counselling and assessment:** routeways counsellors	**Individual vocational guidance:** careers service and vocational guidance officer **Careers education:** tutors, vocational guidance officer and careers service **Educational counselling for refugees and asylum seekers:** refugee council officer and world university service officer **Progression counselling for students with learning difficulties and disabilities:** specialist careers officer **Assessment and support for students with specific learning difficulties:** assessment and support officers	**Transition and application skills [individual and group]:** tutors, vocational guidance officer, careers service and routeway **Progression counselling for students with learning difficulties and disabilities:** specialist careers officers
Specialist guidance			

Figure 4.4 College guidance map. Tutors provide a first-line service and ensure that students have access to advice and guidance on all matters affecting their learning. Guidance officers provide a flexible, comprehensive service which offers an immediate and accessible response to the range of guidance needs.

Student Support at Hertford Regional College

- Learning support for students with learning difficulties and/or disabilities who feel that they need more support than is normally provided by the college. Support is also generally available to students with sensory or physical disabilities, specific learning difficulties and other severe learning needs.
- English and maths workshops for students who have difficulties with spelling and writing English and/or require help with number work.
- Language support is available for all students whose mother tongue is not English.
- Student services are available to provide students with extra help and guidance of a practical or personal nature during their courses.
- Personal tutors to give support both in relation to study and other matters where needed.
- A Students' Union which represents the interest of all students in the college by encouraging sporting and recreational activities and providing financial support for leisure and social events organised by the students.
- Purpose built centres which provide an opportunity for students to meet together in an informal atmosphere. There are also facilities for table tennis, pool, darts, video games and music.
- Sports facilities include a wide variety of sports clubs and access to playing fields, gymnasiums and a sports hall.
- The Careers Information and Guidance Service will help students make choices about their future education, training, employment or career. The services include a career library, computer aided guidance, one-to-one interviews and open workshops. Areas covered include career research, Higher Education, job search strategies, CV preparation and interview skills.

One of the most formalised mechanisms for helping students adapt to college life and feel welcomed is induction, which can last anything from half a day to two weeks.

Reflection

Imagine you are about to start a course in a college. What items would you want to see covered in an induction programme? As you make your list, consider the circumstances of the students we introduced you to in Chapter 2.

The following extracts from FEFC inspection reports show the types of induction programmes in use in colleges. You might wish to compare your ideas for induction with the items listed below:

Induction One
Part-time and full-time students benefit from a well-documented induction
process which is customised to suit individual courses and access centres.
The quality of induction seen was generally good, although the teaching in
some of the sessions was mechanistic and there were few opportunities for
students to participate. Students are provided with a handbook which gives
useful information on their course and college life in general. The handbook also contains a learning agreement which sets out students'
entitlements and obligations whilst on their courses. Signature to this document confirms acceptance of the contents and this document has been
used in student disciplinary hearings.

(FEFC Inspection Report, January 1996)

Induction Two
All new students receive a general induction which is well-organised by student services. A friendly and welcoming atmosphere is created in the main
hall where stalls display the different services available to students. Tutors
take or send their students to make contact with student services. Meetings
are arranged by means of a special booking sheet which also provides a
check on which groups have used the student services. If necessary, tutors
can book follow-up visits to the study centres and counselling services for
their students. All tutors receive training in induction. They are also given
a handbook containing details of all the support and facilities. Similarly,
students receive a handbook which sets out the college's charter and lists the
facilities and staff responsible for each service.

(FEFC Inspection Report, April 1996)

A key deficiency with many induction programmes is that they tend to be
one-off events, whereas the process of induction should carry on throughout
a student's lifetime in the college. That is, at various points in his or her career
in the college, a student will need to be inducted into a new stage, to meet new
tutors and fellow students and so on, or to be reinducted with parts of the college or course long forgotten. Figure 4.5 shows how a college's guidance and
support system should span all aspects of college life from student entry
through to student exit.

THE TEACHER'S APPROACH TO LEARNING

As we noted in Chapter 1, just as the student population in FE is extremely
diverse in terms of its background and prior experience, so too is the teaching
force. This variety provides a reservoir on which the sector can draw to
enhance the learning experiences of its students. For example, a majority of
those teaching in the sector will have had relevant vocational experience before
taking up a career in teaching. Others will still be working within their vocational sectors and perhaps teaching part-time. Some may have taught in

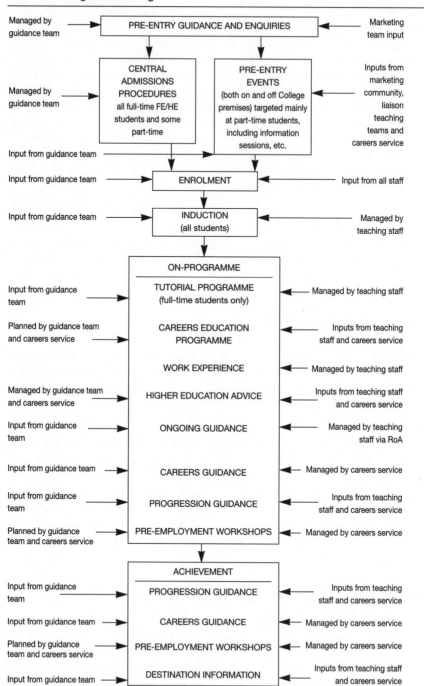

Figure 4.5 Guidance team influence on learner's pathway through college
Source: FEU (1994)

secondary education before moving into the post-compulsory phase and others may have been workplace trainers.

Clearly, this will have an impact on the way in which they approach their teaching, their attitudes to learners, and will underpin their own philosophy of teaching. We now invite you to reflect upon the following series of vignettes of typical lecturers to be found in any college. As you did in Chapter 2 with the student vignettes, we suggest you think about the following questions:

1 What perceptions do you have of each of the lecturers and how his/her previous experience might impact on the students?
2 What do you see as the potential staff development needs of the individual lecturers?

Leslie

Leslie is 49 years old and is head of the hospitality and catering programme area in a medium-sized college. It is a general FE college situated in an attractive town and has a fairly wide rural catchment, mostly covering the tourism, hospitality and agricultural sectors. It offers a wide range of courses, including a substantial A level programme.

Leslie began his career in catering, moving through a succession of jobs until he became head chef in a prestigious hotel. His professional skills were regarded very highly and he won a number of national competitions. When he became tired with the long and unsocial hours associated with hotel work, he decided to move into teaching. He had already had some experience of training younger chefs, which he had enjoyed. So a move into lecturing seemed a natural progression.

He began by doing some part-time lecturing while running a small catering business from home. He successfully completed the City and Guilds FE Teachers' Certificate and decided to take on full-time teaching. As his confidence grew in his new profession he was keen to develop his career. He enrolled on a Bachelor of Education degree at the local university and began to like the idea of part-time study more and more.

When the impact of incorporation began to bite at the college and teaching programmes began to convert to NVQs, Leslie became increasingly dissatisfied with his teaching and more and more interested in developing his own skills as a researcher. He enrolled on a part-time Master's degree and submitted his dissertation on: 'Changing Employment Patterns in the FE sector'. The MA successfully completed, he returned to his teaching with renewed critical reflection but little in the way of career progression. The college introduced a redundancy package, but Leslie was turned down because he was needed to lead the hospitality programme area. He feels he would still like to do some personal academic work but the pressure of increasing student numbers, departmental targets, new vocational qualifications and the administrative burden of running a large programme area preclude it.

Bill

Bill is a lecturer in business studies at a large city college. He joined the college five years ago, having previously worked as an assistant manager at a High Street bank. He started work in retail banking immediately following his completion of a degree in economics. While a junior manager with the bank he was encouraged to take part in a college's Young Enterprise scheme, acting as its business adviser. He enjoyed the experience so much that he seriously began to consider a change of career. He decided to leave the bank and enrolled on a full-time PGCE (FE) course. Having successfully completed it he took up his first teaching appointment at his current college.

He is pleased with his decision and really enjoys teaching, particularly individual tutorial work with students. There are many long serving lecturers in his staff room and he sometimes feels their commitment to the job is not what it might be. Bill always volunteers for new initiatives, is keen to be involved with external agencies and curriculum development. His students achieve well and he encourages them to do so. He feels that there is a lot more that he could do if other members of staff were similarly inclined. However, management, rather than business, is seen as the growth area for the college.

Management is housed in another area of the college and carries more higher-grade posts. The business section runs GNVQ (Business) courses and courses for accountancy technicians and clerical occupations. Bill can see many opportunities for developing business courses but cannot see a way of taking his ambitions forward in the current climate and organisational structure.

Julie

Julie is 33 years old and currently works in 3 different colleges within a large conurbation. She is registered with a national FE staff employment agency and domestic circumstances dictate that she has to take whatever teaching opportunities come along. She is currently teaching: Customer Service skills to Leisure and Tourism students; Licensed Trade NVQs to employees of local licensed houses; and Display and Promotion skills to students on a retail course.

She previously worked in the travel industry and decided to work in education when family commitments reduced the number of hours available for outside work. Julie has taken further qualifications in order to enhance her opportunities for working in the FE sector. She does not like having to work in a peripatetic manner but recognises that this is the only way that she can forge a career in further education. She describes the current arrangements as 'working out of the boot of the car' and says she never knows what she is going to be asked to do next. Nevertheless, she has decided to develop her expertise in the area of basic skills teaching with a view to expanding this aspect of her work. She recognises that this is likely to be an important area for growth within the FE sector and potentially an opportunity for full-time employment.

Isabella

Isabella is 25 years old and is in her first teaching post at a large urban college serving a mixed catchment area. She recently completed a full-time PGCE (FE) course having gained a degree in Spanish and French. Her mother is Spanish and Isabella had considered teaching English in Spain but decided to remain in the UK on completion of her teaching qualification. She had a very positive teaching practice experience in a lively modern languages department, but her first job, in another college, has proved to be a disappointment.

The modern languages department is small and modern languages are not given high priority in the college. A lot of the work involves evening classes for adults wishing to pick up a few useful phrases for holidays on the Costa Brava. The A level group for Spanish is dwindling and its future is uncertain; Isabella is increasingly expected to teach a substantial amount of French, her second language, to students on travel and business courses. She would like to get students involved in European exchange programmes and has ideas of how this might be achieved and about ways in which languages could be expanded at the college. So far, the head of department has been unconvinced by her arguments.

Clifford

Clifford teaches on a range of engineering manufacturing programmes from GNVQ Intermediate to HND level. He has been involved in the development of Modern Apprenticeship programmes in his college and has been industry liaison tutor for second year apprentices since the scheme's inception. Having spent fourteen years of his employed life in the automotive industry, he feels well suited to the job of industry liaison tutor. He has excellent working relationships with a number of local employers and has done a great deal to enhance the college's reputation for providing customised training linked to the needs of industry.

The increased levels of record keeping, monitoring and recording required for the assessment of current qualifications have caused some problems with local employers. Clifford has had to spend a lot of time explaining the new systems and encouraging employers to remain involved. He seems to spend an increasing amount of time chasing record sheets, student performance reports and checking attendance. He feels that this is getting in the way of workshop teaching. He also feels that he needs to update his experience of current practice in the modern automotive industry. If not, he feels that the college will lose its credibility and its market for customised training courses.

Kulwinder

Kulwinder is 28 years old and teaches on a range of health and social care courses at her local college. She left school at 16 with few qualifications and little idea about the type of career she might wish to pursue. She worked in a number of care settings before the manager of the day centre in which she was employed suggested that she might like to attend college in order to help her to work towards NVQ Level 2.

Although initially sceptical, she soon began to enjoy attending the college and completed NVQ level 2 fairly quickly. Once convinced of the benefit of gaining some qualifications and the potential of promotion, she decided to continue with level 3. At 21 she was accepted in a part-time degree programme and managed to juggle the competing demands of full-time employment, part-time study and family commitments. Although the course put considerable stress on Kulwinder's family life, she admits that 'graduation day was one of the happiest days of my life'.

The college in which she currently works has earned an outstanding reputation for its outreach work and Kulwinder particularly enjoys this aspect of her teaching. She has done a great deal to extend the learning opportunities available to women returners and to those for whom previous learning experiences have been negative. She has recently been asked by the vice-principal (curriculum) to join the college's Inclusive College working group. She welcomes the opportunity of enabling others to experience some of the benefits which she has gained from the 'widening participation agenda'.

These vignettes illustrate the diversity of backgrounds and experiences of many of those who teach in FE. Their own experiences will inform and shape their own approaches to teaching and their attitudes to learners.

Chapter 5

Teaching strategies

FLEXIBILITY AND ADAPTABILITY

In the opening chapters of this book, we described the complex world of FE and emphasised the need for teachers to be flexible and adaptable in order to meet the demands that their managers, students and external agencies will put on them. It is worth remembering, too, that the pressures on FE colleges to recruit as many students as possible mean that teaching staff will be faced with some people who have a wide range of learning difficulties. Lumby (2001, p.50) has argued that 'This very comprehensiveness is both a great strength in meeting the needs of learners and a real Achilles heel in communicating what any college is about and in meeting the needs of different groups of learners.'

FE teachers are now seen as 'managers of learning', involved in a range of activities which stretch beyond the day-to-day business of teaching in a classroom or workshop. Young et al. (1995) have proposed that the work of FE teachers has shifted during recent years as follows:

> from subject knowledge to curriculum knowledge
> from teacher-centred pedagogic knowledge to learner-centred pedagogic knowledge
> from intra-professional knowledge to inter-professional knowledge
> from classroom knowledge to organisational knowledge
> from insular to connective knowledge

Instead of being a teacher who is solely concerned with his or her own subject specialism, FE teachers now have to understand how their specialism 'connects' with the rest of the college's curricular provision and how generic (or core) learning can be facilitated through that specialism. In moving to a more learner-centred approach, FE teachers will have to 'manage' the process of learning as a whole and not simply be concerned with transmitting knowledge and skills. As 'managers of learning', teachers will need to seek the help and support of other professionals in their college, including non-teaching staff, and they will be members of course teams. The shift from 'insular' to 'connective' knowledge recognises the way in which FE teachers have to be aware of and build on their students' prior educational experience and their future needs. An FE college represents a transitional stage for many students as they progress from school education through FE and on to work-based training and/or HE.

When they visit colleges, inspectors concentrate, in particular, on the organisation and management of the learning situation and note the strengths and weaknesses of the following:

- level of coherence of schemes of work
- level of teachers' subject expertise
- level of rapport between staff and students
- clarity of aims and objectives
- appropriateness of the pace of learning
- range of teaching techniques in use
- opportunities for students to participate actively
- quality of resources, for example handouts, workbooks, visual aids, etc.
- clarity of assessment criteria
- classroom/workshop management, for example, punctuality of staff and students, behaviour of students
- quality of feedback on students' work
- quality and usefulness of set tasks and appropriateness of coursework
- quality of record keeping to inform students of their progress

The following extracts from inspection reports from the period 1996 to 2000/2001 indicate the range of teaching skills for which the inspectors are looking:

Relationships between teachers and learners are good in all curriculum areas. Students speak positively of the support they get from their teachers and the adult atmosphere in the college. They are well motivated and keen to learn. Teachers recognise that many adults lack confidence at the start of a course and adapt the pace and style of teaching accordingly . . . Teachers often start by reviewing the main points covered in the previous lesson. They then explain to the students how this links to the aims and objectives of the topics to be covered in the current lesson. The more effective teachers ensure that their lessons are pitched at an appropriate level and that students of different abilities are set appropriate tasks. Teachers draw effectively on students' industrial experiences to stimulate interest.

(ALI/Ofsted, 2000/01 Inspection Reports)

Most students work competently and confidently in the hairdressing and beauty therapy salons and develop relevant professional skills . . . However, some of the materials used for teaching are dated; they are not of high quality and show little use of IT in their production.

(FEFC, 1997/98 Inspection Reports)

Most teaching (in Childcare and Health Care) is good . . . In one successful lesson, the teacher creatively used role-play of a child using building
blocks. Students worked in pairs with one student carrying out a detailed
observation of the manipulative movements of the other student. The
teacher expertly extended students' learning during the feedback from the
activity. However, some lesson plans lack sufficient detail and schemes of
work are often lists of topics without reference to the learning activities
which will be carried out.

(FEFC, 1998/99 Inspection Reports)

In construction, a significant proportion of the teaching took place in the
workshops and was of high quality. Underpinning knowledge was taught
using well-designed learning materials and textbooks, but maximum
benefit was not obtained from this development because students had
not been taught the study skills required for independent learning.
Working relationships between students and teachers were excellent
partly due to the respect that students had for the expertise displayed by
their teachers.

(FEFC, 1996d, Inspection Reports)

Many humanities sessions were enriched by the infectious enthusiasm of
teachers who used current references and illustrations to bring subjects
alive. In history sessions, students used computer disk read-only memory
(CD-ROM) databases and computer software to interrogate information
and build up databases of historical facts. Students of English and communications experienced a good range of learning activities which
included a lot of practical work in small groups. In one excellent GCE A
level class, the teacher had prepared a range of resources for group work,
including computers loaded with interactive packages on synthesised
speech. Within a short time, and working through a graded series of exercises, students became aware of the importance of phonemes in the study
of language.

(FEFC, 1996d, Inspection Reports)

CHOOSING A STRATEGY

Students attend colleges to acquire skills, knowledge and understanding
related to their area of study, whether it be English literature, welding, social
care or applied statistics. Separating out the skills, knowledge and understanding components within any one learning encounter is not, of course, a
straightforward process as in most encounters the three are bound together.

Given the underpinning complexity of the learning encounter in terms of
content, there is also the diversity of your potential students to consider. You
are clearly going to need to develop a range of strategies for helping your students to learn effectively. Once you gain some experience as a teacher, you

will find that you can create your own strategies which reflect your personality and are designed to respond to your students' particular needs. Always remember that different strategies work differently for different teachers. You may be the sort of person who will never be comfortable giving a lecture or facilitating a role-play exercise but able to get excellent results from designing group-based problem-solving exercises. Then again, you may shine as a lecturer, providing your students with stimulating talks that capture their imaginations. Gaining confidence as a teacher is important and all teachers tend to stick with the strategies with which they feel most comfortable. Your students, too, as we saw in Chapter 4, have their own preferences when it comes to teaching strategies. There is a danger, therefore, that both teachers and students can settle into a cosy learning relationship in which neither is challenged or pushed into expanding their learning horizons. On the other hand, if the teacher disregards the preferences of the students and sticks to the teaching strategy they feel least happy about, then the learning environment is put under stress and the outcomes may be unsatisfactory for both parties.

In choosing an appropriate teaching strategy, you have to consider four equally important issues:

1 Given a specific curriculum objective to be achieved, which teaching strategy will be most effective for transmitting the necessary skills, knowledge and understanding to your students?
2 How can you ensure that your students will fully participate in the learning process so that they learn for themselves rather than just listening to or watching you demonstrate your learning?
3 Given your knowledge of the group of students, how can you incorporate their prior learning and overcome any barriers to learning they may have?
4 How much time can you allow for this particular curriculum objective?

There are a number of strategies at your disposal and they can be arranged on a continuum (Figure 5.1) that stretches from teacher-centred methods at one end to those methods which encourage students to take more responsibility for their own learning at the other end.

The chart in Figure 5.1 is not judgemental. It is not saying that giving a lecture is wrong or that the best way to teach is to engage students in role plays and problem-solving exercises. It is, however, a means of illustrating how different teaching strategies will affect different learning outcomes.

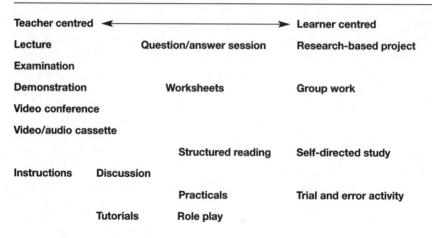

Figure 5.1 Teaching strategies continuum

AIMS, OBJECTIVES, GOALS AND LEARNING OUTCOMES: 'WHAT ARE WE SUPPOSED TO BE LEARNING HERE?'

All students come to their course with preconceived assumptions about its content and will react differently to its separate components. In addition, each student will have certain expectations about how much he or she will gain from the course. The course team has to be aware of such complexities in the student profile when constructing the learning materials and will attempt to cover as many of what it judges to be potential areas of interest. In terms of choosing the inputs or content of a learning programme, it is the teacher or course team, in most cases, who has the main responsibility. Once a learner begins to study, the teacher's control begins to diminish. What goes into a learning programme and what comes out at the other end may not, necessarily, be all that closely related, as Rogers explains:

> The planning agent (teacher-provider) initially determines the goals of the learning process. The agent has in mind certain expected outcomes, the results that will flow from the learning undertaken in changed attitudes and behaviour. However, most of the student participants come with their own intentions, which may or may not be the same as those set out by the agent; they will use the learning opportunity for their own purposes, to achieve their own outcomes. Each of these sets of purposes influences the other. The teacher's intended outcomes to help shape the learners' expectations and the learners' intentions and hopes should affect the formulation of the teacher's intentions. Both sets of proposed outcomes may well be different yet again from the effective outcomes of the educational process. Since those being taught consist of a mixed group of learners, each of whom

responds to the learning in a different way, there will always be a series of unexpected outcomes. The teacher-agent needs to keep these differences in mind when planning the learning encounter.

(Rogers, 1986, p.12)

In the case of competence-based programmes, it would be argued that teaching inputs must be determined by the prescribed competences in the various elements and units of the NVQ or GNVQ, but we would argue that the teaching and learning relationship is more sophisticated than even the purest competence-based approach would assume it to be. And, in most other sorts of programmes, teachers and learners still have some freedom to strive for undetermined outcomes. It is important, therefore, for teachers to be able to identify the aims and objectives of a particular teaching session, albeit with the flexibility to amend their original ideas. Furthermore, there are valuable opportunities here for teachers and students to work together to determine what each wants in the way of learning outcomes and so negotiate a micro-curriculum.

The language of learning can be so complex as to suppress understanding. Indeed, many professional educators and trainers, and particularly academics, are guilty of constructing a highly technical and often impenetrable set of terminology that shuts out teachers and students alike. It is common practice for teachers to set aims and objectives when designing learning programmes, so what is the difference between aims and objectives and learning outcomes? Furthermore, what might be the value of specifying or identifying the outcomes of learning? The following passage from a report of research into learning outcomes in HE is useful here as its central message is equally applicable to FE:

Aims and objectives are primarily the language of course designers. They describe what the course sets out to do and can tend to preserve traditional course structures by discouraging comment and input from other voices: professions, employers, government and students. Learning outcomes, on the other hand, describe what graduates are expected to be able to do and do not relate directly either to courses or to any particular methods of teaching and learning. They can include both knowledge of the subject and the intellectual and personal qualities which are developed as a result of in depth study of a subject. The explicit and detailed nature of the learning outcomes makes it easier for those outside HE, government, employers, etc., to understand the nature of the HE curriculum and to make realistic inputs to its development. Learning outcomes also make it easier for students to understand what is expected of them and to take greater responsibility for their own learning. This can be a means of developing alternative approaches to teaching and learning resulting in greater flexibility and wider participation in HE.

(UDACE, 1991)

Reflection

In this reflection, we hope you will engage in some lateral thinking about learning outcomes from the point of view both of the teacher and the learner. Similar exercises to this are often used in relation to developing communication skills.

Study Figure 5.2 and follow the instructions – you will need a partner to help you. The basic outcome should be for your partner to achieve as close a representation of the original drawing as possible. When you have finished the exercise, you might find it useful to discuss with your partner the following questions:

1 To what extent was the basic outcome achieved?
2 Can you identify any other outcomes of this exercise in terms of (a) your learning and (b) your partner's learning?
3 In terms of the overall outcomes of this exercise, how important was the achievement of the basic outcome?

You could extend this exercise by reversing your roles, though you would, of course, need to use another diagram!

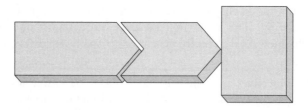

Instructions

1 Study the picture and consider how you would describe it to someone.
2 Sit back-to-back with a friend/colleague who has not seen the picture and give him or her a sheet of paper.
3 Give verbal instructions to enable your partner to draw the picture.
4 When the new picture is complete, examine it to see how closely it matches the original.

Figure 5.2 Reflection exercise

The teaching and learning involved in the exercise you have just carried out will have reflected the personalities, capabilities and learning styles of the two people involved. As the teacher, you will have had to:

- think carefully about the nature of the instructions you supplied;
- communicate those instructions effectively;
- listen carefully to your partner's questions and reactions.

In judging the success of the exercise in terms of how closely your partner managed to reproduce the diagram, you will have considered to what extent each of you contributed to the exercise. Over and above the physical reproduction of the diagram, you may have discussed other outcomes: for example, your partner may have learned that he or she needs to practise following verbal instructions. By simply concentrating on the physical outcome, we can miss a great deal of associated learning which could include generic or transferable skills.

If you look in the index of the overwhelming majority of books about education, at any level, you will be lucky to find more than a handful of entries that have any specific reference to learning outcomes. You may find the word 'objectives' listed in a few and you will certainly find the word 'curriculum' in most. Indeed, you will find whole books devoted to the discussion of what makes up a curriculum, how it is planned and managed, modularised and marketed. This is not to suggest that educationalists have not been concerned with learning outcomes but that the process of learning has been largely seen in terms of what goes in rather than what comes out. Trainee teachers spend a great deal of time constructing lesson plans detailing how they will cover a particular subject in a given period of time. Most curriculum planning takes the form of a stockpot into which ingredients are thrown until the chef decides there are enough to make a decent soup. Some thought will be given to the balance of subjects, the depth to which each should be discussed, and, importantly, the presumed expectations of the potential learners. At some point, the curriculum planners will have identified certain broad aims by which their deliberations and choices are guided. These aims tend to relate to the whole curriculum or large parts of it:

> Not infrequently, such statements reflect philosophical or educational beliefs and values. Statements of aims are generally vague and tend to have little operational value (descriptively or prescriptively) in relation to the planning, development and implementation of curricula. They can, however, act as a 'reference' against which the tenability of more specific statements of intent (e.g. curricula goals and objectives) can be appraised.
>
> (Heathcote, Kempa and Roberts, 1982)

Heathcote et al. found that three recurrent themes emerged when they analysed a range of curriculum aims taken from FE courses:

1 Promotion of the individual's personal and intellectual growth;
2 meeting the needs of the individual in relation to the individual's societal and physical environment;
3 meeting the needs of society itself.

They further found that when curriculum aims were translated into more specific goals, it was to serve two closely connected but alternate functions: the first function involves the teacher acting as an agent for the curriculum planner by teaching directly to tightly defined goals; the second function sees the teacher as a much freer agent who interprets the curriculum planner's goals in the context of each specific group of learners.

The pre-eminence of either function depends, according to Heathcote et al., on the following variables:

1 The amount of direction which the curriculum planner wishes to impose on the implementing teacher.
2 the extent to which the curriculum emphasises student autonomy in relation to learning outcomes.
3 the ability and previous experience of the students for whom the curriculum is intended.
4 the curriculum planner's perception of the constraints imposed and opportunities offered by the subject matter.

We would add a further and, in the light of the competence-based approach, increasingly dominant variable which concerns the teaching or learning system within which the teacher has to function. Heathcote et al. distinguish between the use of curriculum aims as a base from which the curriculum planner exerts control over the teacher who delivers the curriculum, as opposed to a 'staging post' where control passes to the teacher who then translates the aims into more specific objectives. They see the first approach as being objectives-based and the second as being process-based. The distinction here is that the process-based model focuses on the role of the teacher who adopts appropriate pedagogical methods in order to achieve the broad aims of the curriculum. Under the objectives-based model, the activities of the teacher are seen as merely the means to an end, that is the attainment by the students of the specified learning objectives. In the case of distance learning materials, the materials themselves become the main 'agent' of the course team but involve a tutor or 'secondary agent' who interprets the materials for students.

The objectives model of curriculum development in the training field first appeared in the USA with Franklin Bobbitt's *How to Make a Curriculum* in 1924, and was greatly refined in the 1940s by Ralph Tyler, and later in the 1950s and 1960s by R.F. Mager. The attraction of this model is that it systematically defines the skills and knowledge required to accomplish tasks and, in doing so, presents to teachers and trainers clear guidelines for selecting appropriate teaching methods and, most importantly, for designing an assessment programme. As Mager points out:

If you don't know where you are going, it is difficult to select a suitable means for getting there. After all, machinists and surgeons don't select tools until they know what operation they are going to perform . . .

Instructors simply function in a fog of their own making unless they know what they want their students to accomplish as a result of their instruction.

(Mager, 1962)

What is looked for is a change in behaviour on the part of the learner, change that Bloom's Taxonomy (1965), widely adopted by both teachers and trainers, classifies into three domains:

Affective – attitudes and emotions
Cognitive – knowledge and information
Psychomotor – practical or physical skills

Each domain is sub-divided into a hierarchy of categories which demonstrate the different levels at which a learner may operate or be asked to operate. Bloom has been criticised, particularly for separating the cognitive from the affective, and other people have developed alternative taxonomies (see, for example, Gagne, 1988). Despite the criticisms, however, Bloom's domains and categories, when taken together, do provide a useful and fairly straightforward structure of learning. As such, they can be used as a basic template for the teacher when planning learning sessions and can also be used for the purposes of evaluating the effectiveness of a particular session.

The *affective domain* has five categories:

Receiving (taking in messages and responding to a stimulus)

Responding (taking responsibility by responding and seeking to find out)

Valuing (recognising that something is worth doing)

Organising and conceptualising (the individual develops his or her own way of arranging responses to stimuli and develops particular attitudes based on a set of values)

Characterising by value or value concept (bringing together ideas, beliefs and attitudes in a coherent whole)

The *cognitive domain* has six characteristics:

Knowledge (facts, categorisation of facts and knowledge in general, theories and abstractions)

Comprehension (making sense of what things mean and how they relate to each other)

Application (applying knowledge to different situations)

Analysis (breaking down knowledge into its constituent parts to gain a clearer understanding of the whole)

Synthesis (bringing together the separate constituents to create a new whole, which involves making choices)

Evaluation (reflecting on knowledge and making judgements)

The *psychomotor domain*, as developed by Harrow (1972) from Bloom's work, has six characteristics:

Reflex movements (in response to stimuli)

Basic fundamental movements (build upon reflex movements)

Perceptual abilities (used to interpret stimuli and behave accordingly)

Physical abilities

Skilled movements (involve practice)

Non-discursive communication (involves creative and artistic behaviour)

Behavioural objectives have been heavily criticised by many people (see Eisner, 1985) for a number of reasons and, as we discussed earlier, too much emphasis on a predetermined outcome can result in a dangerously narrow approach to learning. All teachers, however, do need to have a sense of what it is they want their students to achieve by the end of a particular session and over a certain period of time. Those 'objectives' might be largely predetermined and written in the form of 'outcomes' (as in the case of NVQs) or they may be framed more loosely but in such a way as to help the teacher give a structure to the learning. On some programmes, it is possible, and often desirable, for the teacher and students to negotiate a set of objectives and for the negotiation itself to be regarded as a central part of the learning process.

So far, we have been talking about 'objectives' for teaching and learning and there has been some reference to 'outcomes'. Teachers also talk about 'aims' and 'goals'. Although there is little point in getting too pedantic about terminology, it might be helpful to separate these terms and use them to differentiate between the distinct elements of a teaching/learning situation. The following example is taken from an Advanced Vocational Certificate of Education (AVCE) course in business and focuses on Unit 4: Human Resources. This unit is broken down into a series of topics all of which have to be covered and for which students need to provide assessment evidence. One of the topics is titled: Recruitment and Selection. The specification states that students need to understand the following:

- Preparing person specifications and job descriptions;
- carefully planning how and when to advertise;
- identifying the strengths and weaknesses of job applications, curriculum vitae and letters of application;
- shortlisting candidates;
- how recruitment interviews are planned, carried out and evaluated;
- the legal and ethical responsibilities relating to equal opportunities.

(Source: OCR, 2000, p.2)

The teacher knows in advance, therefore, what is expected in terms of learning outcomes, but in order to ensure that students achieve those outcomes, the teacher has to construct a teaching plan. This is where aims and objectives come in. We asked a trainee FE teacher to devise a plan for the teaching this section of the AVCE unit. She began by setting down an overall aim, followed by a set of objectives:

Aim: To understand the process involved and the skills required when applying for a job.

Objectives:
1 To understand the recruitment procedures when applying for a job.
2 To respond to a job advertisement.
3 To complete an application form in a clear, accurate and professional manner.
4 To produce a covering letter to accompany the application form.
5 To complete an employer aptitude test.
6 To attend an interview with a personnel officer.

We can see from this that the aim encompasses the topic as a whole whereas the objectives indicate the separate components which the student needs to master in order to fulfil the aim. As this example is taken from an AVCE course, the student may also be expected to demonstrate his or her ability in a number of key skills, for example this particular assignment offers many opportunities for developing communication skills. The teacher may want to extend the prescribed learning outcomes in order to reflect the needs of the students, or to develop the 'wider key skills' of 'problem solving', or 'improving own learning and performance'. Additional outcomes might include, for example:

• developing the students' confidence outside the classroom;
• developing the students' independent research skills;
• improving the level of written work amongst the students in general.

In defining these additional outcomes, the teacher would place them within the context of the course as a whole. An outcome related to the students' research skills would, therefore, be associated with more than one aspect of the assignment. Other outcomes might appear as a result of the teacher (or students) identifying a particular weakness in a previous session which requires attention.

In planning how to take the students through this topic, the teacher might set 'goals'. For example, Objectives 1 to 3 will be covered in three weeks; or one of the objectives will involve a group discussion or activity. It is in the planning where the teacher can be creative, despite the prescriptive nature of the specification. Our trainee teacher decided to divide the content into seven sections and to employ a range of teaching strategies (TS) as follows:

Section 1: general overview
In this section, students are asked to discuss their attitudes to unemployment and the different ways in which people can apply for jobs.

TS: Brainstorm as a group to get initial views; ask students to consider a set of case studies of people seeking work; ask students to choose two job vacancies from the local newspaper and obtain the necessary application forms (use telephone, letters and visit to job centre).

Section 2: the recruitment process
Students learn about how a typical company sets out to recruit staff.

TS: Teacher uses information from an actual company (e.g. Royal Mail) to explain the recruitment process. Teaching aids include OHTs and wipeboard.

Section 3: letters and job specifications
Students learn how to construct a letter of application and interpret job advertisements.

TS: Students have been asked to bring in copies of job advertisements from local newspapers and to select three jobs they could realistically apply for; the students work in pairs to assess the quality of a sample of specimen letters of application; the teacher goes through the key requirements in writing a letter of application; the students work on their own to produce a letter of application for one of the jobs they selected earlier. (These individual letters might be set for homework.)

Section 4: application forms and curriculum vitae
Students learn how to complete an application form and construct a CV.

TS: Students work in groups to assess quality of specimen completed application forms; group discussion about what the applicant needs to do when completing a form; teacher reinforces the requirements by presenting a list on an OHT. The process is repeated for CVs and students use word processors, thereby covering some IT core skills associated with the element.

Section 5: equal opportunities and contracts of employment
Students learn about the legal obligations employers have to adhere to when recruiting staff.

TS: Role play between teacher and student to demonstrate how certain questions could contravene equal opportunities legislation; group discussion of why equal opportunity matters in recruitment; students work in small groups to analyse a sample of contracts of employment; teacher reinforces legal knowledge with handouts.

Section 6: preparing for interviews
Students learn how to prepare for an interview and how to conduct themselves in an interview.

TS: Teacher shows a video of good and bad interviews and students take notes; group discussion of video; teacher reinforces points related to how to prepare for an interview and how to behave as an interviewee.

Section 7: being interviewed
Students take part in mock interviews, acting as both interviewees and interviewers.

TS: Mock interviews held using video cameras and external interviewers brought in; students watch the videos and analyse their strengths and weaknesses; teacher draws together all aspects of the element.

In devising her teaching plan, the trainee teacher was determined to provide her students with a lively and varied learning opportunity; hence she has deliberately chosen a range of teaching and learning strategies.

ASSIGNMENTS

The use of assignments as vehicles for encouraging participative, student-centred learning has been a central feature of college life for many years. Assignments can enable students to see their programme of study as a coherent whole in which all the parts are related to each other and through which they are encouraged to apply their knowledge, understanding and skills. In this way, assignments are an important means for enabling students to engage in learning by doing and for emphasising the integrated nature of their courses. The student-centred nature of assignments and their facility for including both individual and group tasks means that they highlight the process of learning as well as being agents for delivering outcomes of learning. When assignment work is assessed (either by teachers or through student peer assessment, or both), valuable lessons can be learned through a review of the process of learning which took place (see Chapter 6). The common features of assignments are:

- They include an element of independent student activity to be carried out individually or in groups;
- they are based on a realistic scenario;
- they can be of varying length;
- they encourage students to apply knowledge, understanding and skills to meaningful tasks in a realistic situation;
- they allow key skills to be integrated into the learning process and assessed as part of the overall learning outcomes.

Assignments can be created by individual teachers or by course teams who wish to create greater coherence between the modules, units, etc., that comprise the distinctive parts of a course of study. Designing assignments can be divided into three areas:

1 Task – what a student does, often resulting in a product or outcome.
2 Activities – the process used in order to achieve the task.
3 Assessment – the benchmarks or criteria for the product and the process.

For example, if an assignment was built around the design and use of questionnaires, the three areas listed above would translate as follows:

Task	–	devise and use a questionnaire.
Activities	–	select sources and obtain information about questionnaire design; plan the questionnaire; pilot it; amend as necessary; use the amended questionnaire; collect data; evaluate and present data.
Assessment	–	range of methods used in obtaining information; fitness of resulting questionnaire for purpose – language, tone, degree of complexity, etc., depth of analysis; clarity of presentation; adequacy of evaluation.

There is enormous scope when identifying scenarios for assignments for teachers to be creative and to utilise the expertise and ideas of a range of people. When designing an assignment, the following stages should be followed:

1 Choose the unit, topic, etc., you wish to cover.
2 Formulate a scenario, exercise or brief for the students to work within. (Be realistic about the amount of time available to students to cover the work involved.)
3 Correlate possible tasks with evidence criteria that will have to be fulfilled for the purposes of assessment.
4 Identify the key skills that will be assessed through the assignment.
5 Decide if this will be a graded assignment.
6 Write the assignment as a series of tasks with guidance for students.
7 Write assessment guidance (including grading criteria if applicable), indicating the nature of the evidence to be obtained.
8 Design any necessary documentation for assessment purposes, for example grids, question sheets, logs, etc.

By evaluating the implementation of an assignment, the teacher (and or course team) can refine the different elements in order to improve the assignment and ensure its continued applicability and viability. Once a set of effective assignments have been created, the pressure on the teacher to produce teaching materials is reduced and more time can be spent supervising the actual learning process.

Being creative

As early as 1991, the FEU remarked, 'In some colleges a new hybrid of staff (neither conventional lecturer nor support staff job specification) is emerging to take the new roles associated with flexible access to learning and accreditation' (FEU, 1991, p.28). As we discussed in Chapter 4, teachers have to be aware of the different ways in which their students approach learning and try to create a learning environment in which those different approaches can be accommodated. But creativity in teaching involves risk.

The following question and answer section examines the implications for teachers inherent in outcomes-based, student-centred programmes.

What teaching will I need to devise and deliver?

The teaching will have to be designed to contribute to the assignments, in other words, to provide the underpinning knowledge which students will require in order to complete the assignments. This will not always be provided by the teacher, but the teacher may act as a facilitator in pointing the students in the direction of suitable learning resources. You need to check the specifications carefully to see how much teacher support is permitted. In order to gain a distinction grade, at Foundation and Intermediate level, and a higher literal grade at AVCE, students are expected to demonstrate independence in their learning. Teachers need to ask themselves: what do students need to know in order to fulfil the assessment criteria for this unit?

A supplementary question will then be as follows:

Where or from whom can this knowledge be accessed?

The important point here is that there are a wide range of resources and sources from which knowledge can be accessed and the teacher should exploit the interdisciplinary nature of the college environment as well as drawing on resources available through the college's external networks.

How and where will the learning take place?

The answer to this question could be as wide as individual teaching staff wish to make it. If it is accepted that the opportunities for learning are constrained neither by the time nor the place at which it occurs, nor by the age of the candidate, then the opportunities presented by a wide range of diverse contexts and experiences are limitless. However, if teachers subscribe to the view that learning can only take place in classrooms where the teacher stands at the front and talks then it will be extremely difficult to deliver GNVQ or similar programmes effectively.

Examples of work-based learning activities include:

- Work experience placements
- Work shadowing
- Projects undertaken in companies specifically for those companies
- Simulations
- Organising and running events in the college, for example open days, careers fairs, catering and general reception duties.

A 1995 FEFC report indicated that within 75 per cent of GNVQ programmes, supervised work experience on employers' premises was available for students to provide them with the necessary vocational experience (FEFC, 1995). There was some variation in provision across the programme areas, but in the best developed examples assignments had been designed in conjunction with employers. Well-planned work placements allowed students to collect assessment evidence from their experience. In some cases assessments were undertaken by workplace supervisors and later verified by college staff.

There are obvious implications for quality control when parts of the programme are, in effect, being devolved to employers. Issues about the standardisation of assessment are still being resolved. Some colleges have been able to develop effective partnerships with companies by arranging for staff teaching on vocational programmes to have work placements in business and industry. The case study at the end of this chapter illustrates a well-developed partnership model for GNVQ delivery.

What sort of students will be involved?

The current profile for GNVQ/AVCE students is a 16–19-year-old in full-time education. But it should also be remembered that many of these students also have part-time jobs and these can provide rich sources of vocational experience and information on which they can draw.

How will assessment be organised and carried out?

Assessment is continuous throughout the programme and is based on a series of assignments that are completed during the programme plus a series of externally set and marked tests. Initially the tests were not included in the design but were later added in response to criticisms about rigour and in an attempt to confer parity of esteem with A levels.

> One characteristic of GNVQ assessment, which distinguishes it from assessment in most academic qualifications, is that it covers the curriculum outcomes far more comprehensively. All the outcomes reflected in the units must be achieved . . . doing well in one component cannot compensate for a poor result in another . . . and the primary component is the internal assessment which runs throughout a GNVQ.
>
> (Jessup, 1994, p.2)

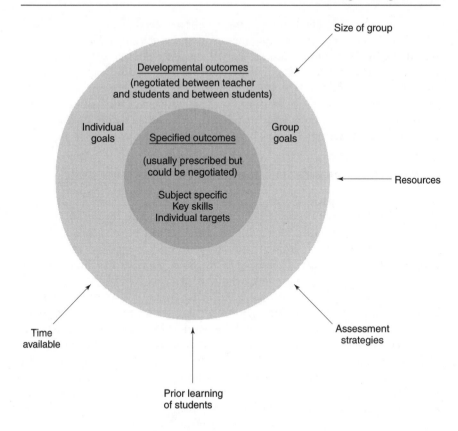

Figure 5.3 Model for effective learning

Evidence for assessment is collected in the student's portfolio. The student has to satisfy the assessment criteria for each unit of the course and has to provide sufficient evidence that this has been achieved. We shall discuss portfolio building more fully in Chapter 6.

Choosing a strategy

It is clear from the GNVQ example above that teaching strategies are chosen for reasons which go beyond being a mechanism for ensuring that the students achieve the subject-specific outcomes. Certainly achievement of those outcomes is vitally important but the teacher also has to ensure that students develop their abilities as learners and build relationships with each other which contribute to an effective learning environment. We can portray this (Figure 5.3) as a model for effective learning.

Once you are clear about the outcomes to be achieved in a session, and have taken account of any constraining factors, you can select one or more teaching strategies. As we noted earlier, those strategies will obviously reflect your preferences as a teacher but you may want to try out different approaches, albeit on a small scale to begin with until you gain confidence in using them. In the following section, we identify the characteristics of a range of teaching strategies and suggest tasks which students can be asked to perform in order to ensure that they participate as fully as possible in the learning situation.

MANAGING LEARNING: HANDLING 'DIFFICULT' STUDENTS

In the opening chapters of this book, we stressed the diversity of college life and, in particular, the need for FE teachers to appreciate that their students will reflect a range of abilities, needs and levels of motivation. Unlike schools, where all the students are legally required to attend, colleges expect their students to attend as a result of acting as responsible adults, rather than from the threat of legal sanction. Some learners, it is true, may be attending courses selected by their employers and, in the case of government-sponsored trainees or apprentices, some students may have their wages reduced for missing classes, but, even in these cases, a college would hope that the students concerned could develop enough maturity to understand the need to fulfil their obligations as course members. All colleges, of course, have to comply with the funding criteria laid down by the relevant funding body (e.g. LSC or SFEFC), part of which puts particular emphasis on maintaining acceptable levels of student retention. This can lead to disputes between teachers and managers in cases where the former wish to remove particularly disruptive students from courses and the latter decide that the need for student retention overrides any difficulties in the classroom. All teachers need to feel that they have the support of their managers when faced with difficult students and should be appraised of their college's disciplinary procedures and policy on exclusions. Indeed, induction programmes for new staff to a college should include a session on this important area and should ensure that teachers have a clear picture of the support structures which exist to help them should the need arise.

It is important for all teachers to realise that some of their students may have problems which require the intervention of specialists and that, as teachers, they are not equipped to deal with such problems beyond the initial stage of encouraging and supporting an individual student to seek help. Deciding where the line falls between those students who need specialist help and those who can be supported within the everyday teaching and learning situation is, however, not a straightforward process. Sue Rees, writing about the 'growing tide' of students with emotional and behavioural difficulties in Norfolk colleges, distinguishes between those students who can be said to be 'sad' and those who are thought of as 'bad':

The former ('sad') sub-group consists of students who are emotionally disturbed in some way. They may be lonely, isolated and have difficulties making relationships, but do not necessarily come to lecturers' attention because they do not cause obvious problems of discipline, etc., during the educational process. The latter ('bad') group may be termed as 'disturbing' rather than 'disturbed'. Their emotional state manifests itself in behavioural problems and they are frequently aggressive and disruptive within the learning environment.

(Rees, 1995, p.93)

The more experience one gains as a teacher, the more adept one becomes at managing the learning process and spotting potential flashpoints. As we discussed in Chapter 4, if teachers demonstrate that they have empathy with their students, they are much more likely to create conditions which are conducive to co-operation with and between their students and in which all parties trust and respect each other. We also noted, however, that the pressures on students in terms of the lives they lead outside college can cause them to display behavioural patterns which appear disruptive in the classroom or workshop. But that pressure may also come from within the college if, for example, a student is struggling to keep up with their written work or if they are being bullied. And, of course, disruptive behaviour may be the students' way of telling a teacher that the sessions are boring, poorly organised or pitched at an inappropriate level. Changes in behaviour can usually be seen as signals of stress or anxiety and the teacher must be able to recognise those signals and act appropriately before the situation gets out of hand.

A key factor in the effective management of any learning situation is for the teacher to involve the students in the whole process. This involves the teacher in an exercise in sharing with students as follows:

1 Discuss with students your expectations (as a teacher) of them and identify their expectations (as students) of you – for example, try to establish a code of practice regarding lateness, the handing in of work, eating/drinking in class, dress codes, etc.
2 Explain to students the nature of what is to be covered in a particular session and how this relates to the rest of their course.
3 Explain clearly (and review at intervals) the assessment procedure you will operate – this includes both the informal (criteria you use to monitor student progress) and the formal (externally imposed criteria for summative assessment) criteria you will employ.
4 Discuss with students the constraints under which you and they must work – for example, presentation of work to satisfy external examiners, coverage of certain elements of a curriculum, the lack of sufficient computers or textbooks, etc.
5 Review your working arrangements as a group, giving students the chance to discuss whether they should be given more time to hand in work or to

receive more support with a particular part of the course – this may require you to recognise any inadequacies in your initial preparation for a course or to accept that you have made mistakes.

By sharing the necessary ingredients of the learning process with students, they are given the opportunity to act responsibly and with the same degree of professionalism as the teacher. At the same time, the teacher has to be prepared to show the same degree of respect to the students and to try not to retreat into a position of isolated superiority when challenged. Working with students does not necessitate a blurring of roles to the point where teacher and student become indistinguishable. Both teacher and students have to recognise the demands of each other's roles and that the teacher, like any manager, has to take responsibility for ensuring that the collective goals of the group are achieved.

The difficulties involved in creating a supportive atmosphere within colleges are illustrated by this extract from a 1996 inspection report:

> Students speak warmly of the helpfulness of teaching staff. A tutorial structure has existed in most parts of the college for some time, but it varies widely in its effectiveness. Some students are unaware that they have personal tutors in addition to their teachers. The college has prepared guidance on the role and responsibilities of personal tutors. Some good practice exists, particularly on access courses. However, on many courses, personal tutors wait for students to present issues to them, and some do not understand their responsibility for guidance. A range of student services, including welfare and counselling, complements the work of personal tutors. The demands for these services are increasing. Staff help students with personal and social problems which interfere with their ability to study effectively, while the welfare service's primary focus is on financial matters.
>
> (FEFC, Inspection Report January 1996)

In her Norfolk study, Rees concludes that strategic planning is required to help teaching and support staff tackle the problem of 'disturbing', 'emotionally disturbed' and 'disruptive' students and suggests that staff development, particularly in 'group management', is a key feature:

> staff will require techniques for dealing with confrontation: for example non-verbal communication methods for use with aggressive students. Personal and social skills are also important, and if these are imparted effectively to staff it is likely that they will find their way successfully into the curriculum. Support groups are desirable, to provide staff with a focus and to maximise communication. By such means it will be possible to generate a positive ethos, to shape staff expectations of behaviour and to manage the general level of discipline in a constructive, staff-oriented way.
>
> (Rees, 1995, p.96)

Team teaching

One of the most stimulating and rewarding ways to teach is to work with a colleague or team of colleagues. Forms of team teaching range from two people taking it in turns to address the class, to larger groups of teachers adopting a variety of roles including facilitating small-group discussion, working on a one-to-one basis with students and co-ordinating project-based activities. Such teaching can be used to counter prejudice along gender and racial lines, and to overcome the difficulties in mixed-ability classes. It can also help stimulate greater responsibility on the part of students who have to learn to co-operate with teachers who display different pedagogical approaches and styles.

A particularly useful role for team teaching is during induction periods when 'ice-breaking' activities can help cement a sense of group identity and community among students and teachers. In their classic text, the *Gamesters' Handbook*, Brandes and Phillips (1985) describe a number of activities, games and strategies which can be used to promote personal development and social cohesion.

Open, flexible and distance learning and the impact of ILT

Distance learning has been available in the UK and throughout the world for much of the twentieth century, beginning with correspondence courses in which there was no contact between tutor and student other than by post. The establishment of the British Open University (OU) in 1969 led to a number of similar institutions being set up around the world. The OU was notable for allowing people to study for undergraduate degrees without any entrance requirements and for combining distance learning via multi-media materials with attendance at residential summer schools. Many FE colleges are designated as study centres for OU students who attend a limited number of face-to-face tutorial sessions in their local areas and some colleges provide courses on study skills (sometimes called 'return to learn') for adults who are considering enrolling with the OU. In a national inspection of open and distance learning delivery in English FE colleges in 2000/2001, the FEFC found that most colleges had some provision and that 55 colleges had more than 1,000 distance learning students (FEFC, 2001b). The courses most likely to be delivered in this mode were book-keeping, security guarding and IT.

The term distance learning has joined a lengthy list of other terms, some of which are used interchangeably. These terms include: flexible learning; flexi-study; resource-based learning; and independent study. Although the expansion of distance learning has been largely aimed at adult learners, some of the techniques involved in the preparation of study materials have been used in schools and the learner-centred approach which drives many (though not all) distance learning programmes has influenced classroom-based and work-based teaching and learning.

Distance learning (and other associated terms, e.g. open, flexible, independent) has been and still is promoted in terms of its ability to provide access to learning to large numbers of people who need the flexibility of being able to study when and where they choose. The European Commission (EC), in particular, and some national governments have extolled the virtues of distance learning for some time. Most distance learning courses are modular and allow a level of learner choice which, though it is increasingly available on more traditional courses, gives people the chance to tailor-make a course to suit their specific needs. Some critics argue, however, that these newer forms of learning have grown in stature and availability as a result of the reduction in spending on staff development, training and adult education in general. Edwards (1993a) takes these arguments a stage further and suggests that the growth of open learning (which he uses as a generic term) reflects the wider societal change that is witnessing organisations shifting from Fordist (mass production lines, labour intensive) to post-Fordist (part-time working, flexible work patterns) structures. He is particularly concerned with the way in which open learning, as used in some industries, can separate employees from each other thus reducing opportunity for critical discussion of shared concerns. Many teachers, in common with managers and other professionals, now gain their professional development through open and distance learning courses which include Masters degrees and even taught Doctorates. Although Edwards's fears deserve constant attention, flexible approaches to course provision and learning are proving to be very popular, particularly with people whose professional and domestic lives allow them little time to study in conventional ways. Well-structured open and distance learning programmes include opportunities, often through residential weekends, for students to come together to share ideas and enjoy the experience of being 'real' students.

If you are involved in teaching on courses which have an open or distance format, you may have the opportunity to prepare learning materials in the form of written, self-study texts, audio cassettes, instructional videos, videoconferencing and interactive computer programmes (see Rowntree, 1990 for a useful handbook). The extent to which you can become proficient in these media will be determined by the amount of training available and the level of resources devoted to this mode of teaching. The development of Information and Learning Technologies (ILT), referred to in Chapter 3, is bound to have a profound effect on the types of media available in colleges and, although one should not get too carried away by the hype surrounding such developments, it is clear that both teachers and students will need to keep abreast of the electronic revolution.

Mayes (2002) argues that ILT and e-learning more generally cannot just be absorbed by teachers and students, rather, these developments require us to ask some fundamental questions about the pedagogical skills needed to properly utilise them (see also Kenway, 2001 and Laurillard, 1993). He says that we need to think about, 'how technology can support the learning cycle, the goal-action-feedback loop that provides a basic model for all learning' (ibid., pp.164–165). One example of the way in which e-learning can be developed comes from the FEFC's 1999/2000 national inspection of the programme area, Business:

> Excellent use is made of Internet and college intranet facilities in one small general further education college in a rural area of the Yorkshire and Humberside region. Full-time GCE A level and GNVQ Advanced business students have assignments, case studies and course notes issued through the college intranet and are directed to a series of Internet business sites to research their assignments. . .The college makes its intranet resources accessible to students from home via an Internet page. Students also use electronic mail to contact each other and teachers. In their lessons, teachers lead lively discussions that draw on students' Internet work.
>
> (FEFC, 2001c, p.12)

On a more specialised level, the FEFC's 1999/2000 national inspection of the programme area, Engineering, reported:

> One college has a high-technology computer-integrated manufacturing centre which is housed in a large glass-sided module within a workshop area. It presents an attractive image of modern manufacturing and is well organised. It is very well equipped with CNC machines, robots, a transportation system, a racking/storage system, and a tensile testing machine with computer printout. There are also 16 computer workstations with computer-aided design (CAD), computer-aided manufacture (CAM) and general purpose software.
>
> (FEFC, 2001b, p.23)

Whilst the use of e-learning and ILT can help make teaching and learning more creative, students (and possibly their teachers) may also benefit in terms of increasing their employability. A recent government analysis of the UK's skill needs reported the following: the proportion of jobs in which computers were essential or very important currently stands at 55 per cent and rising; the proportion of jobs using the Internet stands at 24 per cent and rising; and that by 2003, the UK will be short of 620,000 IT professionals, with e-business being the hardest area to address (PIU, 2001).

Chapter 6

Assessment and recording achievement

THE ROLE OF ASSESSMENT

An important and integral aspect of your work in teaching will be the assessment of your students. In England and Wales in particular, assessment has been the focus of increased interest, and indeed reform, during the past fifteen years or more. These changes have been reflected in an increased emphasis on assessment at each of the key stages of the National Curriculum, and through similar reforms in the area of vocational qualifications and occupational training standards. As we write, a review is being conducted of Curriculum 2000 focusing in particular on the burden of assessment. Assessment is not only a mandatory requirement of examining and validating bodies, for whose qualifications you are preparing students, but you will need to assess in order to maintain a record of students' progress and to assist them in planning their own learning.

Ecclestone (2000, p.144), in a wide ranging analysis of assessment and critical autonomy in post-compulsory education, reminds us that 'ill-formed, and often contradictory, theories of learning and motivation underpin all assessment regimes in different ways'. She gives the example of behaviourism's 'belief in the power of extrinsic motivation through externally set targets, rewards and punishments' which contrasts with the 'humanist belief in people's innate need to learn the need to cultivate intrinsic motivation'. While recognising the many debates about so-called good and bad assessment approaches, Ecclestone calls for formative and diagnostic assessment to be placed 'at the centre of teaching and learning instead of being a separate afterthought, or merely an instrumental process to generate summative targets' (ibid., p.156). In this way, teachers and learners can engage in a community of assessment, a concept which has its roots in the community of practice model described in Chapter 4. Brown (1994) suggests that:

> Assessment, therefore, now has several functions including the diagnosis of causes of young people's success or failure, the motivation of them to learn, the provision of valid and meaningful accounts of what has been achieved and the evaluation of courses and teaching.
>
> (Brown, 1994, p.271)

At the heart of the dilemma for the teacher is the need to provide account-ability across a wide range of learning experiences and programmes of study, to confirm learning, to measure standards and effectiveness, as well as to con-tribute to the personal development of students. When asked, 'Why do we assess students?', a group of trainee teachers gave the following responses:

- It's a measure of feedback for students.
- We do it to grade students.
- Assessment is formative.
- It's for selection.
- It helps us to know if the students have understood.
- To empower the student and teacher to move forward.

The variety of responses indicates the multi-faceted nature of the assessment process. Assessment is now not so much something which is 'done unto' stu-dents but which often involves negotiations with students and sometimes with employers as well. Both its purposes and practice have changed during recent years. Some of these changes are associated with changes to the struc-ture of courses and programmes. The introduction of mandatory assessment within the National Curriculum in the compulsory phase of schooling is mir-rored by similar changes in the post-compulsory sector.

Throughout life, we are both being assessed by and assessing other people, whether it is formally as in the case of a teacher, magistrate, employer or parent, or informally as when we meet someone for the first time or attend a concert. In education and training, assessment is a powerful process, which can both empower people as well as damage them. There are many adults who carry the scars of their encounters with assessment throughout their lives. Some, for example, remember failing the 11+ examination for entry to gram-mar school, whereas others may never forget the agonies of oral spelling tests or being made to write their answer to an arithmetic question on the black-board in front of the whole class. Smith (1989) asserts that both the assessor and the person being assessed need to understand the nature of the assessment process and that:

> The more aware both assessors and assessed become of the relationship between the outcomes of the judgement process and the sources of evidence from which they derive, and the more honest assessors become about the sources of evidence from which their judgements derive, the more equitable and generally acceptable they are likely to be.
>
> (Smith, 1989, p.119)

As we saw in Chapter 3, the introduction of an outcome-based model of voca-tional qualifications has resulted in the measurement of achievement in terms of outcomes, that is through the demonstration of competence, usually within the workplace. Here there is a danger of the assessment dominating the learning process if achievement is measured in terms of outcome and bears scant regard to the process by which these skills are acquired. Assessment for assessment's sake is unhelpful and does little to enhance the learning process. Assessment should be an integral part of learning and should help to identify evidence of achievement as well as inform the design or redesign of learning programmes.

A major contribution to the 'Assessment for Learning' debate has been made by the Assessment Reform Group. Following an extensive review of classroom practice, the group argued that '. . . when carried out effectively, informal classroom assessment with constructive feedback to the student will raise levels of attainment. Although it is now fairly widely accepted that this form of assessment and feedback is important, the development of practice in this area will need a concerted policy-making push' (Assessment Reform Group, 1999, p.1).

Research undertaken by Black and Wiliam (1998, pp.9–11) outlines some guiding principles for effective formative assessment. These stress that: feedback should emphasise the qualities of the work and areas for improvement and not make comparisons with other students' work; students should be trained in self-assessment so that they can see what they need to achieve; students should be provided with opportunities to reflect on their performance; written work and tests should be relevant to learning aims. You may wish to reflect on these features as you begin to design your own assessment strategies.

Similarly, work on theories of learning has also influenced the debate on how we carry out assessment. We have discussed some of these in Chapter 4. Views on the ways in which individuals learn are contested. Broadly speaking, the current debate flows from two theoretical traditions, 'symbolic cognition' and 'situated cognition'. Symbolic processing, it is suggested, separates the learner from the environment, whereas theories of situated cognition place emphasis upon the contexts in which learning takes place. Learning is achieved by 'doing' as well as 'knowing' and by interacting with others through that learning process. 'The focus in understanding learning in this approach (symbolic cognition) is therefore the individual's internal mental processing and the symbolic representations of the mind. In the situated approach human knowledge and interaction are seen as inseparable from the world' (Murphy, 1999, p.ix).

There is insufficient space to pursue these theories in more detail here, nevertheless, it is important to remember that in designing assessment strategies we need, as teachers, to be aware of the different ways in which our students learn, and that we all have particular preferred learning styles.

There are a wide array of assessment techniques that will be discussed in more detail in this chapter. Whichever method is selected 'fitness for purpose' should be the guiding principle. It is important to recognise the purposes of the assessment and what it is designed to measure. Different methods of assessment will be necessary to assess practical skills from those designed to assess a student's ability to engage with a theoretical concept. A catering student's ability to make a soufflé will ultimately have to be assessed by the production of the finished product, not by writing about it. Nevertheless, a written assignment may be used to assess the student's knowledge of the underlying food science theory, or this could be assessed by means of oral questioning. Similarly, intending teachers are assessed on their ability to convert lesson plans into practical teaching activities. Subject knowledge and classroom practice have to be assessed equally but using different techniques.

The focus of assessment should be on the student and the measurement of his or her achievement. Testing as a means of 'catching people out' does little to develop confidence or to identify real learning. Similarly, 'teaching to the test' may simply identify those with good memories or reflect a teacher's ability to spot questions. Most of us will probably remember our attempts to revise only seven out of the ten available topics, in the hope that some of them would 'come up'.

One teacher recently remarked, 'Our business is to help students achieve'. This should be a guiding principle in the design of assessment procedures. Such procedures should be formative and motivational and appropriate in their design for the purpose for which they are intended. Whereas assessment will be used for the purposes of selection, it should always have a strong emphasis on the recognition of achievement. It may now be useful to consider the different types of assessment.

> The term assessment refers to all those activities undertaken by teachers, and by their students in assessing themselves, which provide information to be used as feedback to modify the teaching and learning activities in which they are engaged. Such evidence becomes 'formative assessment' when the evidence is actually used to adapt the teaching work to meet the needs.
>
> (Black and Wiliam, 1998. p.2)

FORMATIVE ASSESSMENT

The purpose of formative assessment is to provide a continuous process, which charts achievement, identifies areas for development and indicates next steps for both teachers and learners. It can be either formal or informal, or a combination of both. Action planning may be a part of the formative assessment process in that students should be encouraged to reflect on what they need to do in order to move their learning on. All colleges now have continuous assessment procedures in place. GNVQ programmes require students to complete portfolios of evidence that testify to the students' achievement of the units of the qualification. In this way they provide a record of achievement but they provide no real feedback on how the student is progressing. They simply record the steps along the way to achieving the full award. The same is true of NVQs. Here individual elements of competence are recorded as they are achieved. The emphasis is on the 'can do' rather than the 'will do'.

A formative assessment should consider the 'will do' in that it should help to inform the next steps of the student's development. As teachers we are constantly involved in formative assessment through informal means, for example the chance remark: 'That's very good, but next time why don't you think about including some conclusions at the end of your report?' We should also encourage our students to reflect upon their performance. We may ask them to consider such questions as:

- 'In which parts of this assignment did I do well?'
- 'In which parts of this assignment did I not do so well?'
- 'How did I manage my time?'
- 'Are there areas which I would wish to improve?'
- 'Do I need to access the Learning Resources Centre?'
- 'Did I work effectively with other members of my team in completing this assignment?'

Ideally, any formative assessment should involve a dialogue between student and teacher. Sometimes this may take the form of a record which may be signed by both parties. See p. 145 for an extract from a student's profile that is designed to provide formative assessment for the student. The emphasis in the student's profile is on what has been learned and on what needs to be learned in the future. The purpose of the assessment should be to improve the learning. Placing a tick or simply writing 'well done' at the end of a piece of work gives little indication of how the piece might be improved further. Tests may be useful in identifying what students know, or do not know, but unless accompanied by some feedback may provide no diagnosis as to the reasons why students do not know. There is always a danger too that some of the correct answers may have been arrived at through guesswork.

One of the most important uses of formative assessment is to establish a student's level of ability in the basic skills of literacy and numeracy. Research by Steve Harris, a lecturer in a college in the West Midlands, found that students on a BTEC National Diploma in Computer Studies had problems with both their written communication and basic numeracy (see Harris and Hyland, 1995). Harris followed up this research by asking delegates to a national conference on BTEC Computer Studies whether his findings were common and found that 'Managerial and financial pressures were forcing tutors to enrol students on the BTEC Computer Studies course who, without the basic grounding, were likely to experience considerable difficulty with parts of the programme' (ibid. p.45). On the basis of his research, Harris's college decided to screen all new full-time students using an ALBSU test and to offer, through its School of Learning Support, a range of support measures including courses for students with learning difficulties and basic skills' drop-in facilities (ibid., pp.46–7).

It is interesting to note that within the current guidance for key skills emphasis is placed on the importance of initial assessment in order to determine the appropriate level at which the student should prepare for key skills. Good practice dictates that this should be the starting point for any programme of study, and that appropriate guidance and induction should be provided for any student embarking upon a course of further education. Inappropriate course choice can be an important factor in student retention.

STUDENT PROFILE

Name:
Programme:
Group:
Date:
Date of last tutorial:

What assessed work has been completed since the last tutorial? (List)

What grades/marks were received? (List)

Do these marks reflect a fair assessment of my performance?

In which assignments do I feel I did particularly well? (You should consider not just the overall grade but if you believe you made a significant improvement on previous work if you succeeded in spite of some practical difficulties.)

In which assignments do I feel I did not do well? (You should consider the possible reasons for this.)

Are there any areas in which I require help?

What are they?

What do I intend to do about this?

What do I want to achieve by the time of the next tutorial?

How shall I achieve this?

Signed . . . . STUDENT
         . . . . TUTOR

SUMMATIVE ASSESSMENT

Summative assessment is used to judge if the aims of a course or programme have been achieved, for example through the setting of a final examination. Examinations often have an important role in selecting or de-selecting those for the next phase of education, for example from FE into HE or from a BTEC National programme to a Higher National programme. Summative assessment has increasingly assumed an important accountability function for colleges, since they are required to provide detailed information on assessment outcomes. There are funding implications too. Bloomer (1997) suggests that, 'current assessment practices are distinctly "product" driven or "outcome" focused, not "process" focused'. Within competence-based qualifications, summative assessment is made to ensure that all units of the qualification have been achieved. In GNVQ programmes the student's portfolio is the collection of work which provides the evidence that the requirements for each unit have been met. This evidence is derived from the coursework assignments. Below are the compulsory and optional units for GNVQ (Intermediate) in Health and Social Care. Each unit is specified in the way outlined in Chapter 3 and evidence must be provided to ensure that all units have been covered. These are checked by the internal assessor, confirmed by an internal verifier, and also scrutinised by an external moderation procedure. Students also have to pass the external tests in the units for which they are specified.

GNVQ HEALTH AND SOCIAL CARE (INTERMEDIATE)

COMPULSORY UNITS

UNIT 1	Health, Social Care and Early Years Provision
UNIT 2	Promoting Health and Well-being
UNIT 3	Understanding Personal Development

OPTIONAL UNITS

UNIT 4	Introducing Human Body Systems
UNIT 5	Planning and Preparing Food for Clients
UNIT 6	Meeting the Needs of Individuals in Care Settings
UNIT 7	Dealing With Hazards and Emergencies
UNIT 8	Child Development and Child Care
UNIT 9	Using Creative Activities in Care
UNIT 10	Human Behaviour in Care Settings
UNIT 11	Practical Caring Skills

(Source: Edexcel)

A more detailed discussion on competence-based qualifications will follow later in the chapter. The important point to note here is that although GNVQ programmes are based on a process of continuous assessment, the mechanism by which this is achieved is through a series of summative assessments. This is even more pertinent in the case of NVQs where candidates will present themselves for summative assessment whenever they consider they can demonstrate competence; that is, through the production of evidence. Evidence may take a variety of forms, for example:

- copies of documents appropriately word-processed;
- artefacts produced in practical classes;
- log books signed by supervisors testifying that certain procedures have been undertaken, for example in retailing, stock rotation.

Essentially the assessment is to verify that the candidate 'can do' what is described in the element.

Although summative assessment plays an important part in assessing students and, it could be argued, is the only means of assessment in competence-based qualifications, ideally this type of assessment should always be underpinned by a diagnostic process that will help students identify how they can improve their performance. Competence-based qualifications attest to candidates' abilities through a series of 'can do' statements; however, there is little scope for indicating how well a candidate 'can do' something over a period of time. As individuals we all know that we can perform a whole range of activities, but that we will perform some of them much better on some days than on other days and under different sets of conditions and circumstances.

As teachers we need to be aware of the range of assessment techniques available to us and to select those most appropriate for the piece of work we are trying to assess. In practice we are likely to adopt a range of approaches within our teaching programmes. Let us now consider some of these different approaches.

Reflection

You may wish to consider the following methods of assessment, which are common across many types of programme. Can you see any specific issues raised by these different assessment methods for your own subject area?

Essays	Short answer tests	Assignments	Practical tests
Presentations	Multiple choice test	Case studies	Portfolios
Oral test	Group work	Simulations	Examinations

ESSAYS

There had been a considerable shift away from essay-type assessment during recent years, particularly within vocational programmes, but criticisms concerning 'lack of rigour' in assessment procedures have led to the inclusion of externally set and marked tests in all GNVQ/AVCE programmes. In GCSE programmes, assessment, which initially included a fair proportion of coursework, has now reverted to a more examination-based assessment, with a corresponding reduction in coursework. The problems associated with essay-type tests are that, as Cohen and Manion (1989, p.286) note, they 'are more difficult to assess reliably. With only one assessor a considerable degree of subjectivity can creep in.' In an examination constructed around essays, within a tightly regulated time frame, there is only a limited capacity to cover the entire syllabus. This may result in some candidates being unable to show their real ability if they have 'spotted' the wrong question. In contrast, those who favour the competence-based approach would argue that this method of assessment ensures complete coverage in that the achievement of every unit must be demonstrated. The essay, on the other hand, gives only partial coverage. Nevertheless, the essay does test students' abilities to organise material, present arguments and to interpret the question in the student's own way. It allows for a degree of creativity and individuality, though this individuality can create problems in the marking. Since no two essays will be alike, it is important to establish clear criteria, in advance, by which the resulting essays can be reliably assessed. In public examinations, the number of candidates can be enormous. It is, therefore, essential that marking is standardised and that it is subject to checks and double-checks.

One approach is to consider what an ideal answer might look like. In setting an essay question you should ask yourself: 'What is it that I want students to be able to demonstrate?' You should also decide what marks you would want to allocate for the style, grammar and syntax. Two illuminating examples spring to mind from a career in FE teaching. One chemistry candidate was referred by the external examiner because of the poor presentation of the written work, including weak spelling and punctuation. The chemistry content, when it could be disentangled from the unstructured answer, was perfectly adequate. The second example occurred during a programme review board. An HND catering student was presented as a fail, but the head of department leapt to his defence stating, 'the boy writes beautifully . . . he's a poet'. The fact that there was very little catering theory included in the answer appeared to have escaped the head's attention. These may be extreme cases but they serve to highlight the importance of setting a fixed analytic grading scheme in advance and of having a clear view of what is expected in the answer. This will avoid some of the pitfalls of impressionistic marking. It is often helpful to indicate a numerical marking scheme for students alongside the question. This will indicate the relative importance of different sections of a question.

You will notice that some assessments are given a numerical rating whereas others may receive a literal grade. The public examination results for GCSE and A level are expressed in literal terms. There is a further element of potential confusion here since what might be a B grade to one marker may be a C to another. It is necessary to have some correlation between a possible numerical score and its literal counterpart, for example 50 to 55 may equate with C. This has to be clearly stated in advance. At GNVQ Foundation and Intermediate level, work is graded on the basis of pass, merit or distinction. There is a clear indication within the specifications of the criteria for each of these levels.

In all externally set and marked examinations there is always some process of moderation. That is, an external examiner or moderator will check a sample of scripts to ensure that marking is consistent across the range of candidates and markers. One useful way of doing this for beginning teachers is to sample a range of scripts and to mark them according to the stated criteria, and then cross-check the results against those of the experienced teacher. Try to identify why differences have occurred.

WRITTEN TESTS

There are other ways of assessing students than through essay writing. These can range from simple questions requiring tick-box answers to those questions that are more unstructured or open ended and require a student to think more deeply about a topic, to analyse, reflect and present arguments. Obviously this form of questioning is far more suitable for some topics than for others. In mathematics, answers will be either right or wrong. For example, the key skill, Application of Number at Levels 2 and 3 is assessed through the following topics:

- interpret mathematical information
- calculate, check and generate results
- interpret, explain and present results

(LSDA, 2001a)

Here is a short-answer test, which might provide some evidence for Application of Number at the appropriate level; for example: 'solve whole number problems involving addition and subtraction'.

Question: Here are the figures for 'Krazy Kuts' hair salon during the last week.

	Mon	Tue	Wed	Thur	Fri	Sat
Cut & Blow-dry	6	10	8	16	25	20
Shampoo & Set	5	8	7	13	21	20
Perm	2	3	2	5	7	10
Tints	4	2	0	4	5	16

(a) How many more perms were sold on Saturday than on Tuesday?
(b) How many 'cut & blow-dry' appointments were made during the week?
(c) On which day were most 'shampoo & sets' carried out?
(d) Which is the least popular treatment?
(e) If the salon decided to close on one day of the week which day should it be? Why?

In designing such questions it is helpful to place them within the context of the students' learning. This is particularly important in the case of vocational programmes where students often find difficulty in relating the theoretical applications of topics to practical situations.

Reflection
Try to think of the opportunities presented for key skills development within your own professional subject area. This is often referred to as mapping. In order to do this, you might use the following planning matrix:

	Opportunities
Communications	Reading, understanding and summarising information
	Using written communication
	Presenting information (orally)
Application of Number	Interpreting mathematical information
	Calculating, checking and generating results
	Interpreting, explaining and presenting findings
Information Technology	Identifying sources and finding information
	Interpreting and exploring information
	Entering and developing information
	Presenting information

There are also plenty of opportunities to develop the wider key skills – 'working with others', 'improving own learning and performance' and 'problem solving' – within post-16 programmes.

Opportunities for key skills development are now signposted within all post-16 qualifications, including those offered in the 'work-based' route. Assessment of key skills has posed considerable challenges for staff, particularly for those who are more accustomed to teaching on academic programmes.

The guiding principle in the assessment of key skills is that evidence should be derived from the work which students are doing in their main programmes of study, academic, vocational, or professional. 'Key skills assignments are not literally key skills assignments at all, but are subject-based assignments that integrate the development and achievement of key skills' (LSDA, 2001a, p.2).

Notice the terminology: the areas are not described as mathematics or English. As a lecturer beginning your work in FE you will need to make these connections in designing your assignments for students. You may have a background in academic mathematics or English and, therefore, you will need to consider the application of your subject knowledge to new contexts.

Highly structured questions are, obviously, much easier to mark than unstructured questions. Multiple choice questions are used by some examination boards and the answers can be pre-coded for ease of marking. In designing such tests care has to be taken in eliminating ambiguity from the possible answers offered since there must only be one 'right' answer. This method of testing purports to offer wide coverage of a syllabus but it offers nothing in the way of analysis or interpretation, dealing primarily with recall. Minton (1991, p.194) suggests that 'Multi-choice objective tests of the kind used by examining boards are best left to experts to compile. Few people have the skills to write them.' They can, however, provide a useful means of checking from time to time on students' learning. They can identify any misunderstandings which might have occurred. However, a balance has to be struck between the amount of time given to testing and that given to real learning. If too much time is spent preparing for tests, including teaching to the test, then this will impede the overall learning process. It can also be demotivating for students. Testing should be seen as part of an overall learning strategy in which there are a variety of assessment methods.

In writing short-answer questions, it is important that the teacher makes absolutely clear what is required; questions should be unambiguous. It is useful to include guidance on marks awarded for each question so that a student can see the relative importance of the questions and plan the timing accordingly.

Here is a short-answer question suitable for NVQ 2 Business Administration. This covers the topic of Reception Duties.

NVQ 2 Business Administration

'Receive and direct visitors'

1. List 3 skills/qualities required by a good receptionist
    i)
    ii)
    iii)

(3 marks)

2. What procedures should be followed when a visitor with an appoint-
    ment arrives at your company?

    (5 marks)

3. What information should be included when leaving messages for mem-
    bers of your company that have been left on the reception
    answerphone?

    (5 marks)

4. Where would you find the following information?
    (a) a copy of the company's Annual Report
    (b) the telephone extension of the Personnel Director
    (c) the nearest first aid box
    (d) the telephone number of a local taxi company
    (e) a brochure of the company's product range

    (5 marks)

Objective tests require very little judgement on the part of the marker because
there may be only one correct answer. Students may be required to fill in missing words from a sentence, for example, or identify places on a map. They are
reasonably easy to write and simple to do. Again they should not be used as
the only means of assessment because they do not allow for creativity.

Here is an example of an objective test which might be used with some
NVQ Level 1 Catering students:

Matching pairs
Draw lines to link the type of pastry with the correct dish

Hot water crust   Apple dumplings
Choux pastry   Sausage rolls
Short crust pastry   Pork pie
Suet pastry   Eclairs
Puff pastry   Plum tart
                           Peach crumble
                           Yorkshire pudding
                           Fruit cobbler

ORAL TESTS

Oral tests are now an integral part of student assessment. Many programmes
often include some form of presentation to a variety of audiences. Presentation
skills are included within the specifications for key skills in Communication.
At level 2, for example candidates would be expected to 'contribute to a discussion' or 'give a short talk'. At level 3, the candidate would be expected to

'make a presentation, about a complex subject' and would be expected to use appropriate visual aids, including 'at least one image to illustrate complex points'.

The assessment of such skills is challenging and can, of course, be highly subjective. The assessor has to be very clear about what is being tested and has to make this known to the candidates. There should be a mark sheet available and it is helpful to have another marker or moderator present in the audience. This can help to eliminate tutor bias. A sample mark sheet might look like this:

	Marks awarded	*Maximum marks allowed*
Content:		20
Structure:		15
Suitability of language for purpose:		10
Clarity of exposition:		15
Accuracy of information:		20
Use of visual aids:		5
Ability to handle questions:		10
Appearance:		5
		100

The relative weightings of the marks can be adjusted according to the purpose of the assignment. If you were assessing students' abilities in public speaking, for example, one might want to include marks for diction or, in the case of a poem, a mark for interpretation.

As with all assessment, feedback is extremely important in this type of activity and it has to be handled with great sensitivity. It is often less threatening to students if they begin by making short group presentations in which each can play a small part before asking them to embark on individual presentations.

ASSIGNMENTS

As we saw in Chapter 5, these are much longer pieces of assessed work and form a very important element in the assessment strategy of vocational education qualifications. The assignment is central to the learning process and should bring together and integrate different components of the programme. Assignments should enable students to learn and develop their knowledge and to practise applying their skills in a vocational context. The assessment is based on the evidence submitted within the assignment. Designing and writing assignments is a complex task and is very different from writing essay questions or short-answer tests. In Chapter 5 we looked at the design of assignments. Every assignment should carry with it a set of grading criteria and students should be absolutely clear as to what is required.

Within GNVQ and AVCE programmes clear grading criteria are expressed within the unit guidance in such a way that candidates know exactly what is required to achieve a pass, merit or distinction grade, or in the case of AVCE, a literal grade, A–E. Full details on GNVQ assessment procedures are available from the awarding bodies and, because they are subject to revision from time to time, readers are advised to ensure that they have the latest available guidance.

The marking of assignments requires co-operation amongst different staff teaching on the programme. If the assignment is to be truly integrative, then it should be jointly designed and written by the course team as well as assessed by them. Coverage of the units will be cross-checked against the evidence provided in the assignment. This evidence may take a variety of forms. Within the same assignment a student may be required to:

- produce some written work, for example to write a report;
- undertake some practical activity, for example, strip down an engine;
- give a short oral presentation, for example, on work experience;
- produce a set of drawings, for example, for a design specification
- record audio tapes;
- complete artwork.

Assessment within vocational programmes may involve using a variety of evidence and need not be done on the basis of paper-based evidence alone. Teachers have sometimes been reluctant to design assignments that will allow students to present evidence in different forms, for example, using tape-recordings, photographs or log books. This may in part reflect the culture of academic teaching where the only acceptable evidence is the production of written work, often under examination conditions. Group work may be seen as tantamount to 'cheating'. There is a further concern which relates to the difficulty of providing valid and reliable methods of assessing work that is not written.

In designing practical assignments it is necessary to strike a balance between the assessment of the finished product/design/result and the skills and knowledge used in achieving that result. For example, what percentage of the marks should be given to manual skills, to the selection of appropriate tools or materials and what percentage to the final product? If a student worked with little regard to health and safety procedures should this invalidate the finished result? All these considerations need to be taken into account in drawing up the grading criteria for an assignment.

One Midlands college has designed an assessment procedure for NVQ Catering which involved the production of a set of photographs indicating 'standard' dishes. Students' practical outputs are judged against the 'photographic standards'. This also helps students to identify what they are aiming for in the finished product.

It is often a useful strategy to show students' pieces of work which have been completed by former students, subject, of course, to those students' agreement. With a teacher's help, students can be encouraged to identify the strengths and weaknesses of different approaches. This is particularly helpful in the case of adult students who may be returning to learning after a considerable break and who may be anxious about the production of assignments. You have already met some of these students in Chapter 2.

You will gather from all of this that the process of assessment and recording achievement is an extremely complex one. The teacher is required to act in a number of different roles, ranging from being purely a marker to being a guide, counsellor and mentor. Some of these roles are potentially conflicting. As a tutor you may know that a student is undergoing a series of personal difficulties, which you feel may have impinged upon the production of a good piece of work. How then are you to assess the work? In terms of a strict 'standards' methodology the work does not meet the criteria. As tutor, you are aware of the reasons why this work may not meet the standards. This brings us back to the fundamental purposes of assessment and the balance between the formative and summative elements. The tutor has to strike a balance between directing the students and 'letting the students go'. In her book, *Adults Learning*, Jenny Rogers writes:

> Some teachers who rightly pride themselves on the standard of their own work, sometimes find their students' mistakes too painful to contemplate, and will often seize the work and do the difficult bits themselves, sometimes under the impression that students are grateful for such professional additions. There may be occasional students too placid to object, but most people feel cheated if someone else does all the hard work for them. They want the satisfaction and sense of achievement of learning to cope for themselves.

> (Rogers, 1992, p.63)

ALBSU (1991) highlights the role of the tutor as the facilitator of learning particularly with adults on open learning programmes. Here a distinction between formative and summative evaluation is a particularly difficult one to draw.

Students may be encouraged to involve themselves in both peer and self-assessment. Peer assessment needs to be handled very sensitively and should not be embarked upon until the teacher has a good knowledge of the group. Guidance should also be provided on the criteria to be applied in making peer assessments. Comments such as 'that was great' or 'that was rubbish' are to be avoided. On the other hand, self-evaluation is an important part of the learning process because only the individual knows his or her objectives in undertaking the programme and should, therefore, be best able to judge whether or not such objectives are being achieved. This may be a new idea to some of your students and they will require guidance in developing techniques of reflection and self-evaluation. You may wish to provide some standard form on which students can record their own evaluation or you may prefer to provide some prompts. As students become more practised they will probably be able to write a short evaluation for each assignment undertaken.

Marshall and Rowland (1993) have drawn attention to the importance of self-evaluation in the learning process and of its role in helping to provide student independence. Students should also be encouraged to discuss their assessments with tutors and there may well be a case for involving students in joint marking with tutors. This can be highly motivational.

In summarising its research findings on assessment and classroom practice, the Assessment Reform Group (1999) emphasises the following key points in ensuring that learning is central to the assessment process. Although its research focused upon learning within the compulsory education phase, the points are valid for learners of all ages.

- the provision of effective feedback to pupils;
- the active involvement of pupils in their own learning;
- adjusting teaching to take account of the results of assessment;
- a recognition of the profound influence assessment has on the motivation and self-esteem of pupils;
- the need for pupils to be able to assess themselves and understand how to improve.

(Assessment Reform Group, pp.4–5)

COMPETENCE-BASED ASSESSMENT

As we saw in Chapter 3, in competence-based assessment the assessor must make judgements concerning the sufficiency of evidence supplied by the candidate. Evidence can take a variety of forms but the assessor needs to be assured of its validity. The assessor will want to make sure he or she has satisfactory answers to the following questions:

- Is this the candidate's own work?
- On how many occasions was this task performed?
- If a 'real-life' situation is unavailable how reliable are those results achieved through a simulation?

The following all provide legitimate forms of evidence. You may wish to consider how you would reliably assess them.

- Displays and presentations
- Practical demonstrations
- Planning and organising events
- Creative use of photographs
- Making and producing models/drawings/paintings
- Group work

- Designing products and services
- Projects undertaken by individuals or groups
- Role-play work

BTEC (1993) suggests that evidence can be divided into two types: perfor-mance evidence and supplementary evidence. Performance evidence is required for each element within each unit and should be derived as far as pos-sible from a 'real' environment. For example, a candidate could be observed welding metal within a workshop situation. The candidate could also be assessed on a finished product. If processes cannot be directly observed by the assessor, then evidence from videotape or audiotape may also be used provid-ing it can be authenticated. Evidence could also be collected by questioning the candidate. There must be sufficient evidence to meet all the criteria for an element.

Often evidence collected to fulfil the criteria for one element may be rele-vant to and provide evidence for the achievement of other elements within the full qualification. It is not necessary to generate a separate piece of evidence for every criterion; the role of the teacher is to help students identify what evi-dence may count towards the achievement of the criteria.

Let us consider an example. 'Maintaining a safe and healthy working envi-ronment' is central to workplace practice and appears as a unit in the majority of occupational qualifications. The achievement of this unit cannot be assessed in isolation because sound and safe working are essential elements of good practice. Evidence of this should permeate the candidate's work across all units of the qualification.

Assessment involves making judgements about the evidence which the candidate provides. This assessment may involve observing a candidate's per-formance in the workplace that is watching the candidate in action. Where performance evidence cannot be assessed, supplementary evidence may be used to infer performance. For example, you may want to question a candidate about certain activities or set some form of written test. However, it should be remembered, when considering performance and supplementary evidence, that 'The two sorts of evidence complement each other. Activities which pro-vide supplementary evidence do not exist in a vacuum. They are designed to support the performance evidence you have collected by confirming the knowledge and understanding of the candidate' (Huddleston, Abbott and Stagg, 1995, p.39).

Competence-based assessment is generally carried out by college staff within the college even for candidates who are in employment, though some-times college staff may go to the employers' premises to carry out assessment. The lack of employer involvement in the assessment of those employees who attend college as part of their NVQ programme raises questions as to what extent competence-based assessment is taking place in the workplace as opposed to a simulated environment. One of the barriers appears to be the lack of trained workplace assessors. NVQs require competence to be demonstrated in a 'realistic environment'; that is, as far as possible under the normal conditions and pressures of the workplace and with the use of appropriate equipment and facilities. Where this is not possible simulated working environments have to be provided. Within colleges, assessment may, therefore, be undertaken in college training restaurants, hairdressing salons or training offices, for example.

For full-time students working towards NVQ accreditation, work placements have to be found in order for them to demonstrate competence to workplace standards. Here assessment may be problematic since it will depend upon the goodwill and co-operation of those employers willing to provide work placements. In some sectors it is extremely difficult to access sufficient placements and there are often competing demands on them. Consistency across work placements may be variable: whilst some may provide excellent opportunities for candidates to demonstrate competence others may be of a poor standard. The Chief Inspector's report (FEFC, 2000d) draws attention to the productive links that some colleges have been able to forge with employers. For example, the 1999–2000 cycle of inspections of engineering within colleges revealed that, 'Colleges often have productive links with industry. They provide specialist courses for employers and benefit from the donation of industry standard equipment' (p.18). However, in construction it was found that, 'Students rarely have their practical skills assessed in the workplace. Few full-time students undertake work experience' (p.16).

There are some key questions upon which you may wish to reflect concerning issues of assessment within the NVQ:

- Who is assessing?
- What is being assessed?
- How valid and reliable is the evidence?
- Is there a consistency of standards across different units/elements of the qualification?
- Where is the assessment being carried out?
- What is the balance between performance evidence and supplementary evidence?
- Do the candidates understand the assessment process?
- How is evidence being recorded?

ASSESSING PORTFOLIOS

Throughout this chapter we have been talking about the centrality of the student's portfolio in assessment within many vocational programmes. Portfolios can be confusing documents for the beginning student, navigating the apparently endless paper trail is a daunting task, particularly if its purpose is not made clear. The portfolio provides the evidence that the student can meet all the criteria set out in the specification for that programme. Let us take a specific example. Within a unit on Business Finance a student may be required to investigate a range of financial products or services suitable for different customer groups, to compare costs and evaluate the benefits. The evidence in the portfolio must demonstrate that the student has collected information from a range of financial services providers, has calculated the costs of certain products for specific customer groups and drawn conclusions from actual data. The evidence should always be suitable for the purpose for which it is provided, and authentic; in other words, it must be the student's own work. It must also be sufficient, that is, it must include all that is required to meet the criteria. If in the example above, the student omitted to include calculations of costings then the criteria would not have been fulfilled.

This may seem relatively straightforward, however the organisation of the material into a coherent portfolio is often problematic. Some organisational techniques can help students to overcome the difficulties. The guiding principles are:

- Appropriate induction, so that students understand clearly the purpose of the portfolio and its role in assessment;
- A clear map through the course indicating exactly where, in which units, and at what time in the programme the pieces of evidence will be produced which will go into the portfolio;
- Copies of the assignment brief should be attached to the front of the student's assignment together with a copy of the assessor's comments and grade awarded;
- Good systems which help students to organise their work, examples include: files with dividers; tracking sheets on which students record where in the file the evidence is located, these should identify for which unit they provide evidence and be signed off by assessors and dated;
- An index, which also contains relevant information about the candidate and the centre.
- Portfolios should be kept up to date; trying to complete them retrospectively is a recipe for disaster.

In the first instance students' work is assessed by the appropriate tutor for the unit. All colleges offering vocational qualifications which include a portfolio assessment must appoint internal verifiers in order to ensure consistency across different markers and across programmes. This is part of the quality assurance system that is required by the awarding bodies, and ultimately by the regulators such as QCA and SQA. In addition, the awarding bodies appoint independent standards moderators to ensure that internal assessment and verification is consistent across different centres, thus ensuring national standards.

If you are involved in the delivery of vocational programmes you should ensure that you keep up to date with developments through your awarding body, or bodies, since you are likely to be teaching on qualifications offered by more than one body. During the past two years there has been substantial change in the qualifications offered and in their methods of assessment. All matters relating to assessment should be referred to the awarding body.

CONCLUSION

You will have reflected that assessment is a complex and a time-consuming business. The nature and forms of assessment in FE have changed considerably during the past ten years. The contexts in which assessment is undertaken have also changed. It is not just a matter for the examination hall but for the workplace too and many other settings as well.

The ways in which grades and marks are applied to assessment have also changed. There is greater emphasis on criterion referencing, that is on what and what has not been achieved, rather than on norm referencing. Norm referencing involves the measurement of an individual's achievement against the achievement of others taking the same test or exam. This is typified by the examination pass list with the marks and positions of candidates shown. You will recall the annual debates over alleged falling standards in GCSEs and A levels because too many candidates appeared to be gaining higher grades. The debate also occurs in the HE sector where too many graduates are allegedly gaining 'good' degrees (see Ainley, 1994). The process of assessment has become more transparent and more emphasis is placed upon the dialogue between the assessor and the assessed. Increasingly, assessment serves a variety of purposes. It helps to identify starting points, and in this sense it is diagnostic. It may help to identify previous learning for which a student may wish to claim credit, as in accreditation of prior learning (APL) procedures. This type of assessment can help to inform the learning plan and avoid unnecessary duplication.

Assessment, in its formative aspects, maintains a record of ongoing progress. This type of assessment aims to improve the quality of what is being achieved and helps to structure learning. On the other hand, summative assessment may be a summary of the formative assessments already carried out of what a student can do at a given time.

In designing assessment plans for our students we will need to ensure a balance of these different types of assessment. We can collect evidence in a variety of ways and over different time periods. We can also collect evidence provided in different contexts; we all know that our students may perform differently on employers' premises from the way that they perform in our practical classes. We should also consider the motivational and personal development opportunities implicit in a negotiated record of achievement or profile.

We should not neglect the opportunities provided by assessment to review our curricula and their organisation, and to judge their suitability for the students for whom they are intended. If we are to talk about assessment for learning, then both teachers and students are engaged in a co-operative venture that should help not only in improving the learning experiences of students but the teaching and support that we offer them.

Part III

Professional development

Chapter 7

Evaluation, reflection and research

The activity of reflection is so familiar, that as teachers or trainers, we often overlook it in formal learning settings ... reflection is a vital element in any form of learning and teachers and trainers need to consider how they can incorporate some forms of reflection in their courses.

(Boud, Keogh and Walker, 1985, p.8)

Stimulated by surprise, they turn thought back on action and on the knowing which is implicit in action ... it is this entire process of reflection-in-action which is central to the 'art' by which practitioners sometimes deal well with situations of uncertainty, instability, uniqueness and value conflict.

(Schon, 1983, p.50)

In this chapter, we examine the benefits which teachers can gain from applying the concept of the 'reflective practitioner' as a means of evaluating and considering their own practice, and by helping their students use the same concept to reflect on their development as learners. Throughout this book, of course, we have been asking you to reflect on your own learning, on some of our ideas, and on your approach to teaching.

Reflection is a natural part of human life but for professionals and students, structured reflection can provide a framework within which they can examine their strengths and weaknesses and identify strategies for improvement. In addition, professionals can use reflection as a bridge to help span what is often regarded as a chasm between the reality of their practice as teachers and the theoretical models and concepts put forward by academics who research education.

Reflection can sometimes turn into 'navel gazing', a pleasant enough pastime for some but not one that will necessarily take the reflector any further forward or cause any changes to his or her practices! This is why we are advocating the need for reflection, whether by teachers or students, to be structured and fully incorporated within the formal framework of a course or teaching career.

Later in this chapter, we discuss ways in which teachers in colleges can build on the reflective process and begin actively to research their practice. By turning one's reflections into ideas for research projects, those reflections can be sharpened and scrutinised, and lead to real and worthwhile policies for improved practices (and policies) for both individuals and institutions.

REFLECTION FOR STUDENTS

In his book *The Enquiring Tutor*, Stephen Rowland, who has taught in both schools and HE, explains his commitment to student-centred learning:

> At the heart of this approach is the view that, both morally and practically, it is worth taking our students seriously. What they have to say about themselves provides us with the most significant information about their own learning, and thus our teaching. If we can give voice to our students' experience, we have come a long way towards understanding our own practice.
>
> (Rowland, 1993, p.6)

There are many ways in which teachers can and will encourage their students to reflect on their learning but, all too often, reflection becomes confused with assessment. As we saw in Chapter 6, constructive feedback that arises out of assessment can, of course, facilitate reflection, but students need to learn how to reflect and come to regard it as a natural process in its own right.

In order to reflect, you have to ask yourself questions, some of which might be difficult or awkward. The identification of those questions may be straightforward if, for example, you have been struggling to write an essay and cannot decide how the story ends, or you may have been cooking and discover that you have left out a key ingredient from the recipe. If, however, you are reflecting on why you find it so difficult to learn how to conjugate verbs in French or how to turn what you have read in a book into a summary using your own words, then the questions you need to ask become more complex. Students, therefore, will have to practise reflection and to do that they need some guidance.

One way of helping students to reflect would be to ask them to analyse themselves as learners. They could, for example, do the exercise at the beginning of Chapter 5 in which you were asked to consider whether you were a 'good' learner. They could use Honey and Mumford's *The Manual of Learning Styles* (1982) to discover whether, by nature, they adopt one of the following learning styles:

Activist (rolls up sleeves and rushes into action)
Reflector (contemplates the problem and considers how to approach)
Theorist (consults 'experts', researches the issues before acting)
Pragmatist (selects the most appropriate form of action given the circumstances)

Whichever method is chosen, however, the student has to learn to reflect in a way which suits his or her own style and needs and the teacher has to create a supportive atmosphere in which this can take place:

> The open teacher, like a good therapist, establishes rapport and resonance, sensing unspoken needs, conflicts, hopes and fears. Respecting the learner's autonomy, the teacher spends more time helping to articulate the urgent questions than demanding right answers … Just as you can't 'deliver' holistic health, which must start with the intention of the patient, the true teacher knows you can't impose learning. You can, as Galileo said, help the individual discover patterns and connections, foster openness to strange new possibilities, and is the midwife to ideas. The teacher is the steersman (sic), a catalyst, a facilitator – an agent of learning but not the first cause.
>
> (Ferguson, 1982, pp.320–1)

We asked a number of students in different colleges to reflect on a recent learning experience. In the first set of examples, three 16-year-old students (two full time and one part time) give their reactions to their tutors' assessments of a piece of work:

GNVQ Group Assignment: a student reflects on how the group worked together

I think the grade is fair because we all really put a lot of work into this. I mean just writing the letters and arranging the company interviews took ages. As usual, Angela did practically nothing, but I think Mrs Bennett [the tutor] knows this because she gave her a lower grade which is only fair anyway. I wasn't too happy about the marks for the oral presentation because I think we did as well as we could have done. I mean, we're not all bloomin' TV presenters! I don't see why we should have so many marks for oral presentation when it's all in the file anyway.

I think Kamal did a brilliant job with the accounts; it really helped our assignment. I am pleased he was given a higher mark for that because he really deserved it. What I especially liked about this assignment was that it really gave us a chance to get together out of college. I mean, in the evenings we used to meet up at someone's house and do all the planning – it was really great. Sharm's Dad gave us lots of help as well, like where we could find out things, and he even brought us some company brochures and reports.

I used to think people in our group were, well, sad until I got to know them through this assignment. Now I know they're OK.

An A level student reflects on the comments she received for an essay on *Hamlet*

I must say I am very disappointed with this mark. I put a lot of effort into this, practically regurgitating all the notes which we had been given. That always seemed to work at GCSE. English was my best subject. If the lecturer can't tell us the answer and give us a decent set of notes, what can he expect? He talks about critical reflection; I don't even know what he means. I don't see how he can expect me to go off and find the stuff when he hasn't told me what to look for. After all, he's paid to teach us and get us through the exam. I don't see why I should have to 'look things up'. Perhaps I should buy a set of those revision notes.

Perming hair: a hairdressing student reflects on an activity in the college's training salon

Well I think that the perm was all right. I mean, not brilliant but all right. Mrs Smith [the tutor] thought it was a pass but she said it wouldn't be fast enough in a real salon. Well it ain't a real salon anyway and the people who come here know that – that's why it's cheap. Anyway, I think Mrs Smith has got it in for me since she caught me using the mousse in the practice salon. I don't care because the gaffer [manager of the salon in which the student works when not at college] thinks I'm OK and that's what matters. He says the college don't know what they're talking about because they don't have to run a business. Anyway, college is a laugh. We have a great time and as long as I just get by that's OK. There was nothing wrong with the perm anyway.

These reflections capture the emotional tensions which formal assessment can engender. In the first example, the experience of learning within a group structure has enabled the student to recognise the strengths and weaknesses of individual group members and to celebrate the social enjoyment to be found in working closely with colleagues. In the second and third examples, we see the students struggling to accept criticism of their work and behaviour. These students instinctively blame the tutor rather than examining their own weaknesses. They may have legitimate reasons for criticising their tutors but unless they are given opportunities to discuss the thinking behind the assessments, they may have difficulty in demonstrating their true abilities. When tutors and learners reflect together about the learning process, both parties can confront each other's level of contribution, thus identifying ways in which that process can be improved.

In the second set of examples, three mature students (one full-time and two part-time) reflect on their individual progress after six months on a course:

Adult basic skills student: 45-year-old Jack has been unemployed for three years

I finally started to understand where I'd been going wrong with maths when I stopped blaming myself for having failed at school. It was this week the penny dropped and I've been here nearly six months. I just sat in class on Tuesday and I heard Brenda [a fellow student] shout at our tutor.

She said, 'I'm really good at some things you know. I might not be any good at these sums you give us but I used to get good marks at school for my writing.' I thought, she's right; just because we're not much cop at maths doesn't mean we're stupid, and then I seemed to lose my fear about what Brenda calls 'sums'.

Information technology student: Frances is a 33-year-old secretary

I still don't really like coming here. I'd rather be at work but my boss wants me to learn about this stuff and I know I need to really. It's not the tutors, they're smashing. Well, I suppose it's the effort of having to concentrate on learning new things when at work I seem to get by so easily and I feel in control. When there's a test I just go to pieces and my husband says he can tell I'm worried about college because I take it out on everyone at home. I'll be glad when it's finished … awful isn't it? I should be grateful for the chance really.

Catering student: Edward is a 27-year-old former policeman who is now training to be a chef

If only I'd done this years ago, I would have been much happier. The course is going well but then I know I've got a good attitude, better than some of the others who are a bit up and down about the whole thing. I can't wait to get into the kitchen and the pressure doesn't bother me at all. I'm much more motivated about this than anything else I've been on and it really makes a difference to your standard of work. I never knew I could learn so fast.

In these examples, their maturity helps the students reflect more deeply on their learning experience and they can relate back to earlier experiences to gain insights into their problems and successes.

CONSTRUCTING A REFLECTIVE DIARY

A 'reflective diary' can take many forms and should be a very personal record so you can be as creative as you wish. You might decide to use a typical diary format, making entries for each day or week in a notebook. You might keep a boxfile or shoebox in which you can store any jottings, cuttings from newspapers, cartoons, photographs and so on. Or, you might keep a very visual record using diagrams or pictures to illustrate your journey through the teaching year. If you feel happier with a more formal structure for the diary, here are some suggestions for dividing the diary into sections to include:

- a record of newly acquired knowledge, understanding and skills that are important to you;

- a commentary on your personal/professional development as you progress through the year;
- a commentary on the interesting (and perhaps contentious) issues and concepts which arise out of your professional experience;
- responses to critical incidents.

Here are two extracts from reflective diaries which show how experienced college teachers record their concerns and queries about their students. The first extract records a teacher's thoughts after an induction meeting with a group of adult students on a 'two plus two' degree course:

> This seems a pleasant enough group. It's a real 'mixed-bag' though. One or two obviously have the impression that they know it all and tend to dominate the rest, mainly through their attempts to monopolise the discussion and to 'name drop' one or two key texts. Mrs Baker is a bit of a worry because she obviously knows quite a lot but is anxious about expressing her opinions. I must remember to let her take a more active role next time. Perhaps I should let her act as a rapporteur for feedback on group work.
>
> Greg seems particularly anxious. I notice he was hovering at the back afterwards waiting to catch me on my way out. Did he really need to check the time of the next class or was there something more important that he wanted to discuss? I noticed that he moved away very quickly when Tony came up.
>
> I must remember that Winifred is repeating this year; I need to keep her interest. I must draw on her knowledge and expertise to help me and the group. It's going to be tough for her because her son is in hospital again. I think I might suggest we plan a group get-together at the local pub or bowling alley to help establish a real group identity.

The second extract is from a catering tutor's diary written after she assessed a group of students working in the college restaurant:

> On the whole, the group performed well with one or two notable exceptions. Ros was late and Chris didn't have his white jacket. Nevertheless, Ranjit, who was maitre d'hotel for the evening, handled the situation very well. I must remember to enter his performance under core skills in his portfolio. His communication skills were particularly appropriate.
>
> The main courses were well presented and service was competently handled. Must remember to tell Gill about her mistake with the cutlery although I don't think she was the only one. Lee should have noticed that the water jugs were empty before the customer had to ask. The dessert trolley was the least well handled. This group are very poor at describing the individual dishes to customers. It's not that they don't know, I think they are too scared to say. I must speak to their communications lecturer. We need to develop some role play situations so that students can practise before they meet real customers.

It may seem daunting to try and find the time to record observations and ideas in this way, but the two extracts above show how a number of important details can be logged by teachers in a relatively short diary-style account.

In the next extract, from a trainee teacher's record of a session with a GNVQ Intermediate class that was being observed by the teacher's tutor, we see an example of how a teacher can reflect on a critical incident:

> It was a disaster, I just totally lost it. I thought I had it all planned and organised and it all went dreadfully wrong. There are some real trouble-makers in this group. I should have realised that, I just wasn't prepared for it. I should have realised that the trouble was starting once the two at the front began banging the cupboard doors. I should have separated them. I can't think why I let them sit together, the whole thing just became worse and there was nothing I could do about it.
>
> I realise that while my attention was being taken by the trouble-makers others were starting to become restless. Then those who were working well were not being given any attention. I really need to think about everyone in the group and not just concentrate on those who are causing trouble. I couldn't believe it when they started throwing the paper darts. Obviously I was an easy target. I knew then I had lost it. My real worry is how I am going to face them next week.

The trainee teacher's tutor also recorded her own reflections on the session she had observed and provided her student with these comments:

A. Opening
Try to be on time and establish control before taking the register. What about the young lady loitering at the door, was she supposed to be in or out of the class? Close the door to show that the class has begun.

B. Introduction
You need to recap on previous class. Make sure everyone is attending before you start. What was that boy doing wandering around? You must ensure that: i) everyone understands the task and is fully prepared and ii) everyone is working through the task. Try to deal with one question at a time. You broke off in the middle of answering one boy's question to answer another. It gives the impression to the group that you are not fully in control. You must deal with the boy at the back who kept shouting. There was a lot of constructive work going on in some parts of the class, try to capitalise on this. Class eventually settled down well to the task.

C. During lesson
Make sure that the troublesome elements are also on the task. Don't leave people too long before checking up on them ... the boy next to me was drawing cartoons.

D. Feedback from activity

Make sure all the class is ready to engage in the activity, people were still writing, others talking amongst themselves. You must draw the whole group together before attempting a de-brief from the exercise. How should you deal with the paper darts incident? The disruption with the cupboard was very unfortunate – one strategy would have been to move the boy away from the cupboard rather than have the confrontation. The class was aware that you were losing control. It is a great pity that those who were working on the task and who had some good ideas were not used more; the disruptive students were really dominating the class. In fact, if you notice, there are only 5, at the most, disruptive students, the rest of the class is fine so capitalise on them.

E. Rounding off

Keep your eye on the time so that you allow sufficient time to draw everything together and reinforce any key points. The lesson didn't have a proper ending but just stumbled to a close.

F. Reflection

What do you feel the students learned from this class?
How would you sum up your classroom management?
What went well?
What did not go well?

Put together, the two sets of reflective notes create a much more meaningful critique of the lesson than if one simply had access to just one person's account. Clearly, the trainee teacher has written his notes from a fairly acute sense of failure and, to some extent, foreboding, given that he will have to meet this same group again. His account gives the impression that the majority of students in the group were behaving badly, that the noise level was high and that he lurched from one crisis to the next. His tutor's notes provide a more coherent account (having been written from the relative calm of the back of the room) by breaking the lesson down into a chronology of pedagogical principles. We learn from this that the trainee teacher apparently arrived a little late for the lesson and so may have created the wrong impression with some students. In addition, we learn that a very small number of students caused the disruptions whereas, for the trainee teacher, it was as if they had completely taken over the proceedings. Finally, the general lack of organisation in the classroom is obviously something which the trainee teacher cannot blame entirely on five so-called 'troublemakers'.

We are, of course, surrounded by examples of people learning, whether at home, at work, in the street, in the pub, or at the football ground. The list is endless. Try to observe your friends, relatives, colleagues and even strangers if you see them in a learning situation and record your observations in your 'reflective diary'. In fact, treat the everyday world as your research laboratory and don't forget to include yourself too!

In Chapters 4 and 5, we discussed some of the theoretical literature related to teaching and learning and tried to show how theory can inform and illuminate the teacher's role. The individual teacher should have the opportunity to contribute to and engage with the theory, and this is where the process of reflection can have real meaning and purpose. For Quicke (1996), theory needs to be balanced with reflective practice, otherwise it is in danger of putting a 'straight-jacket on teacher thought'. He gives three reasons for this:

> First, they (theories) may no longer be relevant. Although conceived originally as a way of clarifying and helping to resolve problems with which common-sense knowledge was no longer adequate to deal, they now address problems which are no longer salient. There may be new agendas in place in relation to which old theories may be obsolete. Second, theories may become reified. This problem is not so much to do with the content of a theory as with the manner in which the theory is held ... Thirdly, theories are not so much irrelevant in terms of the issues they address but are irrelevant as theories. There may be other theories which address the same problems 'better' by constituting them differently or it's possible that common sense has already been informed by such theories. What is required is reflection on existing common sense using ideas from other aspects of common-sense knowledge.
>
> (Quicke, 1996, p.21))

TEACHER AS RESEARCHER

The concept of the 'teacher as researcher' has been promoted for some considerable time, certainly since the 1970s when the work of Lawrence Stenhouse advocated the need for practitioners to become researchers in their own right (see Stenhouse, 1975). In the current climate of change which has swept through FE colleges, the concept is being re-examined for it has the potential to act as a vehicle for enabling college staff to investigate collaboratively the key questions and problems which concern them (see Young et al., 1996). Schon, as part of his advocacy of the 'reflective practitioner', insists that there needs to be a shift away from the type of educational research which appears unconcerned with the realities of practice to research which is grounded in that practice:

> In the varied topography of professional practice, there is the high ground overlooking a swamp. On the high ground, manageable problems lend themselves to solution through the application of research-based theory and technique. In the swampy lowland, messy, confusing problems defy technical solution. The irony of this situation is that the problems of the high ground tend to be relatively unimportant to individuals or society at large,

however great their technical interest may be, while in the swamp lie the problems of greatest human concern. The practitioner must choose. Shall he remain on the high ground where he can solve relatively unimportant problems according to prevailing standards of rigour, or shall he descend to the swamp of important problems and nonrigorous inquiry?

(Schon, 1987, p.3)

FE teachers are familiar with researchers, evaluators and representatives of management consultants who visit their colleges to interview students and staff, collect statistical data and observe teaching and learning. Ironically, however, the concerns of the FE teachers themselves may – though this will be rare – form the focus of this externally generated and externally led research activity. In the main, the teachers are left with their concerns and the external researchers move on to another set of problems. Academics in HE have, of course, their own legitimate reasons for carrying out research and play a crucial role in helping practitioners tackle the theoretical underpinning they need in furthering their understanding of and ability to examine critically the educational context in which they practise. But this relationship can be limited and much of the important work that it generates is hidden from view. There is a need, therefore, for the two communities to work much more collaboratively to ensure the following:

- that research outcomes are disseminated widely and acted upon;
- that teachers and other professionals play a more pro-active part in determining the research questions to be addressed;
- that teachers contribute their professional experience and expertise to the whole of the research process rather than just a small part of it;
- that researchers are made to challenge their research practices and findings through collaborative enquiry and ongoing dialogue;
- that researchers pass on their skills to others and demystify the process of research.

This new relationship cannot, of course, be simply formed in order to meet the needs of one of the partners. It has to be recognised that university education departments are struggling to maintain adequate student numbers at postgraduate level. Gone are the days when the local education authorities and institutions would pay teachers to attend courses and give them time to study. Teachers and other professionals are having to pay their own fees and may, in some cases, be actively discouraged from attending certain courses by their managers. The pressures on college staff to meet retention and attainment targets and meet the demands of external quality assurance means that professional development becomes less of a priority.

From the colleges' point of view, a collaborative relationship with HE should not be driven solely by management priorities or imposed on staff as yet another workload clause in their contracts. Staff who are told on a Monday morning by the college chief executive that they are all to become 'researchers' are unlikely to react positively when a group of academics arrives to begin work. The considerable amount of pedagogical, curricular and policy change that has affected colleges in recent years and the increased emphasis on the role of FE in terms of rising post-compulsory participation rates have presented college staff with a plethora of problems and concerns to be investigated. Given the pressures of workload affecting all staff and the demands of external bodies for information about individual college performance, it will be necessary to ensure that institutions separate routine data gathering and monitoring from a more searching research programme which combines quantitative and qualitative methods and draws on a range of different research traditions and methodologies. At the same time, college staff will need to be supported over a realistic time span in their research activity by both their managers and the academics with whom they are to collaborate.

Andrew Culham, a lecturer at Amersham and Wycombe College in the south of England, sounds a realistic note in relation to teacher researchers when he writes, 'The realities of practitioner research are, in my experience, very different from the optimistic view reported by educational institutions and research journals. With all this "enthusiasm" why is it still difficult or impossible for FE practitioners to conduct research?' (Culham, 2001, p.27). Culham goes on to suggest four key factors affect practitioner research in many colleges:

- lack of time and funding;
- no 'active' research culture within FE;
- no 'value' of research within colleges;
- few opportunities for dissemination.

He calls for 'a greater understanding of the relevance and value of practitioner-based research...embedded within further education philosophy and policy development as part of an active promotion of a college's research effort' (ibid., p.28). Writing in the same publication as Culham, Adam Davey, the Research Co-ordinator at Cambridge Regional College, describes a number of strategies which his college has adopted to try and develop a research culture (Davey, 2001, p.29). They include: evening meetings to hear and debate staff research presentations; a research week involving outside speakers; a teacher fellowship programme which grants teachers a term's sabbatical for research purposes; a funded internal action research programme; and research partnerships with neighbouring colleges.

There are other developments in this area. University departments are seeking to accredit teacher-led research projects within their award-bearing programmes and there are opportunities for colleges and universities to apply jointly for research funding. At the time of writing, the Economic and Social Research Council (ESRC) is funding a major programme of research into teaching and learning across all sectors of education and including work-based learning. One project, which is already underway, is concerned with transforming learning cultures in further education colleges. One of the project's researchers, Denis Gleeson (2001, pp.30–31) explains that the project 'focuses on the nature of learning cultures and of the "turning points" in learners' lives which are amenable to intervention at various levels, for example, through individual support, family learning, teacher involvement, organizational change, community support, work-related experience, and government or policy intervention.'

Despite its long existence and centrality to people's lives and the nation's economic prosperity, the FE sector has not had the attention it deserves from the research community. As Stanton (2000, p.174) notes, 'it is the conventional wisdom that further education is under-researched.' It will be interesting to see the extent to which the Learning and Skills Research Centre (LSRC), established in 2001 as part of the Learning and Skills Development Agency (LSDA) with funding from central government, can redress the balance by ensuring that the FE sector gets some of the attention currently devoted to school-based, and increasingly HE-based educational research. One very practical project which LSDA has developed is the Research and Development Toolkit which comprises units on various aspects of the research process. The Toolkit is delivered by LSDA staff at regional workshops which are designed to be participative and to build on practitioners' existing research experience and abilities.

Chapter 8

Professional development

INTRODUCTION

In previous chapters, we have emphasised the multi-skilled nature of the FE teacher. Given the diversity of FE life and the volatility of curricula within colleges, every FE teacher has to make plans to ensure he or she has access to relevant and appropriate professional development opportunities. Given also that teachers in FE stretch from those who concentrate on basic skills through to those teaching at undergraduate and postgraduate level, the scope of professional development must, necessarily, be broad enough to encompass the wide range of professional needs.

In Chapter 4, we discussed the role that theory plays in developing our understanding of teaching and learning. Your initial teacher training course may have included a study of theoretical concepts and the research underpinning them, but it is important to try and maintain some connection with the developing research field. In addition, you will also need to ensure your specific professional area of expertise is kept up to date. Michael Eraut, who has made a key contribution to our understanding of professional knowledge and competence, sees the 'disposition to theorise' as the 'most important quality of the professional teacher' as once they gain this, teachers will:

> go on developing their theorising capacities throughout their teaching careers, they will be genuinely self-evaluative and they will continue to search for, invent and implement new ideas. Without it they will become prisoners of their early … experience, perhaps the competent teachers of today, almost certainly the ossified teachers of tomorrow.
>
> (Eraut, 1994, p.71)

For Michael Tedder, writing from his experience of teaching in colleges, the concept of professionalism has many meanings in FE:

> Many of us use the term 'professional' regularly to convey a range of meanings among which might be identified the possession of a body of knowledge and expertise, normally accredited with academic or vocational

qualifications, and the awareness of a set of values or a code of conduct that governs our relationship with 'clients', the ethics of our profession. Professionalism also implies a relationship with colleagues that includes responsibility for monitoring the standards in our practice and an acceptance of responsibility or a sense of accountability to the community we serve.

(Tedder, 1994, p.74)

Professional development is itself a concept in need of some clarification. A more familiar term might be staff development, but often, this will tend to refer to largely in-house, short and management-led initiatives rather than activity that is determined by the individual teacher to fulfil personal development goals. Prior to incorporation, staff development in colleges had had a mixed history. As Castling (1996) has shown, the 1970s were a period in which staff development probably meant being sent on an external course for updating related to one's teaching area, whereas in the 1980s, more emphasis was placed on colleges creating internal staff development programmes, often using ideas generated by the Further Education Unit (FEU). Local education authorities (LEAs) also played a key role in the 1980s as they managed government funding targeted at staff development, while Her Majesty's Inspectorate (HMI) ran national conferences for staff development officers. The levels of nationally available funding gradually decreased, however, and post-incorporation staff development is very much seen as a cost to be borne by colleges themselves. It is perhaps worth recording that in its last year (1992), the Grant for Educational Support and Training (GEST) provided £20 million to FE colleges to fund staff development (see Betts, 1996, p.100).

Ofsted and ALI, under their Common Inspection Framework, requires colleges in England to show how 'the professional development of staff contributes to their effectiveness' (ALI/Ofsted, 2001, p.9). Robson (1996) has pointed the danger in assuming that terms such as professional development or staff development privilege the needs of staff, whereas in reality, the inspectors have a more college-centric outlook: 'Staffing needs will be derived from analyses of the college's objectives and staff development activities will be determined less by perceived individual need than by the college's academic and strategic plan' (Robson, 1996, p.3). Thus the majority of activity which falls under the umbrella of professional development tends to be related to servicing an immediate need (e.g. health and safety training, new assessment procedures, FENTO requirements, etc.) or, where it is seen as servicing a long-term goal, as Robson states above, it will be closely tied to the college's strategic plan. There is, of course, every likelihood that some of this activity will complement the professional development needs of some teaching staff, and where a college is prepared to invest large amounts of money, perhaps to retrain teachers or help them develop their professional competence in order to run courses at higher levels, then so-called staff development becomes indistinguishable from professional development.

Staff development tends to take place within the college's own campus and involve only college staff, though an outside speaker might be called upon. Although there are clearly times when a purely internal arrangement is sufficient, there is a real danger that staff and management become too insular if all their staff development is conducted in this way. Castling warns:

> There is the risk of staff becoming bogged down in institutional problems which can obstruct progress, and there may be a lack of fresh ideas which would normally come from working with colleagues elsewhere. There might be a reluctance to resource the input by college staff as fully as that by outside experts, and indeed college staff might not command the respect which would have been accorded to visitors purely because they were from outside. The chief danger is probably insularity. The staff developer managing the programme will need to import wider views, either from their own research or by selecting colleague contributions carefully.
>
> (Castling, 1996, p.80)

Perhaps then staff development should come with a health warning or at least those 'being developed' should recognise that the fix they gain from participating in staff development activities may be less than satisfying. Eraut reminds us that:

> Professionals continually learn on the job, because their work entails engagement in a succession of cases, problems or projects which they have to learn about. This case-specific learning, however, may not contribute a great deal to their general professional knowledge base unless the case is regarded as special rather than routine and time is set aside to deliberate upon its significance. Even then it may remain in memory as a special case without being integrated into any general theory of practice. Thus according to the disposition of individual professionals and the conditions under which they work, their knowledge base may be relatively static or developing quite rapidly. There is little research evidence to indicate the overall level of work-based learning in any profession, but individual examples of both extremes are frequently cited.
>
> (Eraut, 1994, p.10)

As we noted in Chapter 1, there is now a statutory requirement for FE teachers to hold a professional qualification, a privilege they share with their colleagues in HE. To be accepted, the qualification must conform to the standards laid down by FENTO, the National Training Organisation for the FE sector. HE has its own regulatory body for teacher training, the Institute of Learning and Teaching (ILT). Many FE teachers will also hold qualifications related to their area of expertise. For example, lecturers in accountancy, engineering, catering, and law may all have engaged in some form of what Eraut calls initial professional education (IPE) and this may be being 'topped up' by bouts of continuing professional education (CPE) or continuing professional development (CPD). The stage at which these discipline-based professionals will add a qualification in teaching to their curriculum vitae will depend on the nature of their entry to FE. Norman Lucas has argued that this duality of professional role, that is of being at one and the same time a teacher and an expert in a professional or craft/trade area, has dogged the development of a statutory qualification structure:

> Management and staff associations have traditionally united against any statutory professional teaching qualification for further education. Historically lecturers in further education have seen their qualification or expertise in an academic or vocational area as sufficient for teaching. This has placed specialist knowledge of subject or trade above pedagogy. Thus the notion of lecturers being seen as, or seeing themselves as professional teachers with a coherent structure of initial training and professional development has been secondary to a concentration of delivering narrow specialist expertise.
>
> (Lucas, 1996, p.69)

Lucas notes that the number of full-time teachers in FE with a teacher qualification recognised by the DfEE was estimated to be around 60 per cent in 1995, whereas the figure for part-time staff was as low as between 20 per cent and 30 per cent (ibid.). The picture is further complicated by the question of what form of professional development should be required and provided for support staff in colleges whose numbers are on the increase. As we saw in Chapter 1, support staff often perform duties which straddle the boundaries between recognised supportive roles (e.g. technicians operating audio-visual equipment, librarians, etc.) and newer hybrid roles which have a pedagogic dimension (e.g. student counsellors, open learning centre instructors, etc.).

INITIAL PROFESSIONAL EDUCATION FOR FE TEACHERS

As early as 1975, the Haycocks Report recommended that all staff, full- and part-time, should gain a minimum of a Certificate in Education. A number of qualification routes emerged over the years. We provide a brief summary of them here as, at the time of writing, several of these courses will be being adapted to conform to the FENTO standards:

1　Postgraduate Certificate in Education (PGCE): this is a one-year full-time course leading to Qualified Teacher Status (QTS). This course is a statutory requirement for anyone wishing to teach in primary and secondary schools, and is delivered by a local higher education institution (HEI) in partnership with a number of schools. Students spend up to 12 weeks in the HEI and the rest of the year in schools learning to teach 'on the job' supported by a mentor (an experienced teacher within the school) and visits from their HEI tutor. Some PGCEs allow students to carry out their teaching practice in FE colleges. Since 1994, the initial teacher education (ITE) for schools has been controlled by the Teacher Training Agency (TTA) who, in 1996, were charged by the DfEE with the responsibility for improving the standard of ITE that had been criticised by Ofsted, the schools' inspectorate.

2 Certificate in Education (FE): this course, which can be taken in one year full-time or two years part-time, is delivered by colleges in partnership with HEIs or by HEIs on their own. The majority of HEIs delivering this qualification are the 'new' universities reflecting the historical link between the former polytechnics and FE colleges.

3 City and Guilds Teacher's Certificate (7307): this course is delivered by colleges on an in-house basis and is recognised as Part One of the Certificate in Education by some HEIs. Originally known as the Technical Teacher's Certificate when it began life in the 1950s, the 7307 recruited some 10,000 FE teachers per year during the 1990s.

4 City and Guilds Teacher's Certificate (7306): this competence-based certificate is built on the Learning and Development standards identified by the Employment NTO and incorporates the assessor and verifier units referred to in Chapter 1.

5 Related awards: there are a number of other certificates and diplomas which FE teachers can take. These include, for example: the RSA's Diploma in Teaching and Learning in Adult Basic Education and Certificate for Vocational Preparation Tutors; BTEC's Certificate in Management Studies (Education Management); and the City and Guilds' Teaching Basic Skills award.

Young et al. have found that the different routes described above cater for different audiences so that the full-time PGCE courses tended to cater for younger people with more academic qualifications who intended teaching the humanities, English, foreign languages and sciences, whereas the part-time Certificate in Education route attracted older people with work experience in areas such as engineering, electronics, information technology, nursery nursing and careers guidance (Young et al., 1995, p.12).

In the early 1990s, it became clear that FE teachers, who were now responsible for delivering competence-based qualifications, might themselves be subjected to a form of competence-based teacher training. The City and Guilds 7306 had given a taste of things to come. The then Training and Development Lead Body (TDLB), who were responsible for the competence standards for assessors and verifiers of NVQ and GNVQ programmes, developed a set of standards to cover FE more broadly. At the time TDLB was very influential as all college staff involved in teaching NVQs and GNVQs had to achieve the TDLB's so-called D units. In 1994, the government commissioned a 'functional map' of staff roles in FE in England and Wales, which was carried out first by the FEU and then by its successor body, the Further Education Development Agency (FEDA). At the same time, a similar exercise was carried out in Scotland (see

SOEID, 1997). When the map was shown to colleges, it was widely rejected as failing to present the work of teachers in a holistic manner and ignoring the importance of professional judgement and reflective practice (see Lucas, 2002).

Similar concerns had been made about competence-based City and Guilds qualification, the 7306, which some viewed as a device for deskilling FE teachers. Last and Chown, who both tutored on teacher training programmes in an FE college, argued:

> Existing Certificate in Education (FE) programmes provide personal and professional development to the level of first degree study. In our view, teachers who are able to respond effectively to the needs of adult learners in a rapidly changing FE sector require coherent initial professional training to graduate level. Will the adoption of competence-based qualifications in the NCVQ mould help us towards the ambition? Will they at least maintain the current position? Or will they have the effect of removing FE teacher training from HE altogether, with a consequent loss of professionalism to the detriment of the sector?
>
> (Last and Chown, 1996, pp.31–2)

Despite the concerns of the profession, however, the mapping project continued and in 1998, FENTO was established to turn the map into a set of national standards which, in turn, would form the basis of the mandatory teacher training qualification. FENTO has grouped what it calls 'the skills initial teachers should be able to demonstrate' into eight categories as follows:

A   Assessing learners' needs
B   Planning and preparing teaching and learning programmes for groups and individuals
C   Developing and using a range of teaching and learning techniques
D   Managing the learning process
E   Providing learners with support
F   Assessing the outcomes of learning and learners' achievement
G   Reflecting upon and evaluating one's own performance and planning future practice
H   Meeting professional requirement

The teacher training qualification, which equates to NVQ Level 4, is in three stages, all of which are at the same academic level: introduction stage; intermediate stage; and certification stage. An example of how the standards are expressed at each stage can be seen in Figure 8.1, which is taken from category A (Assessing learners' needs). The qualification can be awarded by HE institutions and by other awarding bodies who are accredited by FENTO. At the time of writing, the 46 HE institutions involved in FE teacher training were adapting their courses to meet the FENTO standards. FENTO will assess the course, not the delivery, in order to see if it qualifies for their endorsement.

Introduction Stage	Intermediate Stage	Certification Stage
A1 – identify and plan the needs of potential learners a Acknowledge the previous learning experiences and achievements of learners	**A1** a Acknowledge the previous learning experiences and achievements of learners b Enable learners to review their past experiences in a way that reveals their strengths and needs	**A1** a Acknowledging the previous learning experiences and achievements of learners b Enable learners to review their past experiences in a way that reveals their strengths and needs c Recognise when additional specialist assessment is required and take the appropriate action d Support learners while they deal with unfamiliar circumstances and assist learners to explore and articulate their personal aspirations e assist learners to explore and articulate their personal aspirations f Identify and confirm any exemptions to which learners are entitled g Provide information to, and negotiate with, colleagues to ensure that the learning needs of individuals can be met in a realistic way
A2 – make an initial assessment of learners' needs a Consider and apply a range of assessment techniques b Provide feedback to the learner on the outcome of the assessment and its consequences	**A2** a Consider and apply a range of assessment techniques b Consider a range of selection criteria appropriate to learning programmes c Identify the implications of a disability or learning difficulty for an individual's learning d Assess the experience, capabilities and learning styles of individual learners in relation to the identified learning programme e Prepare for and carry out the initial assessment	**A2** a Consider and apply a range of assessment techniques b Use a variety of methods for assessing the previous learning experiences and achievements of learners including their basic skills and key skills c Consider a range of selection criteria appropriate to learning programmes d Identify the implications of a disability or learning difficulty for an individual's learning e Establish with learners the requirements and limitations of the programme

© Further Education National Training Organization (FENTO)

Figure 8.1 FENTO Standards for Category A: Assessing Learners' Needs

FENTO has a UK-wide remit and has established Advisory Groups for Northern Ireland and Scotland. In Scotland, the Further Education Professional Development Forum has devised its own set of standards and units based on these are included in the TQ(FE) currently delivered by 3 approved HE institutions: University of Stirling; University of Strathclyde; and Northern College in Dundee.

In a small-scale study of FE teachers' perceptions of non-FENTO initial teacher training, Hiller et al (2001, p.41) reported three significant findings:

a) the challenging aspects of initial training may not be acknowledged by teachers until several years after the course;
b) teachers want help to deal with 'difficult' students – regardless of whether the difficulty arises for social, emotional, or cognitive reasons;
c) staff engaged in initial teacher teaching are expected to model good practice.

Perhaps, most importantly, the research also confirmed that initial teacher training should be challenging and allow teachers to explore theory as well as practice.

PATHWAYS TO PROFESSIONAL DEVELOPMENT

Clearly all colleges have their own culture and ethos that may have grown up over a number of years or that may reflect sudden changes introduced by a new senior manager or management team. The level of importance attached to the professional development needs of staff is dependent on that culture so that in some colleges staff may have to fight quite hard to get their real needs met. Jackson et al. (1996), in their study *Managing Careers in 2000 and Beyond*, stress that individual employees cannot afford to wait for their organisations to take the lead in terms of their career development:

> The trend is clearly towards increased demand on people to be proactive in looking after their own careers using their own resourcefulness. This requires continuous information-gathering and analysis, self-assessment, planning ahead for the next few years, and social skills including negotiation and self-presentation.
>
> (Jackson et al., 1996, p.52)

Throughout a career as a teacher in FE, you will probably want a mix of provision to satisfy your professional development needs. As we discussed earlier in this chapter, some of your immediate needs might be covered in staff development activities run within the college.

One of the key mechanisms through which you will be asked to try and identify your professional development needs will be through the college's appraisal system. If the appraisal system in your college is not satisfactory in terms of helping you identify and discuss your professional development needs, you will have to find other means for this. You may, for example, be assigned a mentor. This will most likely be an experienced member of staff who provides ongoing support, advice and guidance, but in some colleges, teachers provide each other with peer mentoring. The process of mentoring has to be nurtured, especially in colleges where individuals feel under pressure to compete with each other and feel at the mercy of externally imposed targets and inspections. From her research on the mentoring of student teachers by experienced staff in FE, Cox writes:

> There is an absence, in further education, of a culture which encourages or even allows open discussion of teaching. In order to have effective mentoring, the mentor and the student teacher must step outside the normal conventions of staffroom discourse and openly discuss, evaluate and reflect on practice. This can be difficult for both parties.
>
> (Cox, 1996, p.41)

She advocates peer or collaborative mentoring because 'In this context, the imbalance of power is less of an issue and the tension generated by the assessment function of the mentor is absent. The discussion of one's own and a collaborative colleague's teaching can be developed in a supportive atmosphere, in a constructive, private dialogue' (Cox, 1996, p.42). As well as helping you to identify and discuss your professional development needs, working with supportive colleagues will also provide tacit doses of professional development as well as enriching one's day-to-day life in college.

Another strategy for considering your professional development needs involves keeping a record of your professional experience in and outside college. This record could take the form of a portfolio, diary or log and could include a combination of examples of your work with students (e.g., teaching plans, assessments, photographs of students' work, etc.) and more discursive accounts of your development as a teacher (e.g., reflections on critical moments, ideas for new ways to teach, etc.). It might also include evidence of your activities related to your area of professional expertise or your links with the local community.

Linked to this notion of recording one's experience is the increasing use of autobiographical writing by teachers throughout all sectors of education. Here, a teacher constructs a narrative of his or her ongoing life as a teacher and uses it to reflect on the extent to which external as well as personal influences determine one's progress and development as a professional. As Bateson argues:

> These resonances between the personal and the professional are the source of both insight and error. You avoid mistakes and distortions not so much by trying to build a wall between the observer and the observed as by observing the observer – observing yourself – as well, and bringing the personal issues into consciousness.
>
> (Bateson, 1984, p.161)

By gaining a better understanding of the personal and the professional, we can then begin to 'map' out our career path and, hopefully, take more control over the nature and scope of the professional development on offer to us. In his highly creative book, *The Man Who Mistook His Wife for a Hat*, the neurologist Oliver Sacks describes a patient of his called Rebecca, a young woman whom he had known for some twelve years and who, after the death of her grandmother, appeared to emerge much more strongly as a person in her own right:

> 'I want no more classes, no more workshops,' she said. 'They do nothing for me. They do nothing to bring me together ... I'm a sort of living carpet. I need a pattern, a design like you have on that carpet. I come apart, I unravel, unless there's a design.' I looked down at the carpet, as Rebecca said this, and found myself thinking of Sherrington's famous image, comparing the brain/mind to an 'enchanted loom', weaving patterns ever-dissolving, but always with meaning.
>
> (Sacks, 1986, p.175)

Some professional development courses now include biographical accounts and portfolios as part of the assessed work submitted by students. There can be problems when personal material of this nature is then used in a public context and Bloor and Butterworth (1996), in their study of the use of portfolios at the University of Greenwich, suggest that these concerns may lead to professionals being less inclined to commit themselves to paper. They stress that the ownership of portfolios must be clarified at the outset.

Clearly, if you are preparing an autobiographical account or portfolio for purely personal use, you will not have the problems of ownership. What you might want to do, however, is to use some of that material as the basis for discussions with friends or colleagues about how well you have managed to address your strengths and weaknesses. As Holloway points out, we need to have our personal constructs challenged, albeit in a gentle and supportive way. 'I know from paying close attention to myself giving accounts in a variety of different settings, that I have a stock of ready narratives to draw on which fit particular situations and which tell me nothing new unless the person I am talking to helps me produce something new' (Holloway quoted in Kehily, 1995, p.28).

Apart from the personal development aspect of building a portfolio or some kind of record of your professional experience, there are important pragmatic reasons for doing so. For example, the practice of the accreditation of prior learning (APL), which we discussed in Chapter 6, is used in a number of HEIs and by professional bodies to give exemption from parts of programmes leading to qualifications. Also, you may find that having some physical evidence of your work will come in useful at job interviews or for promotion panels.

Once you have a 'map' or, at least, some idea of your professional development needs, you may wish to pursue a postgraduate course leading to a diploma or Masters degree, or you may be a member of a professional body that provides professional development courses. All of these may be available within your own college (if it is linked in some way to an HEI) or you may have to find a course elsewhere. Many HEIs now offer flexible ways to gain a postgraduate qualification, for example, by distance learning or residential weekend study, and, as we noted above, some have introduced APL procedures to allow experienced people to be exempted from taking the full set of course modules. The most common postgraduate degrees are: Masters in Education (MEd); Master of Arts (MA); Master of Science (MSc). It is usual to find that these degrees are split into two components: the first part will consist of taught modules, on completion of which a student can gain a diploma; the second part consists of a dissertation or project, on completion of which, along with the taught component, the student will be awarded a Masters degree. A particularly innovative Master's programme is the MSc in Lifelong Learning delivered on-line via the web by the University of Stirling.

Some HEIs have also introduced a structured doctoral programme leading to the Doctorate in Education (or EdD). For this, students take a number of 'taught' modules, some of which will cover research methodology, and have to produce a substantial thesis. As we noted in Chapter 7, some HEIs are developing research links with FE colleges which go beyond the traditional professional development relationship in which FE staff are merely seen as students working towards an accredited qualification. To this end, Masters and EdD programmes often encourage students to conduct action research projects, empirical studies and other forms of analysis based within their professional context.

If you are interested in developing your research potential and feel motivated enough to dedicate some three to five years to one project, you could pursue a research degree (MPhil or PhD). In this case, you would be appointed to a supervisor who has a keen interest in your research ideas and who possibly also carries out research in a similar field. Although all HEIs offer research degrees, it is advisable to gain a good impression of an institution's research rating. All HEI departments are given a rating from 1 to 5, with 5 being the highest and denoting that the department has academics conducting research of national and international excellence. In addition, you should also try to find out which academics are based in the department in which you would be based as there may be someone who has published articles and books related to your research interests. Departments differ, too, in their provision for part-time research students in that some bring students together for seminars and social events and may provide access to information technology. A useful way to begin your investigation of an academic department in an HEI is to visit the institution's library, which will house copies of all Masters dissertations and research degree theses. By looking at a sample of this research output for the department you are interested in, you will gain some idea of the nature and scope of projects the department is able to supervise.

In the 1990s, many colleges seemed to be using the majority of their staff development funds on the TDLB awards, but there were cases where individual staff could get support to pursue a Masters or research degree. In 1987, Suffolk College set itself the target of creating an all-graduate teaching staff from a baseline of 65 per cent. By 1996, that baseline had risen to 95 per cent and stimulated a demand from staff to progress to Masters level. College management, therefore, agreed to second staff to gain Masters degrees. Writing about the Suffolk model, which was linked to the desire to build a research culture in the college, five senior managers reported: 'Implicit in this significant commitment to staff development is a drive towards a quality-led learning organisation. Explicit are the opportunities offered to teaching staff to enhance their professional skills and knowledge base in order to contribute more widely to an expanding economy organisation' (Robinson et al., 1996, p.24). Here we see that the strategic goals of the college are a major driving force behind the decision to invest in long-term professional development programmes but, at the same time, the college has chosen to reach those goals by recognising the individual needs of staff who, in gaining externally accredited qualifications, can enhance their own profiles and have access to high-quality learning which takes them out of their immediate work environment.

If you are a member of a trade union, you should keep in touch with the professional development programmes it offers as well as conferences and discussion group meetings.

Reflection

The following questions and instructions are designed to help you evaluate and identify your professional development needs. You may find them useful during initial training as well as at different stages during your teaching career:

1 Make a list of the skills you would like to gain (or improve) in order to be a more effective teacher. Can you acquire those skills on an in-house staff development programme? If you are on an initial teacher training course, does the course help you develop these skills?

2 Are you comfortable with the curriculum demands imposed on you? Would you feel happier if you could update your skills and knowledge in a particular area of your professional expertise? Have there been recent changes to your professional area (e.g. new legislation, new inventions, changes in information technology, etc.)? Can you cope with these changes?

3 Are you aware of the different organisations which could supply you with information and ideas to support and enrich your teaching? Would you gain by joining a professional body? Are there

people in neighbouring colleges, schools, HEIs, companies, LSCs, LECs and other organisations with whom you should be in contact or with whom you might work in partnership?

4 Will your management support your professional development plans? What will they expect in the form of a proposal (e.g. a written proposal with costings?) and who is the best person to approach first?

5 Have you considered changing direction? There may be opportunities within the college to try a completely new field (e.g. move from teaching into student services) or to set up a new course in a related discipline, or a multi-disciplinary programme.

6 Where do you want to be in five years in terms of your career? Can you identify any professional development issues now so that you can plan your career in advance?

Chapter 9

Networks and support agencies

INTRODUCTION

FE colleges play a significant role in the life of their local communities and beyond; indeed some that specialise in certain courses attract students on a national basis. The range of people who come through the college doors, as we saw in Chapter 2, represents the diversity of the college's geographical, socio-economic and cultural location. Reaching out from the college, the links into the community will include outreach centres for teaching and access-related services, partnerships with local schools and HEIs, and a range of mechanisms for relating to the world of business and industry. As a college lecturer, therefore, you will be constantly aware of the wider world beyond your immediate teaching room.

Part of your duties and responsibilities as a lecturer may include liaising with community groups, representing the college on education–business and lifelong learning partnership committees and so on. In this chapter, we discuss the nature of some of the organisations with whom you may be formally required to liaise and work. We also discuss the ways in which these and other organisations can provide you with valuable support in terms of your teaching and professional development.

TRADE UNIONS AND PROFESSIONAL ORGANISATIONS

Two trade unions have the largest coverage of FE lecturers: NATFHE (the National Association of Teachers in Further and Higher Education); and ATL (the Association of Teachers and Lecturers). Of the two, NATFHE is by far the biggest. Together, these unions form the National Joint Forum which negotiates pay rates on behalf of academic staff in colleges. Manual workers in colleges are represented by UNISON, the GMB and the T&G. In Scotland, lecturers can also join the Educational Institute Scotland (EIS), and there is also a lecturers' trade union in Wales, UNAC (Undeb Cenedlaethol Athrawon Cymru). The Association for College Management (ACM) represents college staff in management positions, though some FE principals also belong to the Secondary Heads Association (SHA).

Since the incorporation of colleges in 1992, NATFHE, ATL and ACM have spent a great deal of their time and resources fighting the imposition by college governing bodies and the national body representing college employers of controversial new teaching contracts. As we discussed in Chapter 1, many college lecturers have a background in a profession or craft-based occupation and may find it useful to maintain a direct link through an appropriate organisation such as, for example, the Institute of Chartered Accountants. Most occupational sectors are covered by a National Training Organisation (NTO). For example, engineering's NTO is Emta, the Engineering and Marine Training Association. NTOs develop training policies and strategies for their sectors and are responsible for devising frameworks for Modern Apprenticeship. From 2002, NTOs will gradually be replaced by Sector Skills Councils (SSCs), overseen by the Sector Skills Development Agency (SSDA).

HIGHER EDUCATION

Another way to maintain links with your professional specialism and/or academic interests is through your local HE institutions whose departments may run seminars that are open to external visitors and may also have arrangements for FE lecturers to become research associates. Departments, schools and Institutes of Education in some HEIs are now encouraging FE staff to have a much closer link with them and will welcome lecturers wishing to pursue research ideas.

As we noted in Chapter 1, some colleges have franchising arrangements with HEIs to run parts of degree courses (see Abramson et al., 1996, and Paczuska, 1999, for a discussion of this aspect of FE's work). The Widening Participation agenda has also further dissolved the boundaries between further and higher education. In 1998–99, the Higher Education Funding Council for England (HEFCE) allocated £1.5 million to encourage universities to work with colleges and other organisations to develop projects for stimulating demand from groups in their communities who were under-represented in higher education. In 1999, HEFCE funds were increased to £5 million plus a further £4 million from the FEFC. Colleges are playing a major role in helping universities to widen participation (through access courses, encouraging their own students to apply to university, holding joint events with universities and so on).

As well as running courses in conjunction with HEIs, some colleges and HEIs have Compact schemes which seek to encourage young people who may not have considered HE to be an appropriate or even realistic option for them to apply to university. Some Compacts, which may be operated through EBPs described below, link university departments to college A level and GNVQ courses or to college-based access courses. Although the idea of Compact appears to very laudable, there are complex issues to be managed when different sectors of education try to work together. Writing about a Compact initiative which has been running in Birmingham since 1987, Bigger notes:

Post-16 Compact is a simple idea with a challenging agenda: to raise achievement and aspiration by enhancing motivation. This produces a drive for quality which requires effort and enthusiasm in all staff. Its effectiveness is strategic and requires support at the highest level through the institution's mission, vision and strategic plan. Some schools and colleges have found this difficult, so the philosophy of the programme is not regularly matched by the reality of implementation: post-16 agendas can reflect survival rather than quality. Looking forward, therefore, the priority is to support institutions in developing quality processes.

(Bigger, 1996, p.164)

BUSINESS AND COMMUNITY-RELATED ORGANISATIONS

There are many different forms of business-related organisation in the UK stretching from national bodies such as the Confederation of British Industry (CBI) and the Institute of Directors to local bodies such as Chambers of Commerce and the Round Table. The locally based organisations often have historical roots in their communities, including those which represent the interests of employees rather than those of employers, such as Trades Councils. The CBI has a regional network of branches that meet regularly for seminars and events at which education and training often feature. There is a wide range of community-based organizations including, for example, charities, voluntary agencies, and single issue groups.

At local level, the one organisation which will have the most direct contact and working relationship with an FE college is the Learning and Skills Council (LSC) or its Scottish equivalent, the LEC (Local Enterprise Company). In 1999, and in anticipation of its plans to harmonise the post-compulsory sector in England, the government established Lifelong Learning Partnerships analogous to what were then TEC areas. These Partnerships bring together all the organisations involved in some aspect of education and training. As such, they overlap, to some extent the work of education–business partnerships (EBPs) that will include representatives from industry and commerce, the LEA, Careers Service, local HEIs, private training providers, voluntary organisations, trade unions, and schools. EBPs began in 1990 at the same time as the Training and Enterprise Councils (TECs) were being established. At that time, most EBPs were set up and largely managed by TECs. In the mind of the then Employment Department, EBPs were the means to formalise the largely ad hoc and voluntaristic links between education and business which have been in existence for many years. The very notion of trying to impose a superstructure on relationships that tended to be organic rather than institutionalised has seemed to some on both sides to be too dictatorial and at odds with the concept of partnership. EBPs have, therefore, developed differently throughout the country ranging from the very successful to those which struggle to get enough people to make meetings quorate.

Where an EBP is successful, the local colleges are likely to be heavily involved. An EBP can provide college staff with an excellent forum for liaising with schools over such matters as managing an effective transition for young people transferring to college at 16 or joint initiatives to raise standards in basic skills. Useful relationships with employers can also be established through an EBP.

The following vignettes illustrate the different ways in which college staff can work together with EBPs.

Chris took over responsibility for running the GNVQ Leisure and Tourism programme in her college. Although she had previously been employed in the travel business, it was some considerable time ago and she felt the need to update her knowledge of the industry. In addition, she was aware that she needed to inform herself about developments in the use of IT in the industry. Her local EBP arranged a week's placement for her with a branch of a national retail travel agent. The placement not only allowed her to gain some 'hands on' experience of the current operation of a travel business but also enabled her to identify work placements for students on the GNVQ programme.

Bob, a lecturer in engineering, was approached by the EBP about the possibility of some of his students undertaking a piece of work for a local engineering company. One of the directors of the company was Chairperson of the EBP and she was anxious to improve the profile of her company, and, at the same time, improve the image of engineering in general by involving students in the company's work. Although initially reticent about the idea, Bob eventually recognised the potential benefits of the link that would allow his students to undertake real tasks to industry standards. Students were given access to the company and completed some of the tasks on site rather than in the college workshops. Bob also had the opportunity of seeing the way in which a small manufacturing company was transforming its production to match new industry standards.

Ranjeep has responsibility for teaching marketing across a range of business courses in his college. For some time, he has been interested in developing a European dimension to the work but has lacked contact with colleges or companies in Europe. The EBP was able to supply the names of several local companies that had links with Europe and the names of local schools involved in European exchanges. Ranjeep followed up these leads and made contact with a vocational school in Belgium that was happy to collaborate in a joint project involving British and Belgian business students. Assignments were developed for a unit on international marketing in which the students exchanged information about their own local economies. Students communicated by fax and e-mail. In future, Ranjeep hopes to extend the project by involving other European partners and, hopes to access some EU funding to finance student exchanges.

Because of the need for local organisations to work together to ensure they make the most of limited resources to finance education and training initiatives, EBPs and similar partnerships rely on individuals who are prepared to put their creative energies to work for the collective good.

Gravatt and Silver (2000, p.121) argue that partnerships are attractive to government because:

- They bring local organisations together to deliver shared goals;
- They are a way of bridging the public and private sector and of harnessing private sector investment to deliver public goals;
- They can be formed – and dissolved – quickly;
- They make it possible to deliver new programmes without the costs of setting up new organisations or of restructuring existing ones.

Writing from their perspective as Registrar and Principal, respectively, of Lewisham College in London, Gravatt and Silver (ibid., p.123) highlight the following reasons why community and business-based partnerships work or not:

WORK	DON'T WORK
Shared purpose	Forced geographically
Conscious acceptance	No trust
Voluntary	No guarantees
Respect difference	Own agendas
Shared values	Forced into frameworks
Outward-looking	Resist change
Allowed to evolve	Over-control by external audit

Gravatt and Silver (ibid., p.126) stress that colleges 'need to tread carefully in the matter of partnerships'. They continue, 'Partnerships help organizations achieve objectives and add value to their activities, but they are not a panacea for all public sector problems. Too many partnerships established too hastily with too many overlapping aims just add to the confusion and complexity that gets in the way of education and training' (ibid.).

The term 'partnership' is, of course, a contested one. Partnership suggests an equal relationship, one entered into willingly. Many of the so-called partnerships that exist in the world of education and training are simply gatherings of people who need to ensure their organisation's needs and agendas are represented. As Field (2000, pp.26–7) argues, 'the discourse of partnership frequently cloaks a profound inequality between the so-called partners'. And the concept of partnership as envisaged by policymakers is a positivist one, that is the partnerships exist to make the delivery of policy objectives run smoothly. It would be interesting to consider what might happen if, for example, the 'partners' at a meeting of a local Lifelong Learning Partnership decided to use their solidarity to challenge the targets and performance indicators imposed on them from on high. Mayo (2002, p.199) explains that there is increasing interest in developing connections between lifelong learning and community capacity building but such connections are particularly problematic:

> Community participants need access to appropriate education and training for capacity building, just as professionals need appropriate education and training, if they are to work with communities in empowering ways. What

'appropriateness' might mean in practice, however, depends upon how capacity-building and empowerment are defined, by whom and according to whose agendas.

(Mayo, 2002, p.199)

At regional level in England, colleges will have links with one of the nine Regional Development Agencies (RDAs) established in 1999 to take forward some of the work previously done by the regional government offices. RDAs are largely responsible for increasing skill levels and the general regeneration of their areas. They control significant budgets, including the Single Regeneration Budget (SRB) and, given the proposals for regional assemblies in England, and the European Commission's desire to see regions gaining greater autonomy, RDAs are clearly in a powerful position. One of their key tasks is to try and even out the differences between participation and attainment in education and training at regional level. For example, the percentage of young people achieving 5 or more GCSEs at Grades A–C in 1998/99 in the South East was 53.8 per cent, compared with 40.8 per cent in the North East (DfES, 2001d).

As we have described earlier in the book, individual college departments, as well as colleges acting as corporate bodies, have direct links with employers for whom they provide an education and training service. Research by the Institute of Employment Studies in 1995 classified college/employer interaction into two types of activities. The first was based around learners (referred to as learner centred) whilst the second (referred to as planning based) was based around planning and advice, and both could be sub-divided as follows (IES, 1995):

Learner centred

Type A: employer-led training and education – company employees or trainees being trained by the college;
Type B: voluntary, work-related activities with full-time or non-employed students – work experience, work shadowing.

Planning based

Type C: advice and information between individual employers and colleges to aid college planning – for example, governing bodies, curriculum advisory groups;
Type D: activities which aid the planning of education and training in the wider community – local working groups, projects, strategic planning.

NATIONAL AND REGIONAL FE BODIES

Prior to the 1992 FHE Act, colleges were affiliated to their local Regional Advisory Council (RAC), a network of which existed throughout the country. These bodies came within the remit of LEAs but were independent of each other and, although they had some activities in common such as running staff development courses, they were very different in terms of their effectiveness. Where RACs did come together was in their contribution to the work of the Further Education Unit (FEU), which was set up in 1977, under the auspices of the then Department of Education and Science, to help promote curriculum development initiatives and co-ordinate and disseminate good practice in teaching and learning. The FEU was particularly active in the late 1970s and early 1980s when it produced reports such as *A Basis for Choice* (1979) and *Vocational Preparation* (1981) which provided guidance and analysis for colleges in dealing with the sudden dramatic influx of recruits to the newly established government-sponsored youth training schemes. Often working alongside the national Further Education Staff College (FESC), which had been set up in 1963 at Coombe Lodge near Bristol, the FEU produced a wealth of literature, much of it based on action research projects involving colleges, which still carries important and useful messages and ideas for today's college lecturers, managers and support staff.

In April 1995, a new organisation, the Further Education Development Agency (FEDA), replaced both the FEU and FESC. In light of the structural changes to the post-compulsory sector described in Chapter 1, FEDA was renamed the Learning and Skills Development Agency (LSDA) in 2000, signaling that it would now represent a much wider constituency. With a head office in London, LSDA also has nine regional development offices in England and one in Wales. LSDA is involved in research, development and policy analysis. It runs two national government-funded support programmes for teachers delivering key skills and vocational GCSEs. Each regional office of LSDA hosts a Learning and Skills Research Network (LSRN) that brings together practitioners from organizations responsible for post-compulsory education and training in the region to share research interests and develop collaborative projects. The establishment of its new research centre (as mentioned in Chapter 8) gives LSDA an even greater influential role and it will be interesting to see how the centre positions itself vis-à-vis the educational research community in HE.

In the 1990s there was a battle between two organisations who sought to claim prime status as the organisation that would represent the FE sector in England and Wales at national level: the Colleges Employers' Forum (CEF) and the Association for Colleges (AfC). The AfC's origins lay in the LEAs which originally controlled the FE sector. In 1996, the CEF and the AfC merged to form the Association of Colleges (AoC). The equivalent in Scotland is the Association of Scottish Colleges (ASC). The AoC and ASC are subscription organisations to which most, but not all colleges belong as members. Once a year, the AoC oversees the Beacon Award scheme which rewards those colleges that have shown excellence in promoting mutually advantageous interdependence between themselves and business, professional and voluntary organisations. For example, one of the winners in 1999/2000 was the Royal Forest of Dean College which had successfully applied for a start up grant from the Basic Skills Agency to pump-prime a plant-based, basic skills training initiative in a local company. Another winner in the same year, the Hugh Baird College on Merseyside, applied for funds to improve its Advanced GNVQ Health and Social Care Programme. The students were called to a meeting and asked for ideas. They said they wanted to become involved in real research that had a real purpose. At the same time, the Health and Social Care Team wanted to make wider links with the local community and, in particular, local health organisations. The co-ordinator for Health and Social Care Programmes at the College approached the co-ordinator at PACE (Pregnancy Advice, Contraception and Education) who had been a regular speaker at the College and together they worked out a plan for the students to conduct research for the organisation in the area of health promotion material. As PACE was also working in conjunction with Liverpool's Hope University, which was working on research into young people and sexual health, the students were offered the opportunity to act as researchers for this larger project.

Given the incorporation of colleges in 1993 and the establishment of bodies such as FEDA and now LSDA, the role of the RACs has become confused and some of them have either dissolved or are on the verge of collapse. Along with colleges, RACs left LEA control in 1992 and some of them have managed to maintain their regional role through the continued support of local colleges. Two examples are the Yorkshire and Humberside Association for Further and Higher Education (YHAFHE) and EMFEC (formerly the East Midlands Further Education Council). In Scotland, the Scottish Further Education Unit (SFEU) performs a similar role to LSDA, while research on FE is also undertaken by SCRE (the Scottish Council for Research in Education).

USEFUL CONTACTS AND SOURCES OF SUPPORT

The following key organisations may prove useful at some time or other during your career in FE. We have listed them with their web site addresses only as these should be more reliable than location addresses. Each of these web sites will also provide links to hundreds of other organisations that may be of use but which we cannot list here for the obvious reasons!

Adult Learning Inspectorate	www.ali.gov.uk
Association of Colleges	www.aoc.org.uk
Association of Scottish Colleges	www.aosc.org.uk
Connexions	www.connexions.gov.uk

British Educational, Communications and Technology Council (Becta)	www.becta.org.uk
Department for Education and Skills	www.dfes.gov.uk
Department of Education Northern Ireland	www.deni.gov.uk
ELWa	www.elwa.org.uk
Learning and Skills Council	www.lsc.gov.uk
Learning and Skills Development Agency	lsagency.org.uk
Northern Ireland Assembly	www.ni-assembly.gov.uk
Ofsted	www.ofsted.gov.uk
Qualifications and Curriculum Authority	www.qca.org.uk
Scottish Executive	www.Scotland.gov.uk
Scottish Further Education Unit	www.sfeu.ac.uk
Scottish Qualifications Authority	www.sqa.org.uk
Trades Union Congress	www.tuc.org.uk
Welsh Assembly	www.wales.gov.uk

References

Abbott, I. and Huddleston, P. (1995) The development of business education: Change or decay, Paper presented to *International Conference on Developments in Business Education*, Liverpool, 18–20 April.

Ainley, P. (1994) *Degrees of Difference*, London, Lawrence and Wishart.

Ainley, P. (2000) Further than where? The place of FE under the Learning and Skills Council, paper presented to the *BERA Annual Conference*, Cardiff, September.

Ainley, P. and Bailey, B. (1997) *The Business of Learning*, London, Cassell.

Ainley, P. and Vickerstaff, S. (1993) Transitions from corporatism: The privatisation of policy failure, *Contemporary Record*, 7:3, pp.541–556.

ALBSU (1991) *Open Learning and ESOL*, London, ALBSU (now Basic Skills Agency).

Aldridge, F. and Tuckett, A. (2001) *Winners and Losers in an Expanding System: the NIACE Survey on Adult Participation in Learning 2001*. Leicester, National Institute for Adult and Continuing Education.

ALI/Ofsted (2001) *Common Inspection Framework*, London, Adult Learning Inspectorate.

Ashworth, P. and Saxton, J. (1990) On competence, *Journal of Further and Higher Education*, 14:2, Summer, pp.3–25.

Assessment Reform Group (1999) *Assessment for Learning. Beyond the Black Box*, University of Cambridge, Assessment Reform Group.

Audit Commission (1985) *Obtaining Better Value from Further Education*, London, HMSO.

Audit Commission/Ofsted (1993) *Unfinished Business – full-time educational courses for 16–19 year olds*, London, HMSO.

Avis, J. (1999) Shifting identity: new conditions and the transformation of practice-teaching within post-compulsory education, *Journal of Vocational Education and Training*, 51: 2, pp. 245–264.

Avis, P., Bathmaker, A. and Parsons, J. (2001) Reflections from a Time Log Diary: towards an analysis of the labour process within further education, *Journal of Vocational Education and Training*, 53:1, pp. 61–80.

Bateson, M.C. (1984) *With a Daughter's Eye*, New York, William Morrow.

Beaumont, G. (1996) *Review of 100 NVQs and SVQs: A Report submitted to Department for Education and Employment*, London, DfEE.

Belenky, M.F., Clinchy, M.B., Goldberger, N.R. and Tarule, J.M. (1986) *Women's Ways of Knowing*, New York, Basic Books.

Berne, E. (1970) *Games People Play*, Harmondsworth, Penguin.

Betts, D. (1996) Staff appraisal and staff development in the corporate college, in J. Robson (ed.) *The Professional FE Teacher*, Aldershot, Avebury.

Bigger, S. (1996) Post-16 compact in Birmingham: School and college links with higher education, in M. Abramson et al. (eds) *Further and Higher Education Partnerships*, Buckingham, SRHE/Open University Press, pp.154–63.

Black, P. and Wiliam, D. (1998) *Inside the Black Box.* London, King's College, London.

Bloom, B.S. (1965) *Taxonomy of Educational Objectives*, London, Longman.

Bloomer, M. (1997) *Curriculum Making in Post-16 Education. The Social Conditions of Studentship*, London, Routledge.

Bloomer, M. and Hodkinson, P. (1997) *Moving into FE*, London, Further Education Development Agency.

Bloor, M. and Butterworth, C. (1996) The portfolio approach to professional development, in J. Robson (ed.) *The Professional FE Teacher*, Aldershot, Avebury.

Blunkett, D. (2001) *Education into Employability: The Role of the DfEE in the Economy*, speech to the Institute of Economic Affairs, 24 January (London: Department for Education and Employment).

Bocock, J. (1996) Take your partners, *Times Higher Educational Supplement*, March 3rd.

Boud, D., Keogh, R. and Walker, D. (1985) *Reflection: Turning Experience into Learning*, London, Kogan Page.

Bradley, J., Dee, L. and Wilenius, F. (1994) *Students with Disabilities and/or Learning Difficulties in Further Education*, Slough, NFER.

Brandes, D. and Phillips, H. (1985) *Gamesters' Handbook*, London, Hutchinson.

Brookfield, S. (1986) *Understanding and Facilitating Adult Learning*, Milton Keynes, Open University Press.

Brown, S. (1994) Assessment: a changing practice, in B. Moon and A. Shelton Mayes (eds) *Teaching and Learning in the Secondary School*, London, Open University/Routledge.

Brundage, D.H. and Mackeracher, D. (1980) *Adult Learning Principles and Their Application to Program Planning*, Toronto, Ministry of Education, Ontario.

BTEC (1993) *Implementing BTEC GNVQs: A Guide for BTEC Centres*, Issue 1, London, BTEC.

Canning, R. (1999) Post-16 education in Scotland: credentialism and inequality, *Journal of Vocational Education and Training*, 51:2, pp.185–98.

Capey, J. (1995) GNVQ *Assessment Review*, Final Report of the review group, London, NCVQ.

Castling, A. (1996) The role of the staff development practitioner in the FE college, in J. Robson (ed.) *The Professional FE Teacher*, Aldershot, Avebury.

CBI (1994) *Quality Assessed, The CBI Review of NVQs and SVQs*, London, CBI.

CEC (1994) *Competitiveness, Employment, Growth*, Luxembourg: Office for Official Publications.

CEDEFOP (1994) *Determining the Need for Vocational Counselling Among Different Target Groups of Young People Under 28 years of Age in the European Community*, Berlin, CEDEFOP.

CEI (2001) 'Evaluation of the DfES key skills Support Programme, Year One'. Coventry, University of Warwick (unpublished)

Clough, P. and Barton, L. (1995) Introduction: Self and the research act, in Clough, P. and Barton, L. (eds) *Making Difficulties, Research and the Construction of SEN*, London, Paul Chapman.

Coats, M. (1994) *Women's Education*, Buckingham, SRHE/Open University Press.

Coffield, F. (1999) Breaking the consensus: lifelong learning as social control, *British Educational Research Journal*, 25:4, pp.545–61.

Cohen, L. and Manion, L. (1989) *A Guide to Teaching Practice*, 3rd Edition, London, Routledge.

Cole, M. (1985) The zone of proximal development: where culture and cognition create each other, in Wertsch, J. (ed) *Culture, Communication and Cognition: Vygotskian Perspectives*, Cambridge, Cambridge University Press.

Cole, M., John-Steiner, V., Scribner, S. and Souberman, E. (1978) (eds) *L.S. Vygotsky: Mind in Society,* Cambridge, Harvard University Press.

Corbett, J. (1997) Transitions to what? Young people with special educational needs, in Tomlinson, S. (ed) *Education 14–19 Critical Perspectives,* London, The Athlone Press.

Corbett, J. and Barton, L. (1992) *A Struggle for Choice, Students with Special Needs in Transition to Adulthood,* London, Routledge.

Cox, A. (1996) Teacher as mentor: opportunities for professional development, in J. Robson (ed.) *The Professional FE Teacher,* Aldershot, Avebury.

Davey, A. (2001) The research culture at Cambridge Regional College, *College Research,* 4:3, p.29.

Davies, P. and Owen, J. (2001) *Listening to Staff,* London, Learning and Skills Development Agency.

Dearing, R. (1996) *Review of 16–19 Qualifications; Summary Report,* London, School Curriculum and Assessment Authority.

DE/DES (1981) *A New Training Initiative: A Programme for Action,* London, HMSO.

Dee, L. (1999) Inclusive learning: from rhetoric to reality, in Green, A. and Lucas, N. (eds) *FE and Lifelong Learning: Realigning the Sector for the 21st Century,* London.

DES/WO (1988) *Advancing A levels* (The Higginson Report), London, HMSO.

DES/ED/WO (1991) *Education and Training for the 21st Century,* London, HMSO.

Dewey, J. (1938) *Experience and Education,* New York, Collier.

DfEE (1997) *Qualifying for Success: A Consultation on the Future of post-16 Qualifications,* London, DfEE.

DfEE (1998) *University for Industry, Pathfinder Prospectus,* Sudbury, DfEE.

DfEE (1999) *Learning to Succeed, Cm 4392,* London: The Stationery Office.

DfEE (2000a) *LSC Council Members Announced, Press Release 442/00,* 16th October.

DfEE (2000b) *Evaluation of the Time Off for Study or Training Legislation,* London, Department for Education and Employment.

DfEE/FEDA (1995) *Mapping the FE Sector,* London, Further Education Development Agency.

DfES (2001a) *Schools – Achieving Success,* White Paper, London, Department for Education and Skills.

DfES (2001b) *Skills for Life. A Guide to Funding Adult Literacy and Numeracy Programmes 2001–02,* London, DfES.

DfES (2001c) *Modern Apprenticeships, The Way to Work,* Report of the Modern Apprenticeship Advisory Committee (Sudbury, Department for Education and Skills).

Dimbleby, R. and Cooke, C. (2000) Curriculum and learning in Smithers, A. and Robinson, P. (eds.) *Further Education Re-formed,* London, Routledge.

Duncan, A. (2001) Realising the possibilities of the National Learning and Skills Network, *Learning and Skills Research,* 5:1, pp. 36–37.

Ecclestone, K. (2000) Assessment and critical autonomy in post-compulsory education in the UK, *Journal of Education and Work,* 13:2, pp. 141–160.

ED (1988) *Employment for the 1990s,* Cm. 540, London, HMSO.

Edexcel (2000) GNVQ *Intermediate Health and Social Care Approved Specifications,* London, Edexcel.

Edwards, R. (1993) Multi-skilling the flexible workforce in post-compulsory education, *Journal of Further and Higher Education,* 17:1, pp.44–51.

Edwards, T., Fitz-Gibbon, C., Hardman, F., Haywood, R. and Meagher, N. (1997) *Separate but Equal? A Levels and GNVQs,* London, Routledge.

Egan, G. (1975) *The Skilled Helper,* San Francisco, California, Wadsworth.

Eisner, E.W. (1985) *The Art of Educational Evaluation,* London, Falmer Press.

Elliott, G. (1996) *Crisis and Change in Vocational Education and Training,* London, Jessica Kingsley.

EMTA Awards Limited (2000) *NVQ/SVQ Level 3 Engineering Design Specification,* Watford, EAL.

Eraut, M. (1994) *Developing Professional Knowledge and Competence,* London, Falmer Press.

Eraut, M., Alderton, J., Cole, G. and Senker, P. (1998) Learning from other people at work, in Coffield, F. (ed) *Learning at Work,* Bristol: The Policy Press.

Evans, K. (1998) *Shaping Futures* (Ashgate: Aldershot).

FEFC (1995) *General National Vocational Qualifications in the Further Education Sector in England. National Survey Report,* Coventry, FEFC.

FEFC (1996a) *Introduction to the Council,* Coventry, FEFC.

FEFC (1996b) *College Responsiveness. A National Survey Report,* Coventry, FEFC.

FEFC (1996c) *Quality and Standards in Further Education in England. Chief Inspector's Annual Report 1995–96,* Coventry, FEFC.

FEFC (1996d) *The Report of the Learning and Technology Committee,* chaired by Sir Gordon Higgonson, Coventry, FEFC.

FEFC (1998) *Chief Inspector's Annual Report, 1997–98,* Coventry, FEFC.

FEFC (1998/99) *College Inspection Reports,* Coventry, FEFC.

FEFC (1999) *Chief Inspector's Annual Report, 1998–99,* Coventry, FEFC.

FEFC (2001) *Chief Inspector's Annual Report, 2000–01,* Coventry, FEFC.

FEFC (2001a) *Quality and Standards in Further Education in England 1999–2000.* Chief Inspector's Annual Report, Coventry, FEFC.

FEFC (2001b) *Open and Distance Learning,* Coventry, FEFC.

FEFC (2001c) *Business,* Coventry, FEFC.

Felstead, A. and Unwin, L. (2001) Funding post compulsory education and training: a retrospective analysis of the TEC and FEFC systems and their impact on skills, *Journal of Education and Work,* 14:1, pp.91–111.

FENTO (2001) *FENTO Project-mapping UK-wide Teaching Standards,* London, FENTO.

Ferguson, M. (1982) *The Aquarian Conspiracy: Personal and Social Transformation in the 1980s,* London, Paladin.

FEU (1979) *A Basis for Choice,* London, FEU.

FEU (1981) *Vocational Preparation,* London, FEU.

FEU (1991) *Flexible Colleges,* London, FEU.

FEU (1994) *Managing the Delivery of Guidance in Colleges,* London, FEU.

FEU, IOE and Nuffield Foundation (1994) *GNVQs 1993–94: A National Survey Report,* London, FEU.

Field, J. (2000) *Lifelong Learning and the New Educational Order,* Stoke-on-Trent, Trentham Books.

Fieldhouse, R. and Associates (1996) *A History of Modern British Adult Education,* Leicester, National Institute for Adult Continuing Education.

Finegold, D., Milliband, D., Raffe, D., Spours, K. and Young, M. (1990) *A British Baccalaureate: Ending the Division between Education and Training,* London, Institute for Public Policy Research.

Freire, P. (1974) *Education: The Practice of Freedom,* London, Writers and Readers Cooperative.

Fuller, A. and Unwin, L. (2001a) From cordwainers to customer service: the changing relationship between apprentices, employers and communities in England, *SKOPE Monograph No. 3,* Universities of Oxford and Warwick.

Fuller, A. and Unwin, L. (2001b) *Context and Meaning in Apprenticeship: Illuminating Workplace Learning,* Paper presented to International Workshop on Context, Power and Perspective: Confronting the Challenges to Improving Attainment at Work, November 8th–10th, University College Northampton.

Furlong, A. and Cartmel, F. (1997) *Young People and Social Change,* Buckingham, Open University Press.

Gagne, R.M. (1988) *Principles of Instructional Design,* New York, Holt, Rinehart and Winston.

Gallacher, J., Leahy, J. and MacFarlane, K. (1997) *The FE/HE Route: New Pathways into Higher Education, Report for SOEID*, Glasgow, Glasgow Caledonian University.

Gibb, J.R. (1960) Learning theory in adult education, in M. Knowles (ed.) *Handbook of Adult Education in the United States*, Washington, DC, Adult Education Association of the USA.

Gleeson, D. (1996) Post-compulsory education in a post-industrial and post-modern age, in J. Avis et al. (eds) *Knowledge and Nationhood*, London, Cassell Education.

Gleeson, D. (2001) Transforming Learning cultures in further education, *College Research*, 4:3, pp. 30–32.

Gleeson, D. and Shain (1999) By Appointment: governance, markets and managerialism in further education, *British Educational Research Journal*, 25:4, pp.545–61.

Green, A. (1997) Core skills, general education and unification in post-16 education, in Hodgson, A. and Spours, K. (eds) *Dearing and Beyond*, London, Kogan Page.

Green, A. and Lucas, N. (1999) From obscurity to crisis: the further education sector in context, in Green, A. and Lucas, N. (eds) *FE and Lifelong Learning: Realigning the Sector for the 21st Century*, London, Bedford Way Papers, Institute of Education.

Griffin, C. (1993) *Representations of Youth*, Cambridge, Polity Press.

Guile, D. and Hayton, A. (1999) Information and Learning Technology: the implications for teaching and learning in further education, in A. Green and N. Lucas (eds) *FE and Lifelong Learning: Realigning the Sector for the Twenty-first Century*, London, Institute of Education.

Guile, D. and Young, M. (1999) Beyond the institution of apprenticeship: towards a social theory of learning as the production of knowledge, in Ainley, P. and Rainbird, H. (eds) *Apprenticeship, Towards a New Paradigm for Learning*, London, Kogan Page.

Harkin, J., Turner, G. and Dawn, T. (2001) *Teaching Young Adult*, London, Routledge/Falmer.

Harris, S. and Hyland, T. (1995) Basic Skills and Learning Support in Further Education, *Journal of Further and Higher Education*, 19:2, Summer, pp.42–6.

Harrow, A.J. (1972) *A Taxonomy of the Psychomotor Domain*, New York, McKay.

Heathcote, G., Kempa, R. and Roberts, I. (1982) *Curriculum Styles and Strategies*, London, Further Education Unit.

Hill, R. (2000) A study of the views of full-time FE lecturers regarding their college corporations and agencies of the FE sector, *Journal of Further and Higher Education*, 24:1, pp.67–76.

Hiller, Y., Harkin, J., Blair, T., Cowhig, T., Dunbar, D., Smith, O. and Wilson, S. (2001) Teachers' perceptions of the effectiveness of initial training, *Learning and Skills Research*, 50:1, p.41.

Hodkinson, P. (1996) Careership: The individual, choices and markets in the transition into work, in J. Avis et al. (eds) *Knowledge and Nationhood*, London, Cassell Education.

Hodkinson, P. (1998) How Young People Make Career Decisions, *Education and Training*, 40:6, pp.303–6.

Hodkinson, P. and Issitt, M. (1995) *The Challenge of Competence*, London, Cassell Education.

Hodkinson, P., Sparkes, A.C. and Hodkinson, H. (1996) *Triumphs and Tears: Young People, Markets and the Transition from School to Work*, London, David Fulton.

Hodson, A. and Spours, K. (1997) *Beyond Dearing, 14–19: Qualifications, Frameworks and Systems*, London, Kogan Page.

Hodgson, A. and Spours, K. (1999) *New Labour's Educational Agenda*, London, Kogan Page.

Hodgson, A. and Spours, K. (2001) Part-time work and full-time education in the UK: the emergence of a curriculum and policy issue, *Journal of Education and Work*, 14:3, pp.373–8.

Hodkinson, P. (1997) Neo-fordism and teacher professionalism, *Teacher Development*, 1, pp.69–81.

Honey, P. and Mumford, A. (1982) *The Manual of Learning Styles*, Maidenhead, Peter Honey.

Huddleston, P. (1996) *An Evaluation of the Contribution made by the FE Colleges to the Delivery of Rover Group's Integrated Engineering Development Scheme*, Centre for Education and Industry, University of Warwick.

Huddleston, P. (2000a) Enterprise and its transfer to combat social exclusion (ENTRANCE): UK National Implementation Report. Report on a project funded under the auspices of EC Framework IV, TSER programme. (unpublished).

Huddleston, P. (2000b) Uncertain Destinies. A study of recruitment and retention on GNVQ Intermediate programmes in 4 West Midlands colleges. (unpublished).

Huddleston, P., Abbott, I. and Stagg, P. (1995) *Introduction to GNVQs: A Practical Guide*, London, UBI/ED.

Hyland, T. (1994) *Competence, Education and NVQs: Dissenting Perspectives*, London, Cassell Education.

IES (1994) *Implementing NVQs: The Experience of Employers, Employees and Trainees*, Sussex, Institute of Employment Studies.

IES (1995) *Employers' Use of the NVQ System*, Sussex, IES.

Istance, D. and Williamson, H. (1996) *16 and 17 year olds in South and Mid-Glamorgan not in Education, Training or Employment (status zero)*, Swansea, Mid-Glamorgan Training and Enterprise Council.

Jackson, C. et al. (1996) *Managing Careers in 2000 and Beyond*, Sussex Institute of Employment Studies.

Jaques, D. (1992) *Learning in Groups, 2nd Edition*, London, Croom Helm.

Jarvis, P. (1987) *Adult Learning in the Social Context*, London, Croom Helm.

Jessup, G. (1994) *GNVQ: An Alternative Curriculum Model*, London, NCVQ.

Johnston, R. (1999) Adult learning for citizenship: towards a reconstruction of the social purpose tradition, *International Journal of Lifelong Education*, 18:3, pp.175–90.

Johnstone, J.W.C. and Rivera, R.J. (1965) *Volunteers for Learning: A Study of the Educational Pursuits of Adults*, Hawthorne, New York, Aldine.

Jones, A.M. and Hendry, C. (1994) The Learning Organisation: adult learning and organisational transformation, *British Journal of Management*, 5:2, pp.153–162.

Kehily, M.J. (1995) Self-narration, autobiography and identity construction, *Gender and Education*, 7:1, pp.23–31.

Kennedy, H. (1997) *Learning Works: Widening Participation in Further Education*, Coventry, FEFC.

Kenway, J. (2001) The information superhighway and postmodernity: the social promise and the social price, in Paechter, C. et al. (eds) *Knowledge, Power and Learning*, London, Paul Chapman.

Kidd, R. (1973) *How Adults Learn*, Chicago, IL, Follett.

Knowles, M. (1978) *The Adult Learner: A Neglected Species*, Houston, TX, Gulf.

Knox, A.B. (1977) *Adult Development and Learning: A Handbook on Individual Growth and Competence in the Adult Years*, San Francisco, CA, Jossey-Bass.

Kolb, D.A. (1984) *Experiential Learning*, Englewood Cliffs, NJ, Prentice Hall.

KPMG Peat Marwick (1994) *COSH and obstacles to employers implementing NVQs and SVQs*, Sheffield, Employment Department.

Last, J. and Chown, A. (1996) Competence-based approaches and initial teacher training for FE, in J. Robson (ed.) *The Professional FE Teacher*, Aldershot, Avebury.

Laurillard, D. (1993) *Rethinking University Teaching*, London, Routledge.

Lauzon, A.C. (1989) Educational Transition: A Qualitative Study of Full-time Married Male Students, *International Journal of University Adult Education*, XXVIII:2, pp.34–46.

Lave, J. (1995) *Teaching as Learning in Practice*, Sylvia Scribner Award Lecture, Division

C, Learning and Instruction, American Educational Research Association, Annual Meetings, San Francisco, California.

Lave, J. and Wenger, E. (1991) *Situated Learning*, Cambridge, Cambridge University Press.

Lipsig-Mumme, C. (1997) The politics of the new service economy, in James, P., Veit, W.F., and Wright, S. (eds) *Work of the Future*, London, Allen and Unwin.

LSC (2001a) *Summary Statistics for FE Institutions 1999/2000*, Coventry: Learning and Skills Council.

LSC (2001b) *Funding, Post-16 Funding Arrangements for 2002/03*, Circular 01/13, Coventry: Learning and Skills Council.

LSC (2001c) *Centres of Vocational Excellence*, Circular 01/14, Coventry: Learning and Skills Council.

LSDA (2001a) *Key Skills, LSDA Information Pack*, London, Learning and Skills Development Agency.

LSDA (2001b) *Writing Assignments. Good Practice Guide.* London, Learning and Skills Development Agency.

LSDA (2002) *LSDA Response to Hefce's Consultation on HE enrolments in the FE Sector*, London, Learning and Skills Development Agency.

Lucas, N. (1996) Teacher Training Agency: is there anyone there from further education?, *Journal of Further and Higher Education*, 20:1, Spring.

Lucas, N. (1999) Incorporated colleges: beyond the Further Education Funding Council's Model, in Green and Lucas, *op cit.*, pp.42–68.

Lucas, N. (2002) Unpublished PhD, University of London.

Lucas, R. and Lammont, N. (1998) Combining work and study: an empirical study of full-time students in school, college and university, *Journal of Education and Work*, 11:1, pp.41–56.

Lumby, J. (2001) Managing Teaching and Learning: diversity and innovation, *College Research*, 4:3, pp.50–52.

Mayes, T. (2002) The technology of learning in a social world, in R. Harrison, F. Reeve, A. Hanson and J. Clarke (eds) *Supporting Lifelong Learning, Volume 1, Perspectives on Learning*, London, RoutledgeFalmer.

McGiveney, V. (1996) *Staying or Leaving the Course: Non-completion and Retention of Nature Students in Further and Higher Education*, Leicester, National Institute for Adult Continuing Education.

Mclure, R. (2000) Recurrent funding, in A. Smithers, and P. Robinson (2000) (eds) *Further Education Re-formed*, London, Falmer Press.

Mager, R. (1962) *Preparing Instructional Objectives*, San Francisco CA, Fearon.

Marshall, L. and Rowland, F. (1993) *A Guide to Learning Independently*, 2nd Edition, Buckingham, Open University Press.

Maslow, A (1968) *Towards a Psychology of Being*, New York, Van Nostrand.

Mayo, M. (2002) Learning for active citizenship: training for and learning from participation in area regeneration, in F. Reeve, M. Cartwright and R. Edwards (eds) *Supporting Lifelong Learning, Volume 2, Organising Learning*, London, RoutledgeFalmer.

Miller, H.L. (1964) *Teaching and Learning in Adult Education*, New York, Macmillan.

Minton, D. (1991) *Teaching Skills in Further and Adult Education*, London, City and Guilds/Macmillan.

Morris, M., Nelson, J., Rickinson, M., Stoney, S.M. with Benefield, P. (1999) *A Literature Review of Young People's Attitudes Towards Education, Employment and Training*, Research Report 170, Nottingham, Department for Education and Employment.

Moser, C. (1999) *A Fresh Start: Improving Literacy and Numeracy*, London, Department for Education and Employment.

Moser, C. (1999) *Report of the Working Group, A Fresh Start: Improving Literacy and Numeracy*, London, DfEE.

Munroe, A., Rainbird, H. and Holly, L. (1997) *Partners in Workplace Learning*, London, UNISON.

Murphy, P. (ed.) (1999) *Learners, Learning and Assessment*, London, Paul Chapman/Open University.

Nash, I. (1992) Alliance calls for A level reform, *Times Educational Supplement*, 14 February.

National Audit Office (2001) *Improving Student Performance: How English Further Education Colleges Can Improve Student Retention and Achievement*, London, HMSO.

National Institute for Adult and Continuing Education (2001)

NSTF (1999) *Delivering Skills for All, Second Report of the National Skills Task Force*, Sudbury, Department for Education and Employment.

NCVQ (1995) *GNVQ Assessment Review*, Final report of the review group chaired by Dr John Capey, London, NCVQ.

OCR (2000) *Intermediate GNVQ Business*, Approved Specifications. Coventry, OCR.

Osborne, M., Cloonan, M., Morgan-Klein, B. and Loots, C. (2000) Mix and match? Further and higher education links in post-devolution Scotland, *International Journal of Lifelong Learning*, 19:3, pp.236–52.

Paczuka, A. (1999) Further Education and Higher Education: the changing boundary, in A. Green and N. Lucas (eds) *FE and Lifelong Learning: Realigning the Sector for the Twenty-first Century*, London, Institute of Education.

Payne, J. and Storran, J. (1995) *Further and Higher Education Progression Project Final Report*, London, Division of Continuing Education, South Bank University.

Pearce, N. and Hillman, J. (1998) *Wasted Youth*, London: IPPR.

Piaget, J. (1970) *Genetic Epistemology*, New York, Columbia University Press.

PIU (2001) *In Demand: Adult Skills in the 21st Century*, London: Performance and Innovation Unit, Cabinet Office.

Pring, R. (1997) Aims, values and the curriculum, in S. Tomlinson (ed.) *Education 14–19 Critical Perspectives*, London, The Athlone Press.

QCA (1998) *Disapplication of the National Curriculum at Key Stage 4 Using Section 363 of the 1996 Education Act for a Wider Focus on Work-related Learning. Guidance for Schools*. London, QCA.

QCA (1999a) *Consultation on Flexibility within the National Qualifications Framework*, London, QCA.

QCA (1999b) *Improving the Value of NVQs and other Vocational Qualifications: Consultation Documents*, London, QCA.

QCA (2001a) *QCA Review of Curriculum 2000 – Report on Phase One, July, 2001*, London, QCA.

QCA (2001b) *QCA Review of Curriculum 2000 – Report on Phase Two, December*, 2001, London, QCA.

Quicke, J. (1996) The reflective practitioner and teacher education: an answer to critics, *Teachers and Teaching: Theory and Practice*, 2:1, pp.11–22.

Raffe, D. (1997) The Scottish experience of reform: From *Action Plan* to *Higher Still*, in Hodgson, A. and Spours, K. (eds) *Dearing and Beyond*, London, Kogan Page.

Raffe, D., Spours, K., Young, M. and Howieson, C. (1998) The unification of post-compulsory education: Towards a conceptual framework, *British Journal of Educational Studies*, 46, pp.169–87.

Raggatt, P. and Williams, S. (1999) *Government, Markets and Vocational Qualifications*, London, Falmer Press.

Randle and Brady (1997) Further education and the new managerialism, *Journal of Further and Higher Education*, 21, pp.229–238.

Rees, S.A. (1995) Students with emotional and behavioural difficulties: coping with a growing tide, *Journal of Further and Higher Education*, 19:2, Summer, pp.93–7.

Rees, G., Gorard, S., Fevre, R. and Furlong, J. (2000) Participating in the Learning Society: History, place and biography, in F. Coffield (ed.) *Differing Visions of a Learning Society*, volume 2, Bristol, The Policy Press.

Richardson, W., Woolhouse, J. and Finegold, D. (1993) *The Reform of Post-16 Education and Training in England and Wales*, Harlow, Longman.

Richardson, W., Spours, K., Woolhouse, J. and Young, M. (1995) *Learning for the Future, Initial Report*, London, Institute of Education and Centre for Education and Industry, University of Warwick.

Riddell, S., Wilson, A. and Baron, S. (1999) Captured customers: people with learning difficulties in social markets, *British Educational Research Journal*, 25:4, pp.545–61.

Robinson, J.E., Such, S., Walters, C., Muller, D. and Stott, D. (1996) Researching in further education: an illustrative study from Suffolk College, in M. Young et al. *College as Learning Organisations: The Role of Research*, Unified 16+ Curriculum Series, Number 12, London, Institute of Education.

Robinson, P. (1996) *Rhetoric and Reality: Britain's New Vocational Qualifications*, London, Centre for Economic Performance.

Robson, J. (1996) (ed.) *The Professional FE Teacher*, Aldershot, Avebury.

Robson, J. (1998) A profession in crisis: status, culture and identity in the further education college, *Journal of Vocational Education and Training*, 50:4, pp.585–607.

Rogers, A. (1986) *Teaching Adults*, Milton Keynes, Open University Press.

Rogers, A. (1994) *Teaching Adults*, Buckingham, Open University Press.

Rogers, J. (1992) *Adults Learning*, 3rd Edition, Buckingham, Open University Press.

Rowland, S. (1993) *The Enquiring Tutor*, London, Falmer Press.

Rowntree, D. (1990) *Teaching Through Self-Instruction: How to Develop Open Learning Materials*, London, Kogan Page.

Ryan, P. and Unwin, L. (2001) Apprenticeship and the 'Training Market', *National Institute Economic Review*, No.178.

Sacks, O. (1986) *The Man Who Mistook His Wife For a Hat*, London, Pan Books.

Sanderson, B. (2001) Branding education, *RSA Journal*, 3:4, pp.22–5.

Satir, V. (1983) *Conjoint Family Therapy*, 3rd edn, Palo Alto, CA, Science and Behavioural Books.

Schon, D. (1983) *The Reflective Practitioner: How Professionals Think in Action*, New York, Basic Books.

Schon, D. (1987) *Educating the Reflective Practitioner*, San Francisco, CA, Jossey-Bass.

Scottish Office (1994) *Higher Still: Opportunity for All*, Edinburgh, HMSO.

SEU (1999) *Bridging the Gap: New Opportunities for 16–18 Year Olds Not in Education, Employment or Training*, London: The Stationery Office.

Shattock, M. (2000) Governance and Management, in Smithers, A. and Robinson, P. (eds) *Further Education Re-formed*, London, Falmer Press.

Skinner, B.F. (1968) *The Technology of Teaching*, New York, Appleton-Century-Crofts.

Smith, J.J. (1989) Judgements in educational assessment, *Journal of Further and Higher Education*, 13:3, pp.115–19.

Smith, R.M. (1982) *Learning How to Learn: Applied Theory for Adults*, New York, Cambridge University Press.

Smithers, A. (1993) *All Our Futures: Britain's Education Revolution*, London, Channel Four Television.

Smithers, A. and Robinson, P. (eds.) (2000) *Further Education Re-formed*, London, Falmer Press.

Spours, K. (1995) *The Strengths and Weaknesses of GNVQs: Principles of Design, Learning for the Future*, Working Paper 3, London, Institute of Education and Centre for Education and Industry, University of Warwick.

Squires, G. (1987) *The Curriculum Beyond School*, London, Hodder and Stoughton.

Stanton, G. (2000) Research, in Smithers, A. and Robinson, P. (eds) *Further Education Re-formed*, London, Falmer Press.

Stenhouse, L. (1975) *An Introduction to Curriculum Research and Development*, London, Heinemann.

Taubman, D. (2000) Staff relations, in Smithers, A. and Robinson, P. (eds) *Further Education Re-formed*, London, Falmer Press.

Tedder, M. (1994) Appraisal and professionalism in colleges, *Journal of Further and Higher Education*, 18:3, Autumn, pp.74–82.

TES 2 (1995) Drama out of a crisis, 20 September, London, *Times Educational Supplement*.

TES (1996) Perils of penguin-like star gazing, 9 February, London, *Times Educational Supplement*.

THES (1998) Doubts over who foots the bill for the University of Industry, Editorial, *Times Higher Education Supplement*, 20th November.

Tomlinson, J. (1996) *Inclusive Learning: Report of the Learning Difficulties and/or Disabilities Committee*, London, The Stationery Office.

Tough, A. (1971) *The Adult's Learning Projects*, Toronto, Ontario Institute for Studies in Education.

UDACE (1991) *What Can Graduates Do?* A Consultative Document, Leicester, UDACE.

Unwin, L. (1993) Training credits: The pilot doomed to succeed, in W. Richardson et al. (eds) *The Reform of Post-16 Education and Training in England and Wales*, Harlow, Longman.

Unwin, L. (1994) I'm a real student now: access to and the use of library services by distance learning students, *Journal of Further and Higher Education*, 18:1, Spring, pp.85–91.

Unwin, L. (1995) *Staying the Course: Students' Reasons for Non-completion of Full-time Education Courses in South and East Cheshire*, Middlewich, South and East Cheshire Education–Business Partnership, 42 pages.

Unwin, L. (1997) Reforming the work-based route: problems and potential for change, in A. Hodgson and K. Spours (eds) *Dearing and Beyond*, London: Kogan Page.

Unwin, L.(1999a) 'Flower Arranging's Off but Floristry is On': Lifelong Learning and Adult Education in Further Education Colleges, in Green, A. and Lucas, N. (eds) *FE and Lifelong Learning: Realigning the Sector for the 21st Century*, London:

Unwin, L. (1999b) *Jungle Trekking: Vocational Courses and Qualifications for Young People*, Skills Task Force Research Paper 10, Sheffield, Department for Education and Employment.

Unwin, L. and Edwards, R. (1990) The tutor-learner relationship: making sense of changing contexts, *Adults Learning*, March, pp.197–9.

Unwin, L. and Wellington, J. (2001) *Young People's Perspectives on Education, Employment and Training*, London, Kogan Page.

Usher, R., Bryant, I. and Johnston, R. (2002) Self and experience in adult learning, in R. Harrison, F. Reeve, A. Hanson and J. Clarke (eds) *Supporting Lifelong Learning*, Volume 1, London, RoutledgeFalmer.

Vygotsky, L.S. (1978) *Mind in Society*, Cambridge, Cambridge University Press.

Wildemeersch, D. (1989) The principal meaning of dialogue for the construction and transformation of reality, in S.W. Weil and I. McGill (eds) *Making Sense of Experiential Learning*, Milton Keynes, SRHE/Open University Press.

Wilmot, M. and McLean, M. (1994) Evaluating flexible learning: A case study, *Journal of Further and Higher Education*, 18:3, Autumn.

Young, M. (1993) A curriculum for the 21st century? Towards a new basis for overcoming academic/vocational divisions, *British Journal of Educational Studies*, 40:3, pp.203–222.

Young, M., Lucas, N., Sharp, G. and Cunningham, B. (1995) *Teacher Education for the*

Further Education Sector: Training the Lecturer of the Future, London, Institute of Education, University of London.

Young, M., Guile, D., Lucas, N. and Unwin, L. (1996) *Colleges as Learning Organisations: The Role of Research*, Post 16 Curriculum Series Number 12, London, Institute of Education, University of London.

Young, M. and Leney, T. (1997) From A-levels to an Advanced Level curriculum of the future, in A. Hodgson and K. Spours (eds) *Dearing and Beyond*, London, Kogan Page.

Further reading

PART I FURTHER EDUCATION IN CONTEXT

Chapter 1 Where will I teach?

Gray, D. and Griffin, C. (2000) (eds) *Post-compulsory Education in the New Millennium*, London, Jessica Kingsley.

Green, A. and Lucas, N. (1999) (eds) *FE and Lifelong Learning: Realigning the Sector for the Twenty-first Century*, London, Bedford Way Papers.

Smithers, A. and Robinson, P. (2000) (eds) *Further Education Re-formed*, London, Falmer Press.

Usher, R., Bryant, I. and Johnston, R. (1997) *Adult Education and the Post-Modern Challenge*, London, Routledge.

Chapter 2 The student body: who will I teach?

Ball, S., Maguire, M. and Macrae, S. (2000) *Choice, Pathways and Transitions Post-16*, London, Routledge.

Corbett, J. and Barton, L. (1992) *A Struggle for Choice, Students with Special Needs in Transition to Adulthood*, London, Routledge.

Field, J. and Leicester., M. (2000) (eds) *Lifelong Learning: Education across the Lifespan*, London, Falmer.

Hayton, A. (1999) (ed) *Tackling Disaffection and Social Exclusion: Education Perspectives and Policies*, London, Kogan Page.

Hodgson, A. (2000) (ed) *Policies, Politics and the Future of Lifelong Learning*, London, Kogan Page.

Pearce, N. and Hillman, J. (1998) *Wasted Youth, Raising Achievement and Tackling Social Exclusion*, London, IPPR.

Chapter 3 Diverse curricula: what will I teach?

Barr, J. (1999) *Liberating Knowledge: Research, Feminism and Adult Education*, Leicester, NIACE.

Bloomer, M. (1997) *Curriculum Making in Post-16 Education: The Social Conditions of Studentship*, London, Routledge.

Evans, K. (1998) *Shaping Futures, Learning for Competence and Citizenship*, Aldershot, Ashgate.

Hodgson, A. and Spours, K. (1999) *New Labour's Educational Agenda*, London, Kogan Page.

Raggatt, P. and Williams, S. (2000) *Government, Markets and Vocational Qualifications*, London, Falmer.

PART II TEACHING AND LEARNING

Chapter 4 Approaches to learning

Ainley, P. and Rainbird, H. (1999) (eds) *Apprenticeship: Towards a New Paradigm for Learning*, London, Kogan Page.
Boud, D. and Garrick, J. (1999) (eds) *Understanding Learning at Work*, London, Routledge.
Evans, K., Hodkinson, P. and Unwin, L. (2002) (eds) *Working to Learn: Transforming Workplace Learning*, London, Kogan Page.
Harrison, R. et al. (2002) (eds) *Supporting Lifelong Learning, Volume 1, Perspectives on Learning*, London, Routledge.
Gardner, H. (1993) *Frames of Mind: The Theory of Multiple Intelligences*, London, Fontana.
Paechter, C., Preedy, M., Scott, D. and Soler, J. (2001) (eds) *Knowledge, Power and Learning*, London, Paul Chapman.

Chapter 5 Teaching strategies

Curzon, L.B. (2000) *Teaching in Further Education*, 5th edition, London, Continuum.
Deer, R., Deer, L. and Wolfe, M. (2001) (eds) *Informal Learning with Young People*, London, RoutledgeFalmer.
Edwards, T., Fitz-Gibbon, C., Hardman, T., Haywood, R. and Meagher, N. (1997) *Separate but Equal? A Levels and GNVQs*, London, Routledge
Harkin, J., Turner, G. and Dawn, T. (2001) *Teaching Young Adults*, London: RoutledgeFalmer.
Rogers, J. (2001) *Adults Learning*, Milton Keynes, Open University Press.
Mortimore, P. (1999) (ed) *Understanding Pedagogy and its Impact on Learning*, London, Sage.
Simpson, O. (2000) *Supporting Students in Open and Distance Learning*, London, Kogan Page.
Stephenson, J. (2001) (ed) *Teaching and Learning On-line*, London, Kogan Page.
Wallace, S. (2001) *Teaching and Supporting in Further Education*, London, Learning Matters.

Chapter 6 Assessment and recording achievement

Ecclestone, K. (1994) *Understanding Assessment: A Guide for Teachers and Managers in Post-compulsory Education*, Leicester, NIACE.
Hargreaves, A. (1989) *Curriculum and Assessment Reform*, Milton Keynes, Open University Press.
McKelvey, C. and Peters, H. (1993) *APL: Equal Opportunities for All*, London, Routledge.
Weedon, P., Winter, J. and Broadfoot, P. (2001) *Assessment*, London, RoutledgeFalmer.
Wolf, A. (1995) *Competence-based Assessment*, Buckingham, Open University Press.

PART III PROFESSIONAL DEVELOPMENT

Chapter 7 Evaluation, reflection and research

Carr, W. and Kemis, S. (1986) *Becoming Critical*, London, Falmer Press.

Grubb, W.N. and Ryan, P. (1999) *The Roles of Evaluation for Vocational Education and Training*, Geneva, International Labour Office.

Moon, J. (2000) *Learning Journals*, London, Kogan Page.

Wellington, J. (2000) *Educational Research: Contemporary Issues and Practical Approaches*, London, Continuum.

Silver, H. (1999) *Researching Education: Themes in Teaching and Learning*, Bristol, The Policy Press.

Young, M. et al. (1996) *Colleges as Learning Organisations: The Role of Research*, Unified 16+ Curriculum Series, No. 12, London, Post-16 Centre, Institute of Education.

Chapter 8 Professional development

Eraut, M. (1994) *Developing Professional Knowledge and Competence*, London, Falmer Press.

Hodkinson, P. and Issitt, M. (1995) (eds) *The Challenge of Competence*, London, Cassell Education.

Hoyle, E. and John, P. (1995) *Professional Knowledge and Professional Practice*, London, Cassell.

Mahoney, P. and Hextall, I. (2000) *Reconstructing Teaching: Standards, Performance and Accountability*, London, RoutledgeFalmer.

Squires, G. (1999) *Teaching as a Professional Discipline*, London, Falmer.

Woodward, I. (1996) (ed) *Continuing Professional Development*, London, Cassell.

Chapter 9 Networks and support agencies

Crowther, J., Martin, I. and Shaw, M. (1999) (eds) *Popular Education and Social Movements in Scotland Today*, Leicester, NIACE.

Index

A2 units 51
Accreditation of Prior Learning (APL) 23, 66, 160, 186
Accrington and Rossendale College 16
achievement 12, 140–61
action planning 143
activities 130–1, 137, 172
adaptability 116–18
administration 20
adolescence 84–91
Adult Guidance Networks 9
adult learning 71–5, 82–4, 92–8
Adult Learning Inspectorate (ALI) 7, 24–5, 48, 178
Adult Literacy and Basic Skills Unit (ALBSU) 144, 155
Advanced (A) levels 24, 41–4, 51–2; assessment 149; curriculum 55, 61; reflection 167–9
Advanced Extension Award (AEA) 52
advanced studies 69–71
Advanced Subsidiary (AS) levels 41, 43, 51, 55
Advanced Vocational Certificate of Education (AVCE) 41, 51, 57–9; assessment 148, 154; curriculum 61; teaching strategies 126–7
Advisory Groups 185
affective domain 97, 125
age factors 29–30, 82–4
agricultural colleges 3, 18
aims 120–9
Ainley, P. 12
Amersham and Wycombe College 175
andragogy 93
Applied A levels 57
appraisal systems 184–5
approaches to learning 79–115

area costs 12
assessment 130, 132, 140–61
Assessment Reform Group 142, 156
assignments 129–34, 142–3, 153–6
Association for College Management (ACM) 190, 191
Association for Colleges (AfC) 196
Association of Colleges (AoC) 196–7
Association of Scottish Colleges (ASC) 196
Association of Teachers and Lecturers (ATL) 190–1
attendance 29
Audit Commission 9
autobiography 185–6
average level of funding (ALF) 9
Avis, J. 20
Awarding Bodies 41, 51–3, 160–1

banking concept 81
Baron, S. 31
barriers to learning 80, 87–8, 98–101
Barton, L. 32
Basic Skills Agency 74
Bateson, M.C. 185
Beacon Award 197
Beattie Committee 19, 31
behaviourism 80, 92, 95, 140
Belenky, M.F. 83
Belgium 49
Berne, E. 103–4
Bigger, S. 191–2
Black, P. 142
Blair, T. 5
Bloom, B.S. 97, 125–6
Bloomer, M. 21, 47, 86–7
Bloom's Taxonomy 125
Bloor, M. 185–6
Blunkett, D. 11–12, 16

Bobbitt, F. 124
Bocock, J. 17–18
Brandes, D. 137
British Broadcasting Company (BBC) 73
British Council 31
Brookfield, S. 92
Brown, S. 140
Brundage, D.H. 92
business organisations 192–5
Business and Technology Education Council (BTEC) 41, 44, 49; assessment 144–6, 156; awards 55; First/National Diplomas 58; national awards 56; qualifications 181
Butterworth, C. 186

Cabinet Office 8
Callaghan, J. 7
Cambridge Regional College 175
Canada 92, 99
Canning, R. 50
Capita 73
Careers Service 8
Cartmel, F. 85–6
Castling, A. 178–9
CEDEFOP 87
Centres of Vocational Excellence (CVEs) 16
Certificate for Pre-Vocational Education (CPVE) 54, 58
Certificates in Education 181–2
Chambers of Commerce 192
Chief Inspectors 17, 27, 31
China 84
Chown, A. 182
City and Guilds (C&G) 23, 55; Teacher's Certificates 181–2
civil rights movement 84
class system 72, 75
Clough, P. 32
Coats, M. 91
cognitive domain 97, 125
Cohen, L. 148
Colleges of Art and Design 3
Colleges Employers' Forum (CEF) 196
Common Inspection Framework 25
Common Inspection Framework 178
communities of practice 97–8, 140
community organisations 192–5
Compact 191–2
competence-based approach 80–1, 121, 124; assessment 156–8; qualifications 147, 181–2
competitiveness 46
computer-aided design (CAD) 139

computer-aided manufacturing (CAM) 139
computer-based learning 47
conditions of service 19–20
Confederation of British Industry (CBI) 42, 192
connective knowledge 116
Connexions 8–9
Conservative governments 4, 6–7, 26, 41
consumerism 81, 84–5
contracts 19–20
Corbett, J. 32
core skills 42, 65, 116, 170
correspondence courses 80, 137
counsellors 108
course choice 144
coursework 51, 53, 62
Cox, A. 183
creativity 131–3
Culham, A. 175
curriculum 39–41, 43, 87–9; advanced 51–2; Curriculum 2000 42–3, 61, 140; diversity 39–78; general 51–4; planning 123

D units 23
Davey, A. 175
Davies 21
day-release provision 63
Dearing Review 41–2, 57
Dee, L. 31
Delors, J. 71
Denmark 49
Department for Education and Employment (DfEE) 56, 72–3, 180
Department for Education and Skills (DfES) 8, 24, 47; curriculum 62–3, 73–4; networks 196
Department for Employment and Learning (Delni) 9
Department for Trade and Industry (DTI) 8
Department for Work and Pensions 8
dependency 93
Dewey, J. 81, 102
diaries 169–73, 185
difficult students 134–9, 171–72, 184
disadvantage 12
dispositions to learning 86–7
distance learning 124, 137–9
diversity 28–32, 39–78
domestic environments 98–9
drop-in centres 48
Duncan, A. 47–8
Dundee Northern College 184

E-Envoys 8
e-learning 48, 138–9
Ecclestone 140
Economic and Social Research Council
    (ESRC) 175
EdExcel 41
Education Acts 6, 29, 54
Education and Learning Wales (ELWa) 8,
    24, 62
Education Maintenance Allowances (EMAs)
    30
Education Reform Act 5–6
education–business partnerships (EBPs)
    192–3
Educational Institute Scotland 190
Edwards, A. 19–20
Edwards, R. 104, 138
effective learning model 133
Egan, G. 108
ego states 103–4
Elton, B. 101, 103
emotional and behavioural difficulties
    134–5
employers 84–5, 134, 157
Employment Rights and Responsibilities
    (ERR) 56
Employment Service 8
EMTA Awards Ltd 64
Engestrom, Y. 98
England assessment 140; college numbers 3;
    curriculum 39–41, 43, 47, 50; funding
    6–9, 13; general education 51; higher
    education 5; inspections 24–6;
    performance figures 10; residential
    colleges 32; staff 21, 23; students 29–30;
    younger learners 84
Enterprise and Lifelong Learning
    Department (ELLD) 8
entrepreneurialism 26
environmental factors 86–7, 98–9
Eraut, M. 97, 177, 179
essays 148–9
Estyn see Her Majesty's Inspectorate
European Commission (EC) 31, 71, 138,
    195
European Social Fund (ESF) 16, 36, 74
European Union (EU) 13, 49, 87
evaluation 165–6
Evans, K. 86
evening classes 63
evidence 157
examinations 51–2
experiential learning 81

familial systematic perspective 99
family support 88, 90
feeder courses 89
Felstead, A. 4, 10
Field, J. 48, 71–2, 194
financial issues 88–90
First Diplomas 58
flashpoints 134
flexibility 81, 116–18, 137–9
Fordism 138
formative assessment 143–4
Foundation Degrees 70–1
France 46, 49
franchises 69–70
Freire, P. 81
full-cost courses 18
Fuller, A. 97
funding 5–6, 9–15, 24; curriculum 49–50,
    63; formula 12; methodology 74;
    professional development 176; research
    175–6; students 32; teaching strategies
    134
Furlong, A. 85, 86
Further Education Development Agency
    (FEDA) 180, 196–7
further education (FE) colleges 10–11, 57;
    adult education 75; age ranges 82–4;
    distance learning 137; flexibility 116;
    higher education 69–71; nature/scope
    3–8; networks 190; NVQs 64;
    qualifications 182; research 173; teachers
    102; types 3
Further Education Funding Council (FEFC)
    5, 6–8, 12–13; curriculum 39;
    inspections 49, 117–18, 139; NVQs 65;
    organisations 17–18; qualifications 9–10,
    44; reports 132; staff 19; students 31;
    support services 110–11; vocational
    qualifications 55
Further Education National Training
    Organisation (FENTO) 23, 178–80,
    182–4
Further Education Professional
    Development Forum 185
Further Education Staff College (FESC) 196
Further Education Unit (FEU) 42, 178,
    181, 196
Further and Higher Education (FHE) Act
    5–6, 69, 196

Gagne, R.M. 95–6
gender issues 90–1, 100
General Certificate of Education (GCE) 51

General Certificate of Secondary Education
(GCSEs) 29, 47, 51–5, 149
general education 39, 51–4
General National Vocational Qualifications
(GNVQs) 23, 52–3, 55; Advanced 41,
52, 57–8; assessment 143, 146–7, 148–9,
154, 181; establishment 57–62; reflective
diaries 171; reflective practice 167;
teaching strategies 131–2
General Teaching Council 23
generic skills 42, 116
Germany 46, 49
Gibb, J.R. 92
Gleeson, D. 6, 21, 27, 176
goals 120–9
governing bodies 27
grading 25–6, 148
Grant for Educational Support and Training
(GEST) 178
Gravatt 193–4
Green, A. 42, 203
Griffin, C. 84
group learning 105–7
guidance 108–9, 111–12, 155
Guile, D. 48, 98

Harkin, J. 86, 97
Harris, S. 144
Harrow, A.J. 126
Haycocks Report 180
Hayton, A. 48
Heathcote, G. 123–4
Her Majesty's Inspectorate (HMI) 24, 178
Hertford Regional College 110–11
hierarchy of needs 96
Higginson report 47
High Peak College 5
higher education, professional links 191–2
Higher Education Funding Council
(HEFC) 5, 8, 13
higher education (HE) 52, 57, 69–71;
provision 4–5; research 174, 176;
students 17
higher education institutions (HEI) 180–2,
185–7
Higher National Certificate (HNCs) 69, 71
Higher National Diploma (HNDs) 69, 71
Highlands and Islands Enterprise 8
Hill, R. 19
Hillier, I. 184
Hodgson, A. 41, 52
Hodkinson, H. 85
Hodkinson, P. 85, 86–7

Holloway, W. 186
homework 85
Honey, P. 166
Hope University 197
horticultural colleges 3
Huddersfield Technical College 3
Hugh Baird College 197

Illich, I. 44
incorporation 6, 24, 26
independent self-study 93
Individual Learning Accounts (ILAs) 72, 73
individualised learning 39, 106
Individualised Student Record (ISR) 9–10
induction 111, 137, 159, 170
Information and Communications
Technology (ICT) 30, 106
Information and Learning Technology (ILT)
47–9, 86, 137–9
initial professional education (IPE) 179–84
initial teacher education (ITE) 181
inspections 24–7, 48–9, 110–11; assessment
158; reports 117–18, 139
Institute of Employment Studies 195
Institute for Learning and Teaching (ILT)
179
Institutes of Lifelong Learning 71
insular knowledge 116
Internet 86, 139
Istance, D. 30

Jackson, C. 184
Japan 46
Jaques, D. 106–7
Jarvis, P. 81
job titles 22
job-related training 39, 63–8
Johnstone, J.W.C. 93
Joint Information Systems Committee
(JISC) 47

Kennedy, H. 4
Kennedy Report 31
Key Skills 42, 150–3
Key Skills Support Programme (KSSP) 62
key stage 4 29, 37, 53–4
Kidd, R. 83, 92, 102, 106
Knowles, M. 93
Knox, A.B. 92
Kolb, D.A. 80–1, 95

L units 23
labelling 101–2

Labour governments 4, 8, 26–7, 41, 72
labour market 88, 90
Last, J. 182
Lauzon, A.C. 99
Lave, J. 21, 97–8
Leadership College 23
LearnDirect 13, 72
learning activities 195; approaches 79–115;
    areas 39–40; centres 72; cycle 81, 95;
    difficulties 18–19, 31–2, 144; experiences
    167–9; outcomes 120–9; programmed
    80; styles 87–8; support 22–3, 32–3, 110;
    theory 92–8
Learning Resources Centres 48
Learning and Skills Council (LSC) 7,
    10–13, 16; networks 190; students 30
Learning and Skills Development Agency
    (LSDA) 5, 42, 62; networks 196–7;
    reflection 176
Learning and Skills Research Centre (LSRC)
    176
Learning and Skills Research Network
    (LSRN) 196
Leeds College of Technology 16
leisure courses 39
Leney, T. 51
Lewisham College 194
lifelong learning 47, 62, 71–3
Lifelong Learning Partnership 194
lifestyles 87
literacy 47, 74, 108, 110
local education authorities (LEAs) 5–6, 10,
    12; Conservatives 26; networks 192,
    196–7; professional development 178;
    students 30
Local Enterprise Companies (LECs) 6, 192
Local Learning and Skills Councils (LLSCs)
    36, 50–1, 67, 74
Lowestoft College 3
Lucas, N. 6, 10, 180
Lumby 116

McClure, R. 10
McGiveney, V. 100, 108
Mackercher, D. 92
McLean, M. 81
Mager, R.F. 124–5
Major, J. 5
management of learning 134–9
managerialism 20–1
mandatory units 64
Manion, L. 147
Manpower Services Commission (MSC) 42

marketing 31
marketisation 20–1
marriage 84
Marshall, L. 156
Maslow, A. 96–7
mature students 83, 90, 99–100, 168–9
Mayes 138
Mayo 194
Mechanics Institutes 3
mentors 185
Miller H.L. 92
Minister for e-Commerce and
    Competitiveness 8
Minister of Higher and Further Education,
    Training and Employment 9
Minton, D. 151
Modern Apprenticeships 8, 43–4, 55–6;
    curriculum 66, 68; frameworks 191;
    learning approaches 97
modularisation 41
Morris, E. 16, 43
Moser report 47
motivation 54, 59, 95–7; assessment 140;
    learning approaches 106; students 32–8;
    teaching strategies 134
multiple choice questions 150
Mumford, A. 166

National Assembly for Wales see also Welsh
    Assembly 8
National Association of Teachers in Further
    and Higher Education (NATFHE) 20,
    190–1
National Audit Office (NAO) 55
national base rate 12
National Council for Education and
    Training 8
National Council for Industry Training
    Organisation (NCITO) 57
National Council for National Training
    Organisations (NCNTO) 189
National Council for Vocational
    Qualifications (NCVQ) 43–4
National Curriculum 29, 37, 47; assessment
    140–1; curriculum 54
National Diplomas 58
National Framework 55
National Institute for Adult Continuing
    Education (NIACE) 74–5
National Joint Forum 190
National Learning Targets 11, 70
National Qualifications Framework 44–5,
    58, 71

National Skills Task Force (NSTF) 55–6
National Training Organisation (NTO) 53,
    56, 66; networks 191; reflection 179, 181
National Vocational Qualifications (NVQs)
    23, 29, 43–4; assessment 143, 147,
    151–2, 154, 157–8, 181; curriculum
    55–6, 58, 63–8, 74
needs 32–8, 96
networks 190–8
New Deal 8, 73
non-vocational courses 39
Northern Ireland Advisory Groups 185;
    college numbers 3; curriculum diversity
    50; funding 5, 9; inspections 25; staff 23
Northern Ireland Assembly 9, 41
Northern Ireland Office 5, 73
numeracy 47, 74, 108; assessment 144;
    learning approaches 110

objectives 120–9
OCR 55
off-the-job training 56
Office for Standards in Education (Ofsted)
    7, 9, 24–5; curriculum 48; professional
    development 178
Open College Network 55, 73
open learning 137–9
Open University (OU) 69–71, 137
Optimum 72
optional units 64–5
oral tests 152–3
overseas students 31
Owen, J. 21

part-time students 108
part-time teachers 19
part-time work 85, 87, 90; teaching
    strategies 132, 138
partnerships 54
pass rates 52
Patten, J. 57
pay 20
peer assessment 155–6
peer groups 87, 89–90
performance 20, 157
Performance and Innovation Unit (PIU) 8
Performing Arts colleges 3
Phillips, H. 137
Piaget, J. 81
planning-based activities 195
Poll Tax 6
polytechnics 5
portfolios 54, 58, 61–2; assessment 158–60;

curriculum 65; professional development
    185–6; reflection 170
post-16 education and training (PCET)
    7–8, 11–12
Postgraduate Certificate in Education
    (PGCE) 180–1
postgraduate teaching courses 186–7
postmodernism 100
practitioner research 165, 173–6
Probations Service 8
professional development 74, 177–89
professional organisations 190–1
programme weighting 12
progression 87, 89
prospectuses 83, 108–9
proximal development zone 98
psychomotor domain 125–6
Pupil Referral Unit 54

qualifications 9–10, 23, 41; assessment 141,
    147, 161; curriculum 43–4, 51–4;
    professional development 178; statutory
    requirements 178; teachers 181–2;
    vocational 55–6
Qualifications and Curriculum Authority
    (QCA) 42–5, 51, 62; assessment 160;
    general education 52; vocational
    qualifications 56
Qualified Teacher Status (QTS) 180
Quicke, J. 173
quotations 88–90

Raffe, D. 50
record of achievement 60
record-keeping 140–61
recruitment 84
Rees, S.A. 100, 134–6
reflection adult learning theory 94–5;
    approaches to learning 80, 84; assessment
    147, 150; barriers to learning 98–9;
    curriculum diversity 50–1, 75; gender
    issues 91; GNVQs 61; learning outcomes
    122; NVQs 67; professional development
    188–9; student needs/motivation 33–8;
    student support services 110;
    teacher–student relationship 104–5
reflective practice 165–76
Regional Advisory Council (RAC) 196–7
Regional Development Agencies (RDAs) 8,
    13, 195
Related Vocational Qualifications (RVQs)
    55–6
research 165, 172–6

Research and Development Toolkit 176
residential courses 32, 99–100
responsiveness 16–19
Return to Learn programme 73
Riddell, S. 31
Rivera, R.J. 93
Robson, J. 21, 178
Rogers, A. 96, 120–1
Rogers, J. 155
Round Table 192
Rowland, S. 156, 166
Royal Forest of Dean College 197
Royal Society of Arts (RSA) 13, 181

S levels 52
Sacks, O. 186
Sanderson, B. 13
scaffolding 98
Schedule 2 9–10
Schon, D. 81, 171–2
School Curriculum Assessment Authority
    (SCAA) 44
Scotland 16-19 curriculum 41; Advisory
    Groups 183; college numbers 3; funding
    6, 8–9; higher education 5; inspections
    24–5; qualifications 179–80; residential
    colleges 32; special needs 19; staff 23;
    students 31; trade unions 188
Scottish Credit and Qualifications
    Framework 44
Scottish Enterprise 8
Scottish Executive 8, 73
Scottish Further Education Funding
    Council (SFEFC) 6, 8, 24
Scottish Further Education Unit (SFEU) 62
Scottish Office 6
Scottish Qualifications Authority (SQA) 44,
    50, 62, 159
Scottish Vocational Qualifications (SVQs)
    43, 56, 63–8
Secondary Heads Association (SHA) 191
Secretaries of State 11, 16, 43, 57
Sector Skills Councils (SSCs) 53, 191
Sector Skills Development Agency (SSDA)
    191
self-assessment 155–6
self-directed learning 93
self-study support 20
senior management 188
service philosophy 26
Shain 21, 27
Sherrington 186
Silver 191–2

simulated work environments 66–7
Single Regeneration Budget (SRB) 195
sixth form colleges 3, 5, 10, 57
Skinner, B. F. 80
Smith, J.J. 141
Smith, R.M. 92
Social Exclusion Unit 8
Social Inclusion and Learning Technologies
    Team 47
socialcultural activity theory 98
South Birmingham College 16
South East Essex College 16
South-east Derbyshire College 14–15
Sparkes, A.C. 85
special needs 18–19, 32
specialist designated colleges 3
Spours, K. 41, 52, 58, 62
Squires, G. 44, 69, 74
staff development 113–15, 138, 177–89
staffing 19–23
Standards Fund 13
Stanton, G. 176
status zero problem 30
Stenhouse, L. 173
stereotypes 100
strategies 118–20, 133–4
student-centred learning 166
students, age ranges 82–4; difficult 134–9,
    171–2, 184; diversity 28–31; group
    learning 105–7; mature 83, 90, 99–100,
    168–9; motivation 32–8, 54, 59; range
    79; reflective practice 166–9; support
    services 107–11, 136; teacher relationship
    101–5; younger 29–30, 84–91, 168
summative assessment 146
supplementary evidence 157
support services 107–11, 136, 190–8
Sweden 49

tasks 130
Taubman, D. 6
Teacher Training Agency (TTA) 181
teachers IPE 180–4; learning approaches
    111–15; reflective diaries 169–73; student
    relationship 101–5, 133, 135–6; training
    23, 180–2
Teaching Qualification (Further Education)
    (TQFE) 23
teaching strategies (TS) 116–39
team teaching 137
Technical Certificates 55–6
technical colleges 63
Technical and Vocational Education

Initiative (TVEI) 54
Tedder, M. 177–8
tertiary colleges 3
testing 149–53
timetables 88–9
Tomlinson Committee 31
Tough, A. 92–3
trade unions 20, 188, 190–1
Trades Councils 192
Training Credits 73
Training and Development Lead Body
   (TDLB) 23, 181, 188
Training and Employment Agency 9
Training and Enterprise Councils (TECs)
   6–8, 12, 192
Training Standards Council (TSC) 7
transactional analysis (TA) 103
tutors 108, 110, 136; reflection 167–8, 171
Tyler, R. 124

undergraduate studies 69–71
Union Learning Fund 72–3
Union of Textile Workers 73
UNISON 73
unit-based qualifications 59–60
United Kingdom 84–5, 137, 139
United States 46, 48, 80; learning outcomes
   124; learning theory 93, 98; younger
   learners 83–4
universities 52, 69–70
University of Derby 5
University of Greenwich 186
University for Industry (UfI) 13, 72
University of London Examinations and
   Assessment Council (ULEAC) 41
University of Stirling 184
University of Strathclyde 184
Unwin, L. 4, 10, 97, 104

Usher 100

vignettes 33–8, 84; approaches to learning
   113–15; group learning 105; learning
   theory 93; networks 193
vocational education 39, 54–69, 141
Vygotsky, L. 98

Wales 3, 5–6, 100; assessment 140;
   curriculum 39–41, 47, 50; funding 8–9;
   inspections 24–5; residential colleges 32;
   staff 23; students 29; trade unions 190
web sites 25, 197–8
Welsh Assembly *see also* National Assembly
   for Wales 41
Welsh Funding Council 5
Wenger, E. 21, 97–8
Wildemeersch, D. 106
William, D. 142
Williamson, H. 30
Wilmot, M. 81
Wilson, A. 31
women 90–1, 100
word processing 86
work 85, 87–8, 90; assessment 157–8;
   experience 99–100, 132; learning 29, 54,
   131–2, 179; placements 66; teaching
   strategies 132; training 80
Workers' Educational Association (WEA) 71
written assessment 142–3, 150–3

Young, M. 39–41, 51–2, 98; networks 181;
   teaching strategies 116
younger students 29–30, 84–91, 168
Youth Service 8
Youth Training Scheme 42

zone of proximal development 98